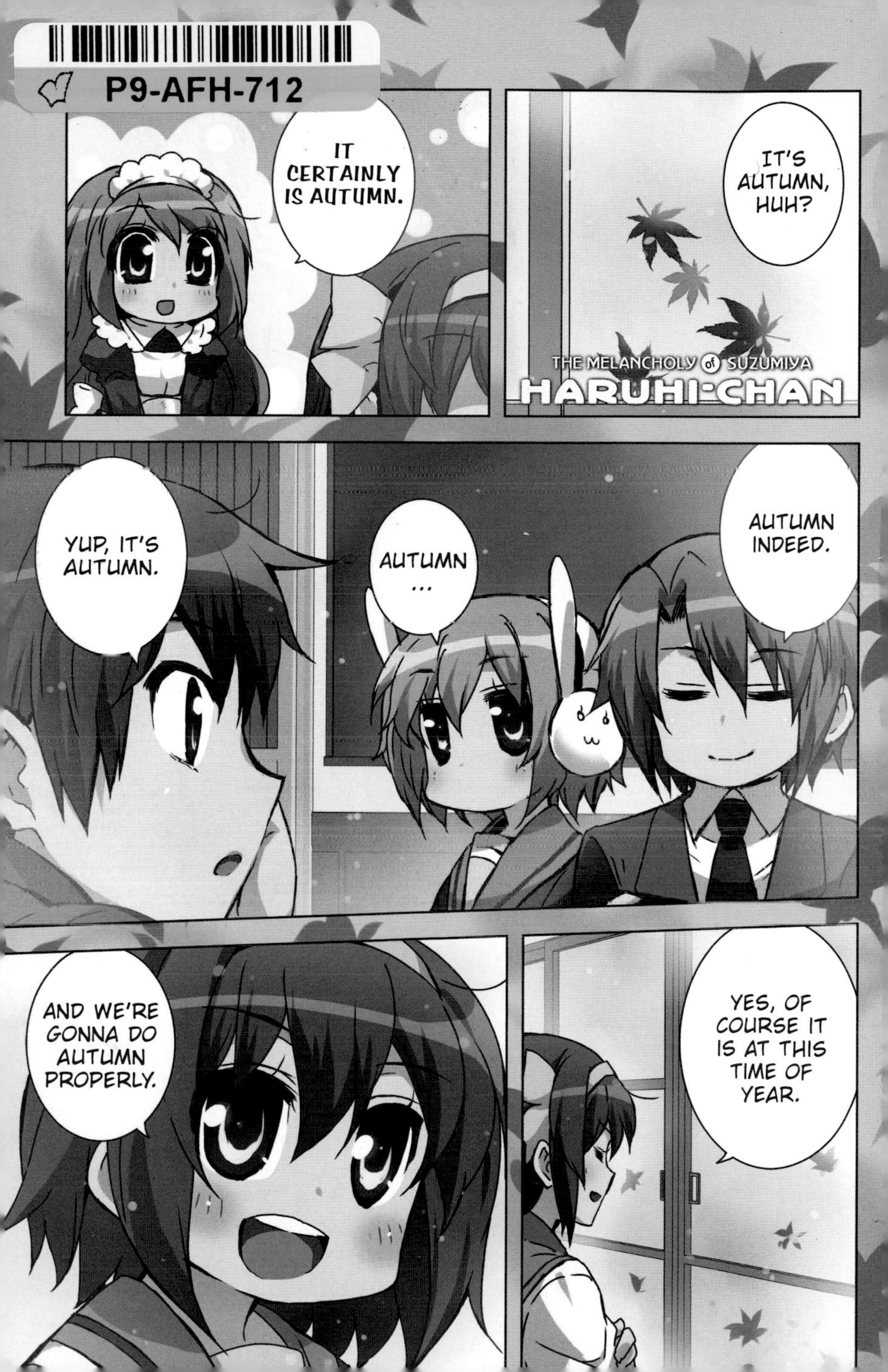
IT'S AUTUMN, HUH?
THE MELANCHOLY of SUZUMIYA
HARUHI-CHAN
IT CERTAINLY IS AUTUMN.
AUTUMN INDEED.
AUTUMN ...
YUP, IT'S AUTUMN.
YES, OF COURSE IT IS AT THIS TIME OF YEAR.
AND WE'RE GONNA DO AUTUMN PROPERLY.

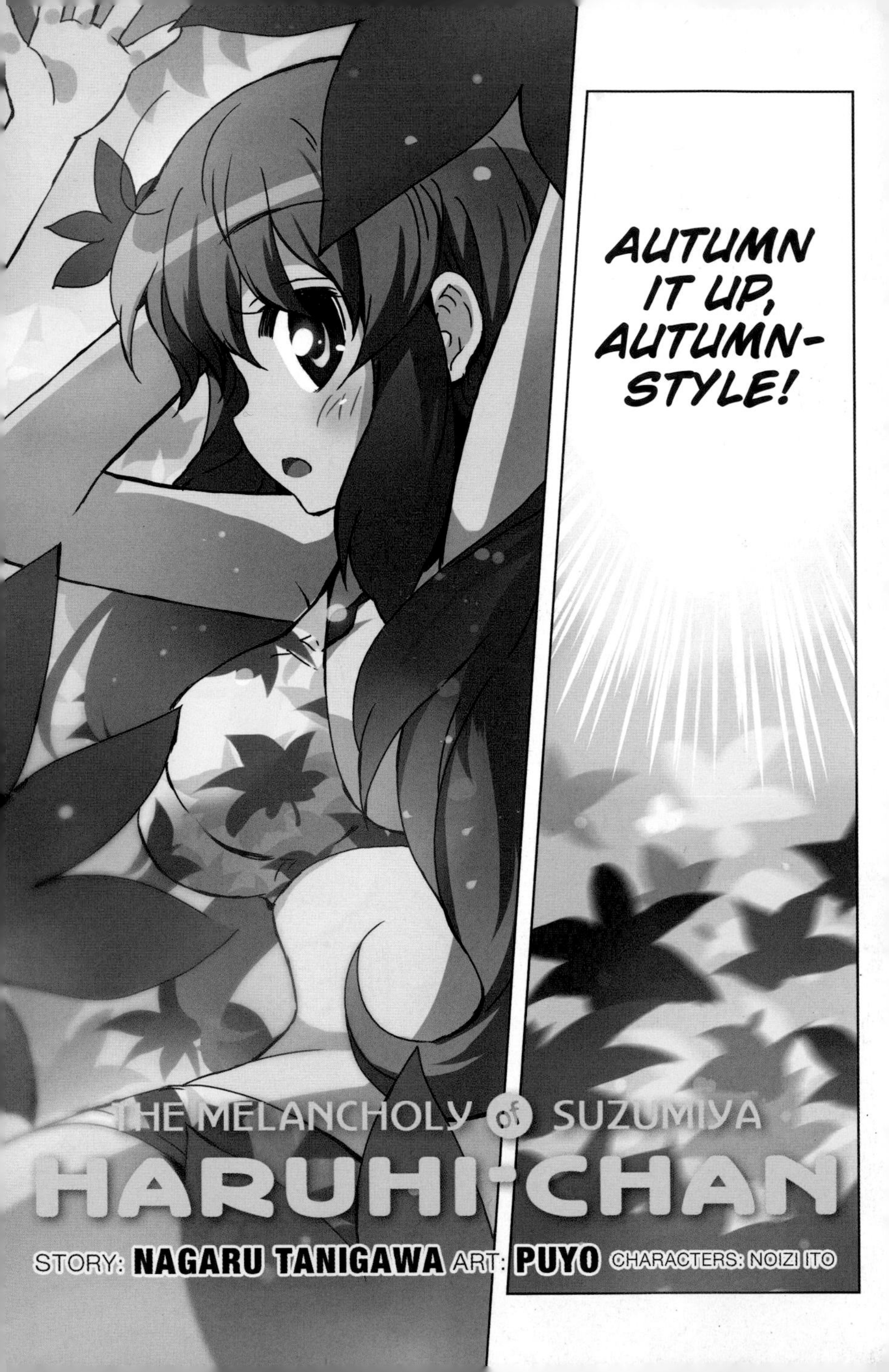
AUTUMN IT UP, AUTUMN-STYLE!
THE MELANCHOLY of SUZUMIYA
HARUHI-CHAN
STORY: NAGARU TANIGAWA ART: PUYO CHARACTERS: NOIZI ITO

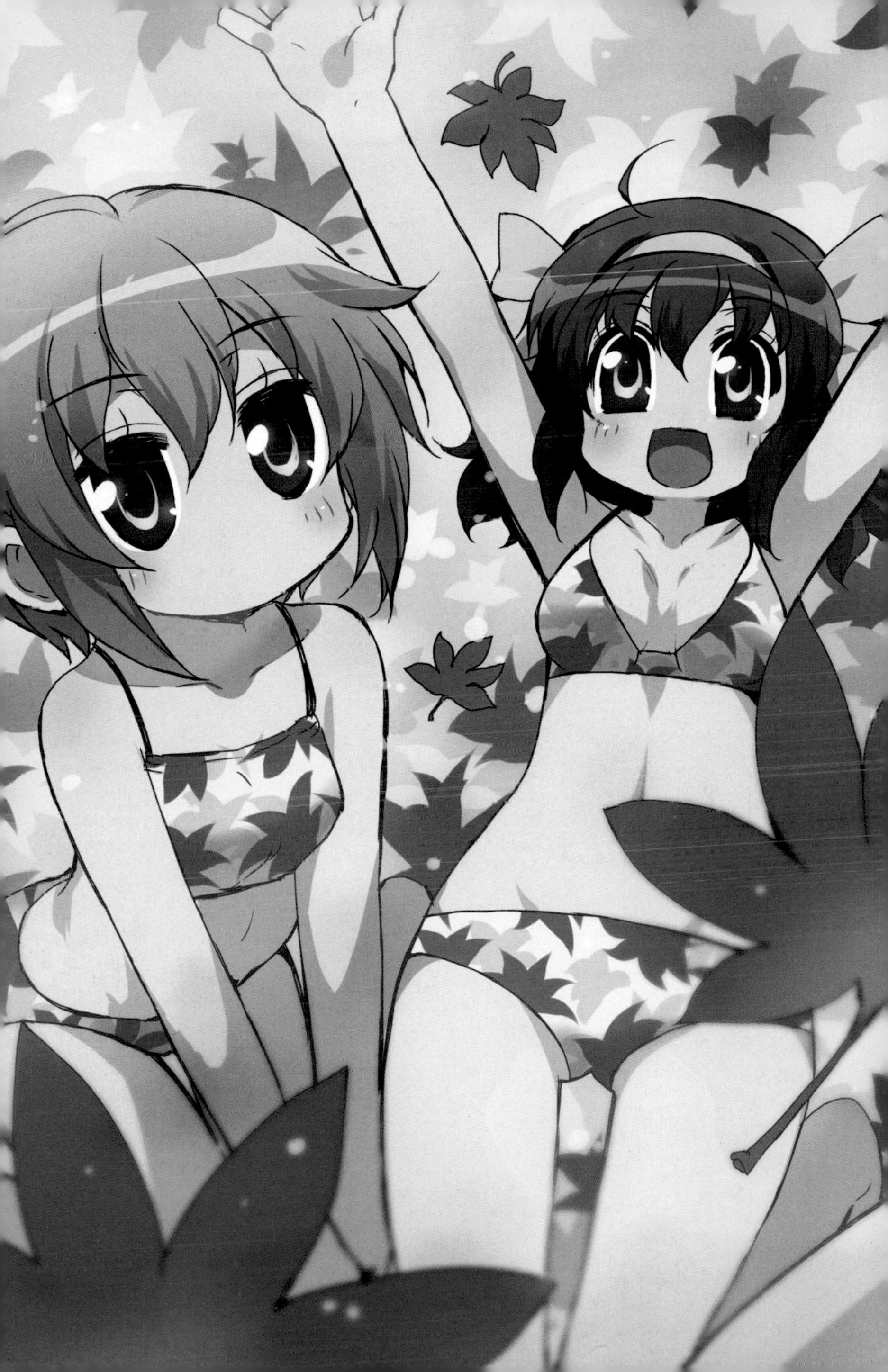

The Melancholy of Suzumiya
Haruhi-chan
07

# INDEX

# THE MELANCHOLY of SUZUMIYA
# HARUHI-CHAN
## The Untold Adventures of the SOS Brigade

THIS IS FICKSHUN, VILLAIN!

STORY: **NAGARU TANIGAWA** ART: **PUYO** CHARACTERS: NOIZI ITO

SHUDDER ガク SHIVER ブルル

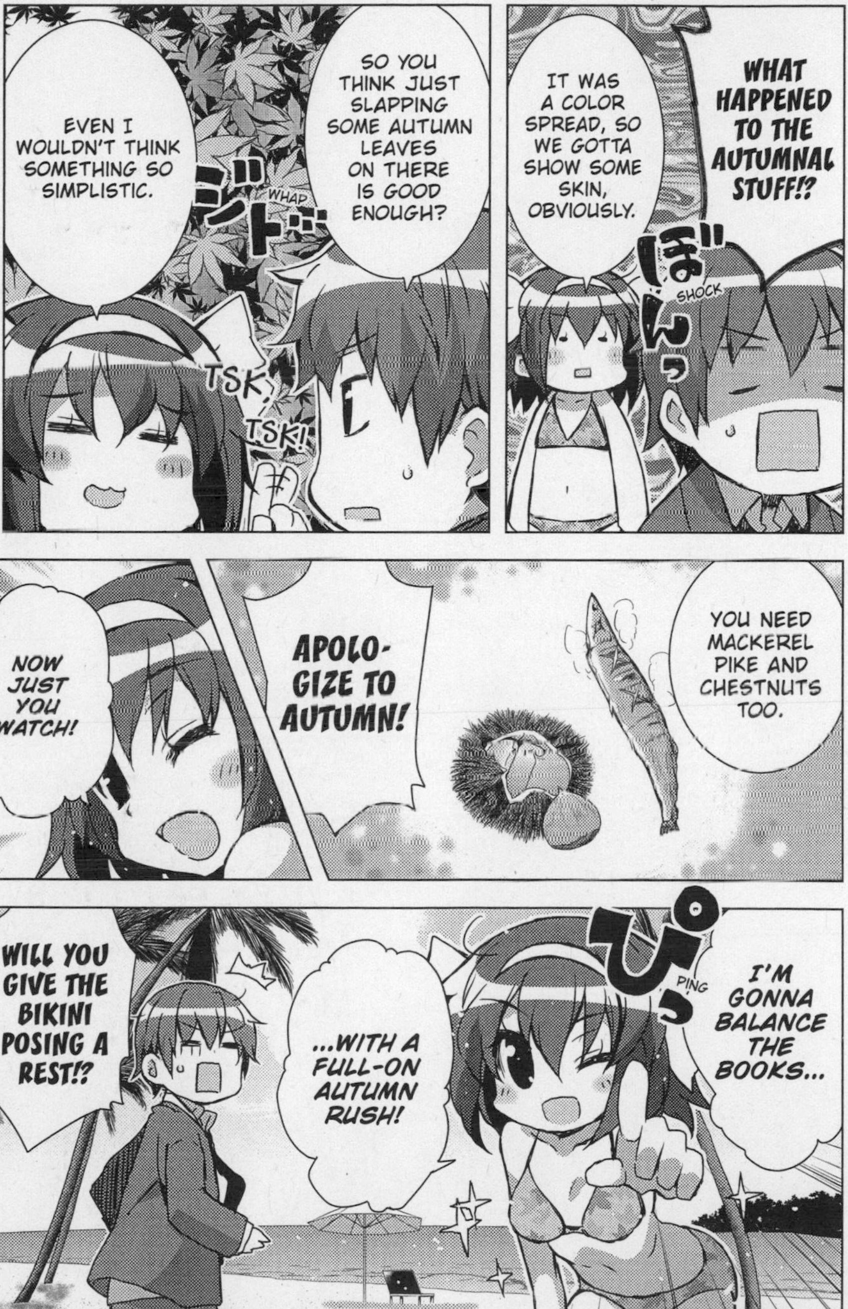
WHAT HAPPENED TO THE AUTUMNAL STUFF!?
IT WAS A COLOR SPREAD, SO WE GOTTA SHOW SOME SKIN, OBVIOUSLY.
SHOCK
SO YOU THINK JUST SLAPPING SOME AUTUMN LEAVES ON THERE IS GOOD ENOUGH?
WHAP
EVEN I WOULDN'T THINK SOMETHING SO SIMPLISTIC.
TSK, TSK!
YOU NEED MACKEREL PIKE AND CHESTNUTS TOO.
APOLO-GIZE TO AUTUMN!
NOW JUST YOU WATCH!
I'M GONNA BALANCE THE BOOKS...
PING
...WITH A FULL-ON AUTUMN RUSH!
WILL YOU GIVE THE BIKINI POSING A REST!?

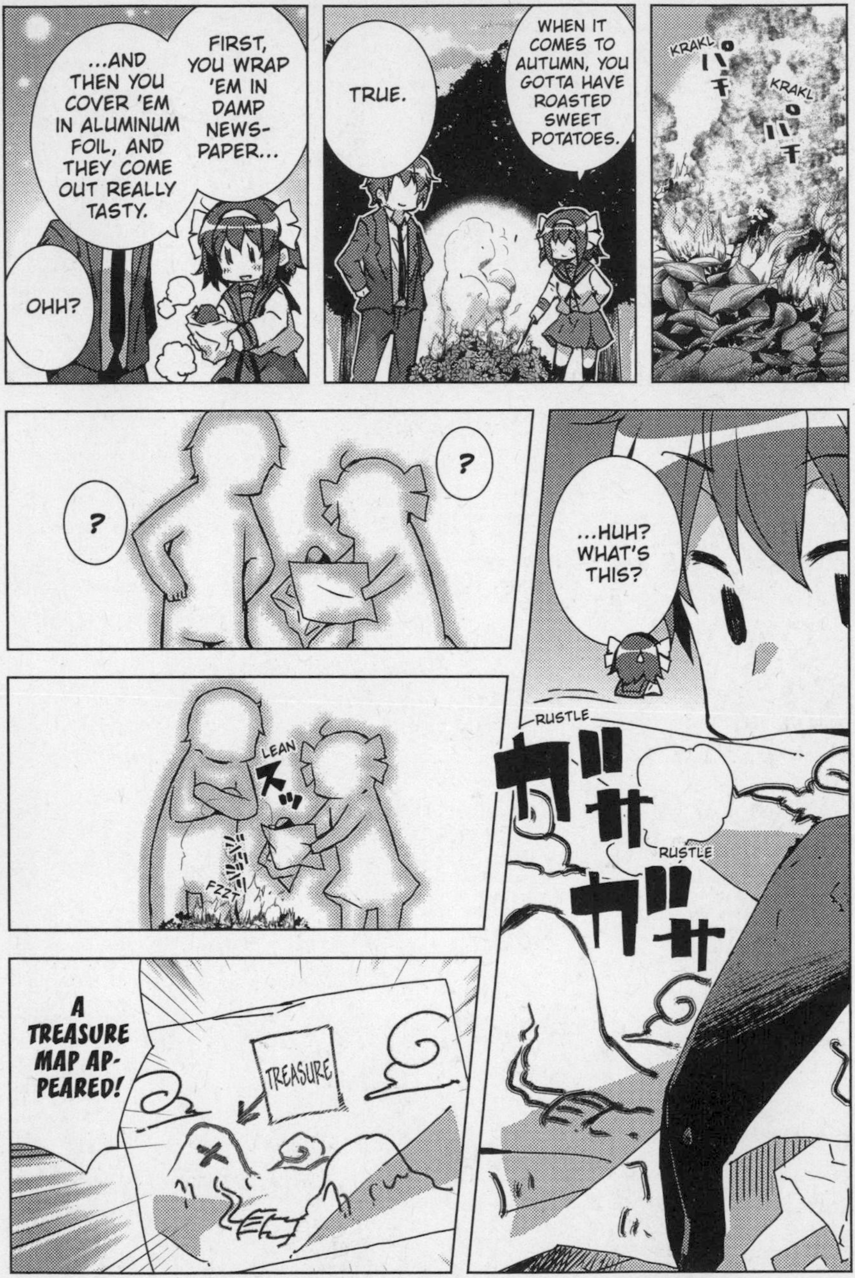
KRAKL
KRAKL
WHEN IT COMES TO AUTUMN, YOU GOTTA HAVE ROASTED SWEET POTATOES.
TRUE.
FIRST, YOU WRAP 'EM IN DAMP NEWS-PAPER...
...AND THEN YOU COVER 'EM IN ALUMINUM FOIL, AND THEY COME OUT REALLY TASTY.
OHH?
...HUH? WHAT'S THIS?
RUSTLE
RUSTLE
?
?
LEAN
FZZT
A TREASURE MAP AP-PEARED!
TREASURE

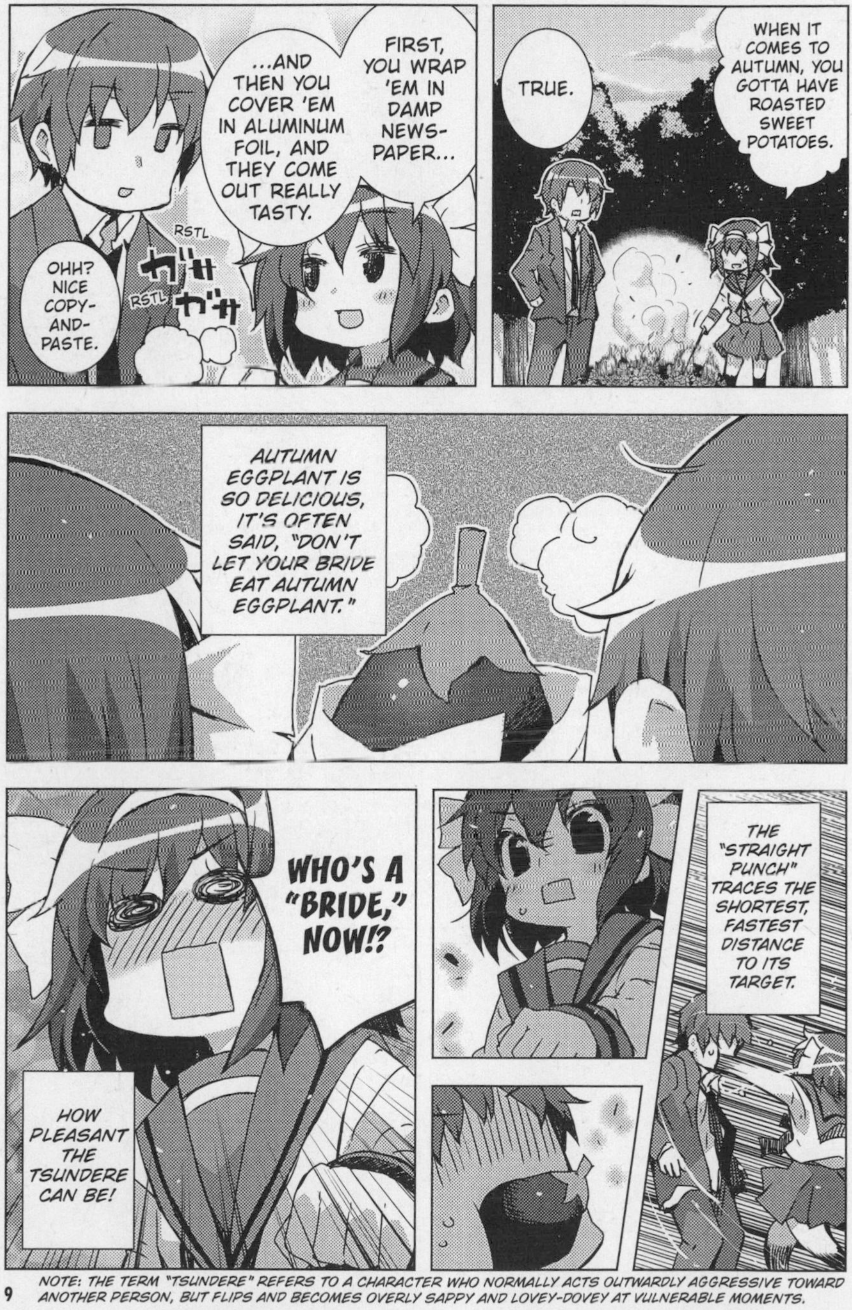
WHEN IT COMES TO AUTUMN, YOU GOTTA HAVE ROASTED SWEET POTATOES.
TRUE.
FIRST, YOU WRAP 'EM IN DAMP NEWS-PAPER...
...AND THEN YOU COVER 'EM IN ALUMINUM FOIL, AND THEY COME OUT REALLY TASTY.
RSTL
ガサ
RSTL
ガサ
OHH? NICE COPY-AND-PASTE.
AUTUMN EGGPLANT IS SO DELICIOUS, IT'S OFTEN SAID, "DON'T LET YOUR BRIDE EAT AUTUMN EGGPLANT."
THE "STRAIGHT PUNCH" TRACES THE SHORTEST, FASTEST DISTANCE TO ITS TARGET.
WHO'S A "BRIDE," NOW!?
HOW PLEASANT THE TSUNDERE CAN BE!

*NOTE: THE TERM "TSUNDERE" REFERS TO A CHARACTER WHO NORMALLY ACTS OUTWARDLY AGGRESSIVE TOWARD ANOTHER PERSON, BUT FLIPS AND BECOMES OVERLY SAPPY AND LOVEY-DOVEY AT VULNERABLE MOMENTS.*

# AUTUMN OF ART

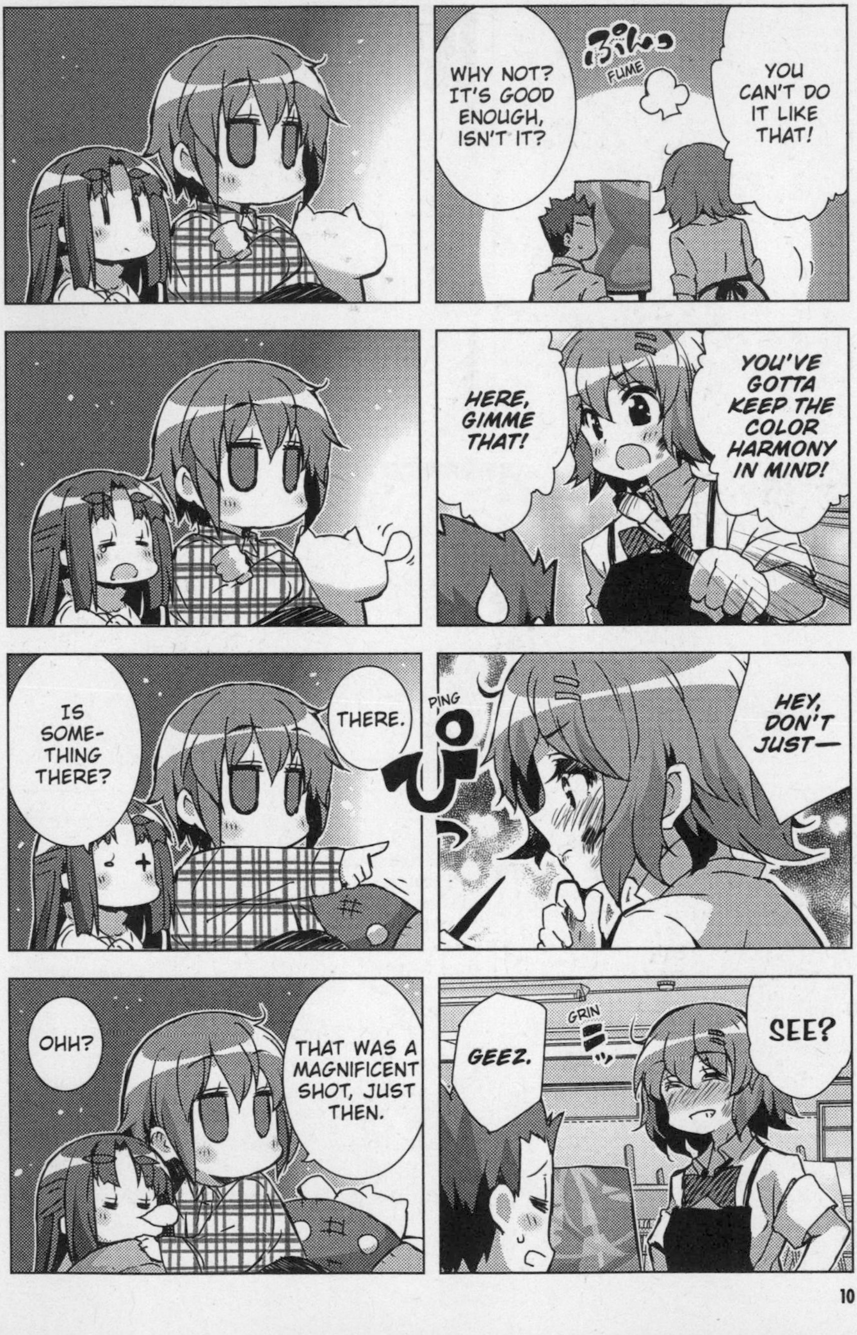
YOU CAN'T DO IT LIKE THAT!
ぷんっ
FUME
WHY NOT? IT'S GOOD ENOUGH, ISN'T IT?
YOU'VE GOTTA KEEP THE COLOR HARMONY IN MIND!
HERE, GIMME THAT!
HEY, DON'T JUST—
PING
THERE.
IS SOMETHING THERE?
SEE?
GRIN
GEEZ.
THAT WAS A MAGNIFICENT SHOT, JUST THEN.
OHH?

# AUTUMN OF ATHLETICS

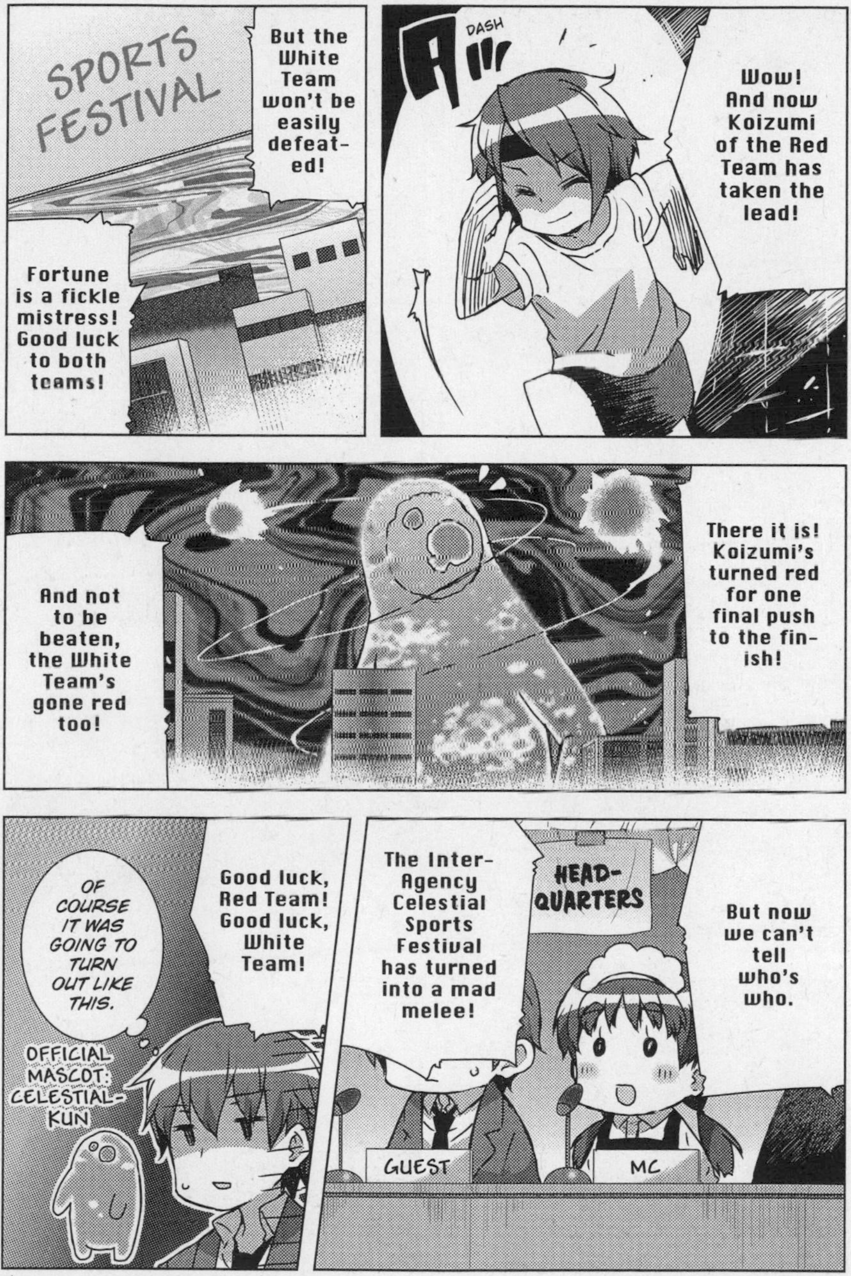

Wow! And now Koizumi of the Red Team has taken the lead!
DASH
But the White Team won't be easily defeat-ed!
SPORTS FESTIVAL
Fortune is a fickle mistress! Good luck to both teams!
There it is! Koizumi's turned red for one final push to the fin-ish!
And not to be beaten, the White Team's gone red too!
But now we can't tell who's who.
HEAD-QUARTERS
The Inter-Agency Celestial Sports Festival has turned into a mad melee!
MC
GUEST
Good luck, Red Team! Good luck, White Team!
OF COURSE IT WAS GOING TO TURN OUT LIKE THIS.
OFFICIAL MASCOT: CELESTIAL-KUN

# AUTUMN OF READING ①

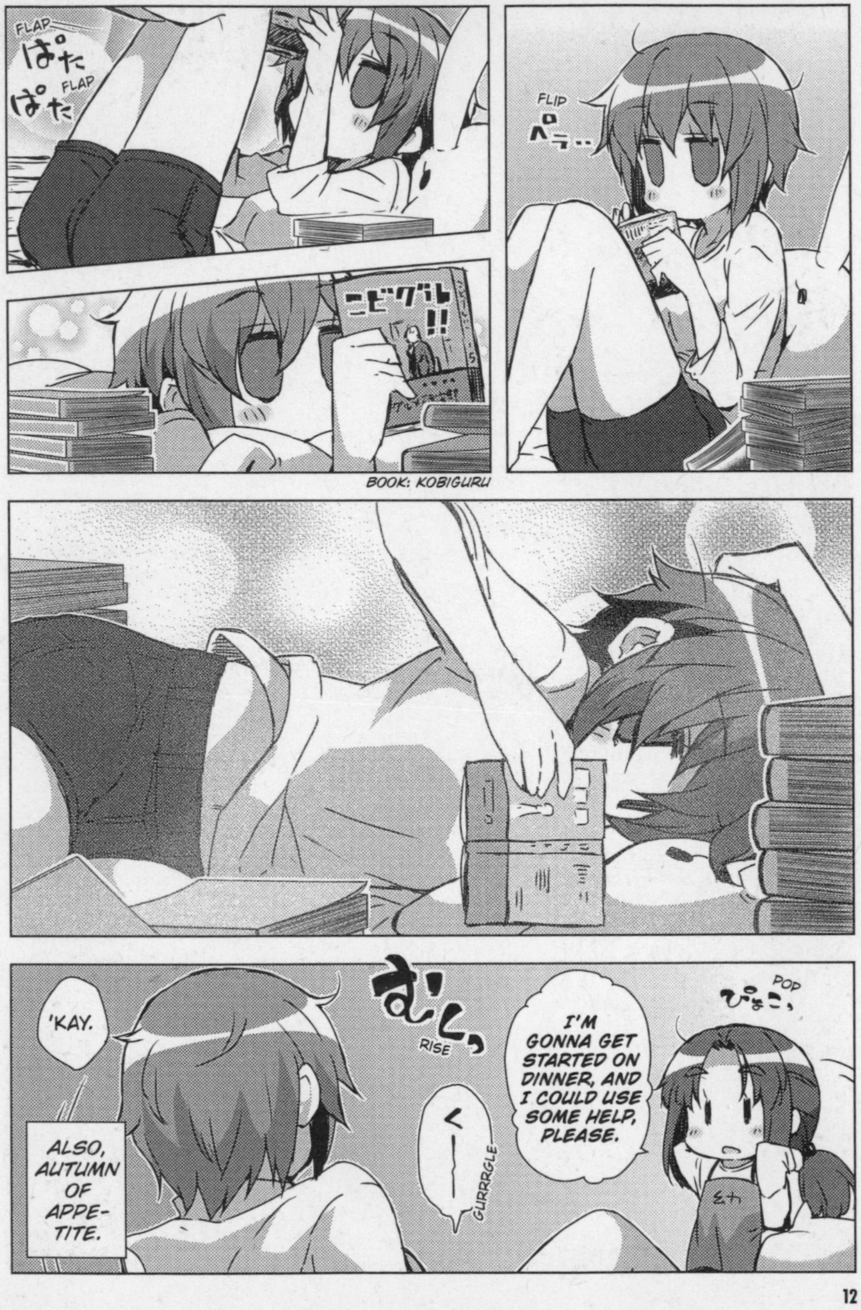
FLIP
ペラ…
FLAP
ぱた
FLAP
ぱた
BOOK: KOBIGURU
POP
ぴょこっ
I'M GONNA GET STARTED ON DINNER, AND I COULD USE SOME HELP, PLEASE.
くーー
GURRRGLE
むくっ
RISE
'KAY.
ALSO, AUTUMN OF APPE-TITE.

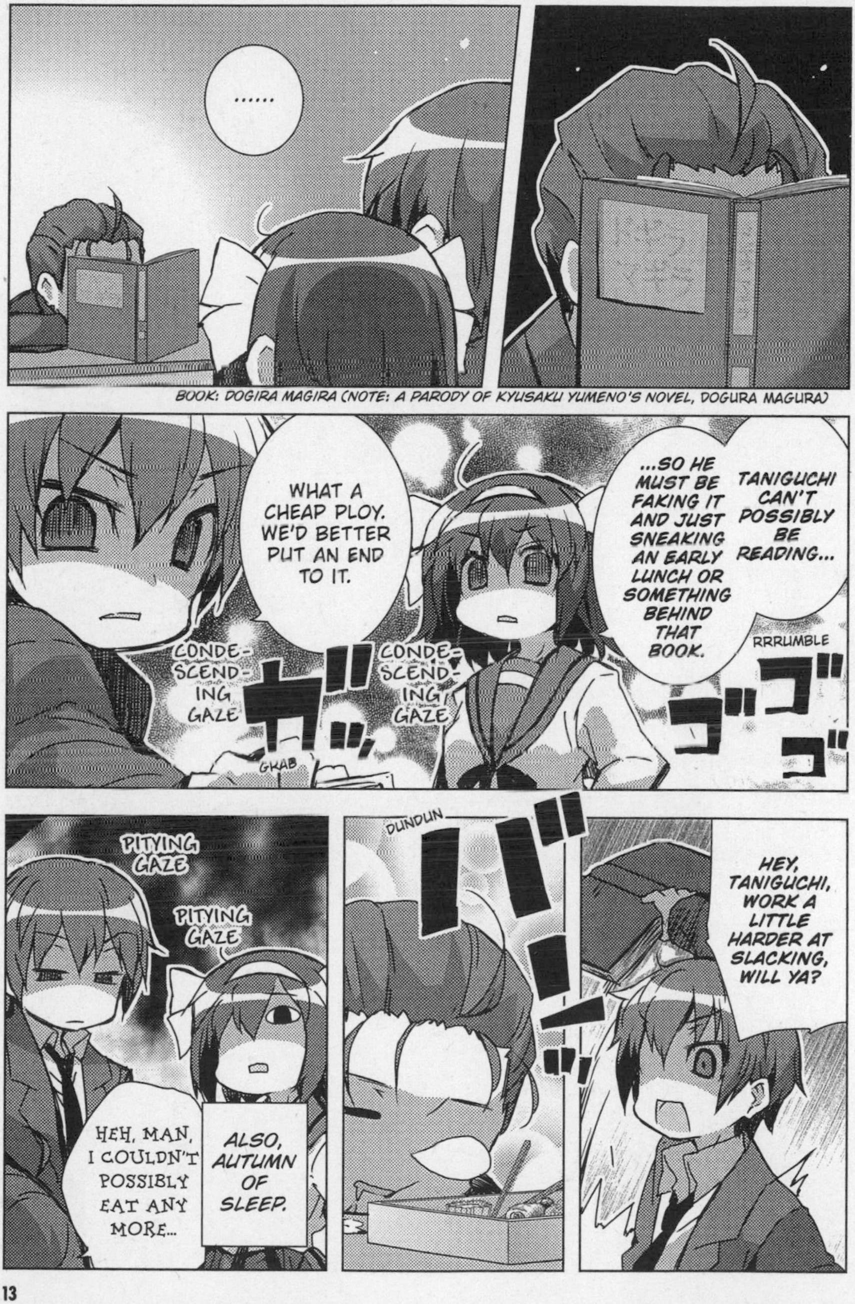
......
BOOK: DOGIRA MAGIRA (NOTE: A PARODY OF KYUSAKU YUMENO'S NOVEL, DOGURA MAGURA)
TANIGUCHI CAN'T POSSIBLY BE READING...
...SO HE MUST BE FAKING IT AND JUST SNEAKING AN EARLY LUNCH OR SOMETHING BEHIND THAT BOOK.
RRRUMBLE
CONDE-SCEND-ING GAZE
WHAT A CHEAP PLOY. WE'D BETTER PUT AN END TO IT.
CONDE-SCEND-ING GAZE
GKAB
DUNDUN
HEY, TANIGUCHI, WORK A LITTLE HARDER AT SLACKING, WILL YA?
PITYING GAZE
PITYING GAZE
ALSO, AUTUMN OF SLEEP.
HEH, MAN, I COULDN'T POSSIBLY EAT ANY MORE...

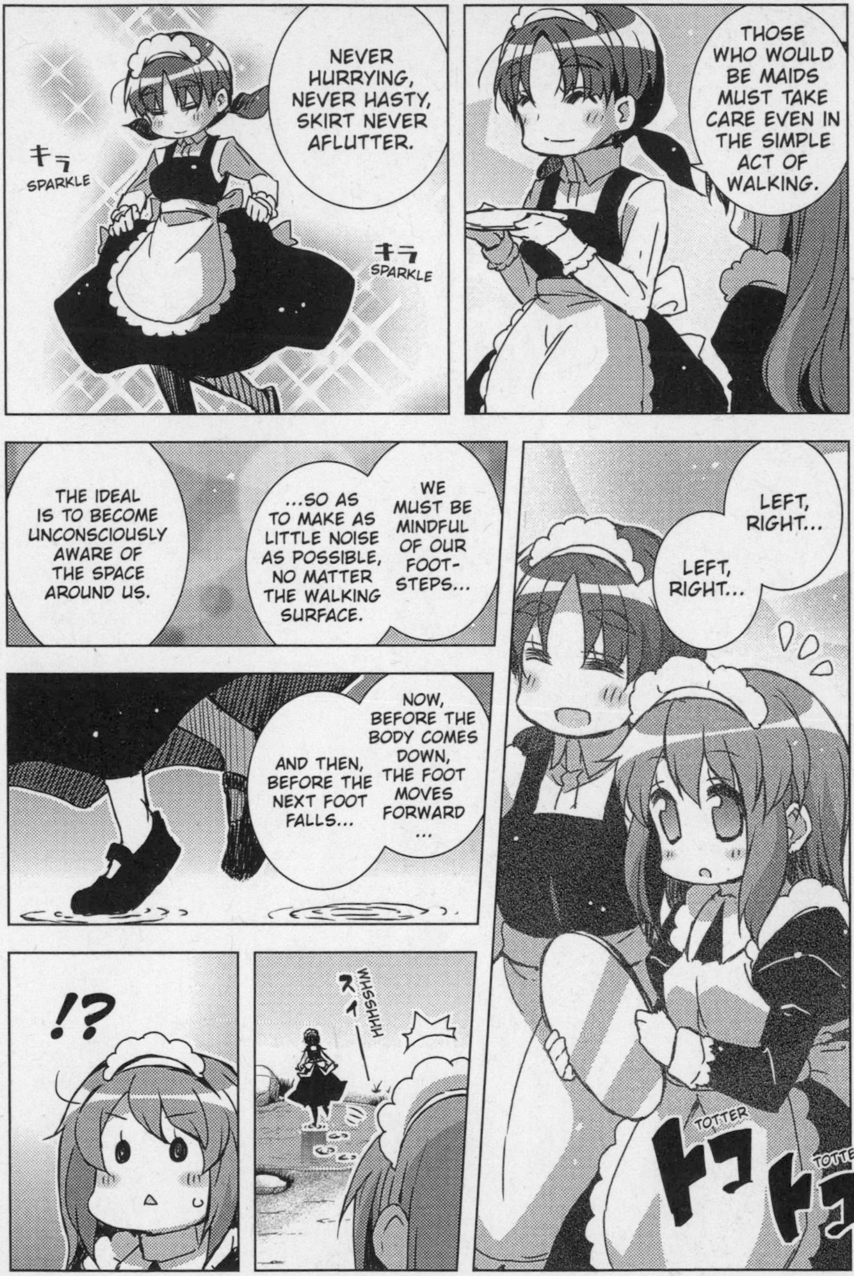
THOSE WHO WOULD BE MAIDS MUST TAKE CARE EVEN IN THE SIMPLE ACT OF WALKING.
NEVER HURRYING, NEVER HASTY, SKIRT NEVER AFLUTTER.
キラ
SPARKLE
キラ
SPARKLE
LEFT, RIGHT...
LEFT, RIGHT...
トコ
TOTTER
トコ
TOTTER
WE MUST BE MINDFUL OF OUR FOOT-STEPS...
...SO AS TO MAKE AS LITTLE NOISE AS POSSIBLE, NO MATTER THE WALKING SURFACE.
THE IDEAL IS TO BECOME UNCONSCIOUSLY AWARE OF THE SPACE AROUND US.
NOW, BEFORE THE BODY COMES DOWN, THE FOOT MOVES FORWARD ...
AND THEN, BEFORE THE NEXT FOOT FALLS...
スイ
WHHSHHH
!?

# AUTUMN OF APPETITE ③

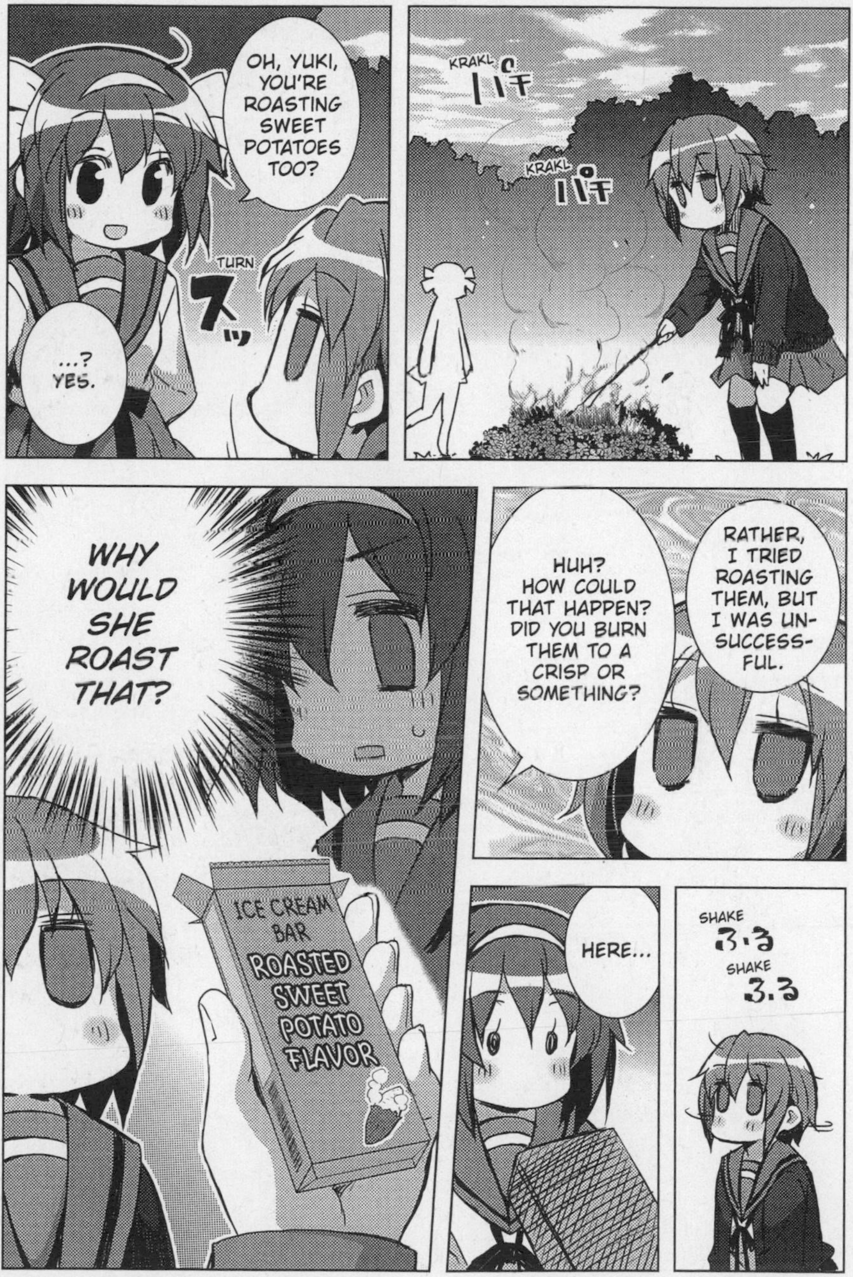
KRAKL
パチ
KRAKL
パチ
OH, YUKI, YOU'RE ROASTING SWEET POTATOES TOO?
TURN
スッ
...? YES.
RATHER, I TRIED ROASTING THEM, BUT I WAS UN-SUCCESS-FUL.
HUH? HOW COULD THAT HAPPEN? DID YOU BURN THEM TO A CRISP OR SOMETHING?
SHAKE
ふる
SHAKE
ふる
HERE...
WHY WOULD SHE ROAST THAT?
ICE CREAM BAR
ROASTED SWEET POTATO FLAVOR

# AUTUMN OF ROMANCE

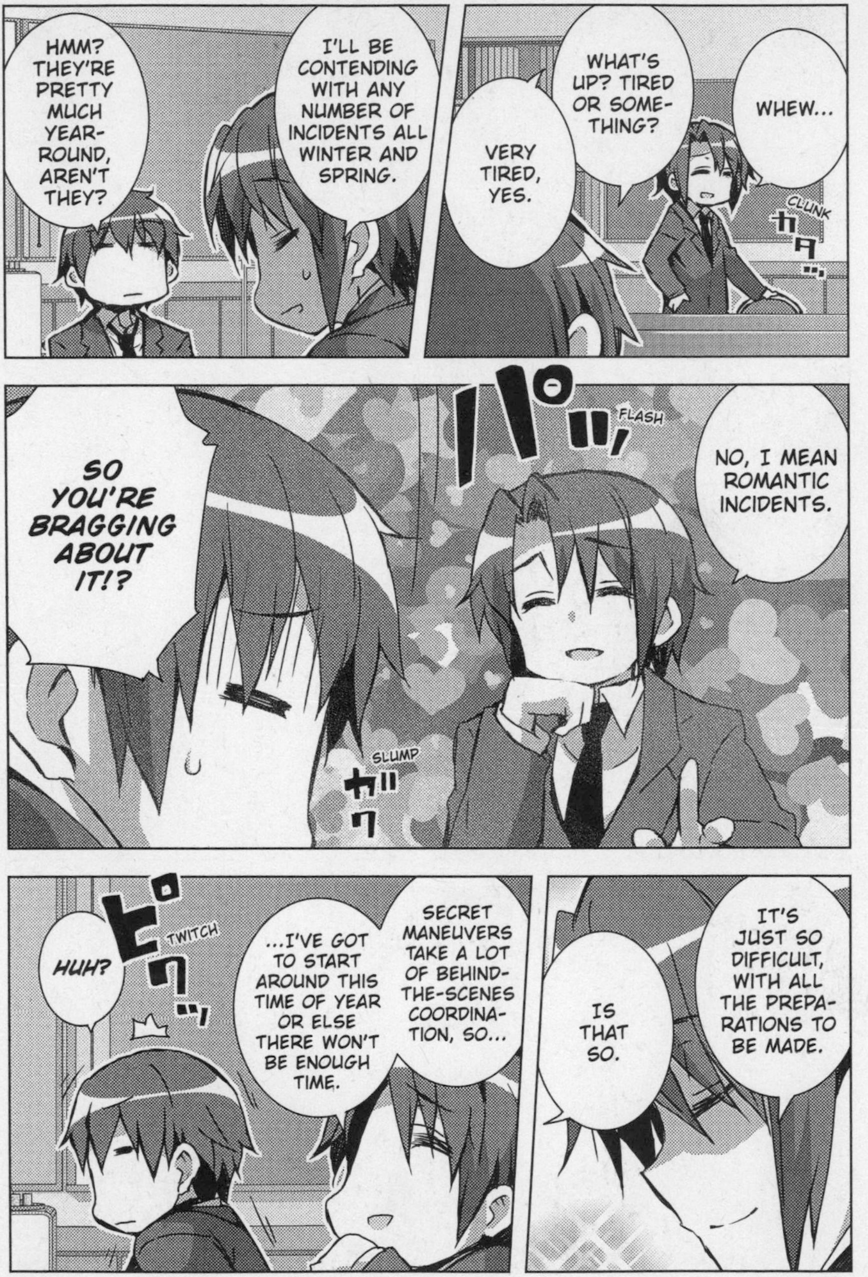
WHEW...
CLUNK
WHAT'S UP? TIRED OR SOME-THING?
VERY TIRED, YES.
I'LL BE CONTENDING WITH ANY NUMBER OF INCIDENTS ALL WINTER AND SPRING.
HMM? THEY'RE PRETTY MUCH YEAR-ROUND, AREN'T THEY?
NO, I MEAN ROMANTIC INCIDENTS.
FLASH
SLUMP
SO YOU'RE BRAGGING ABOUT IT!?
IT'S JUST SO DIFFICULT, WITH ALL THE PREPA-RATIONS TO BE MADE.
IS THAT SO.
SECRET MANEUVERS TAKE A LOT OF BEHIND-THE-SCENES COORDINA-TION, SO...
...I'VE GOT TO START AROUND THIS TIME OF YEAR OR ELSE THERE WON'T BE ENOUGH TIME.
TWITCH
HUH?

## AUTUMN OF SECRET MANEUVERS

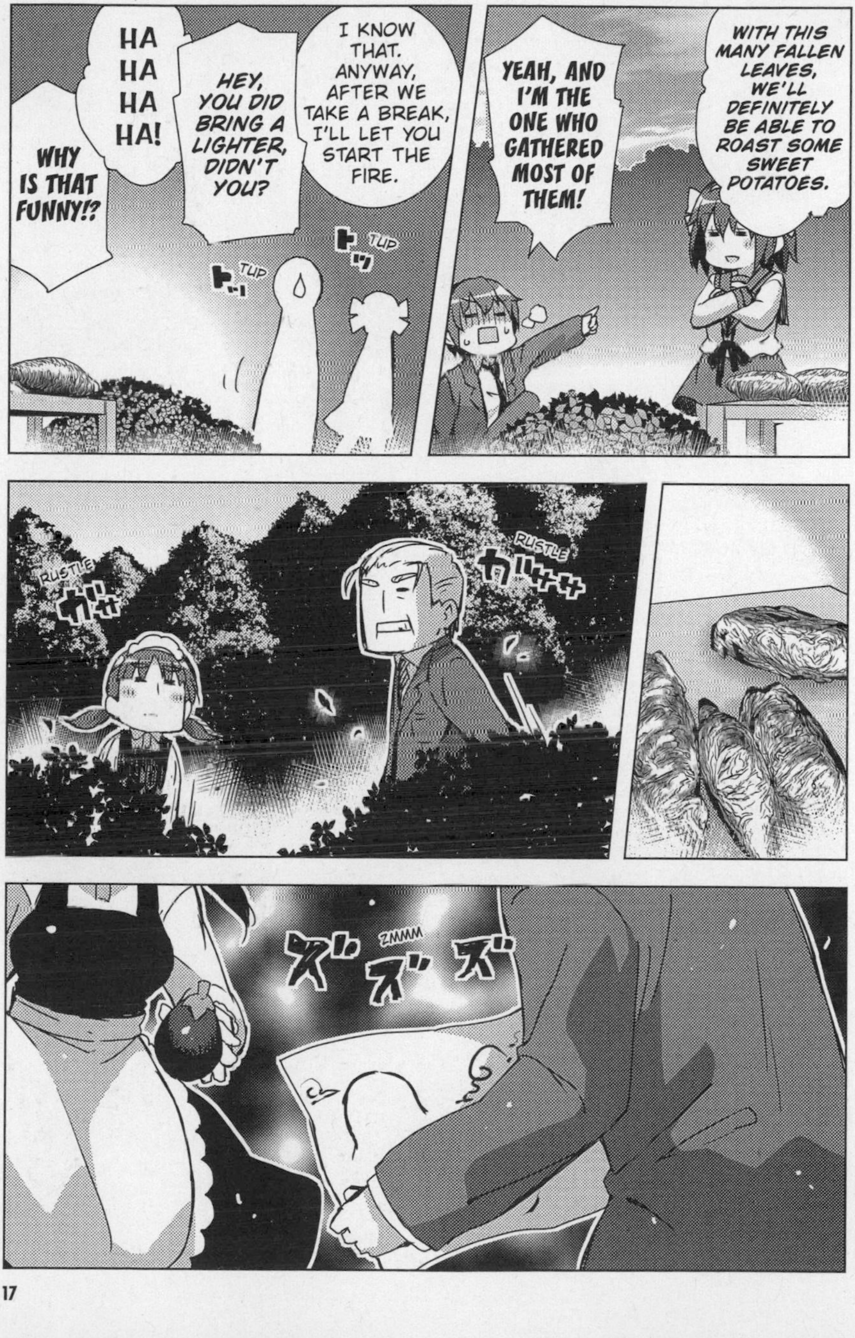
WITH THIS MANY FALLEN LEAVES, WE'LL DEFINITELY BE ABLE TO ROAST SOME SWEET POTATOES.
YEAH, AND I'M THE ONE WHO GATHERED MOST OF THEM!
I KNOW THAT. ANYWAY, AFTER WE TAKE A BREAK, I'LL LET YOU START THE FIRE.
HEY, YOU DID BRING A LIGHTER, DIDN'T YOU?
HA HA HA HA!
WHY IS THAT FUNNY!?
TUP
TUP
RUSTLE
RUSTLE
ZMMM

# AUTUMN OF LEAVES

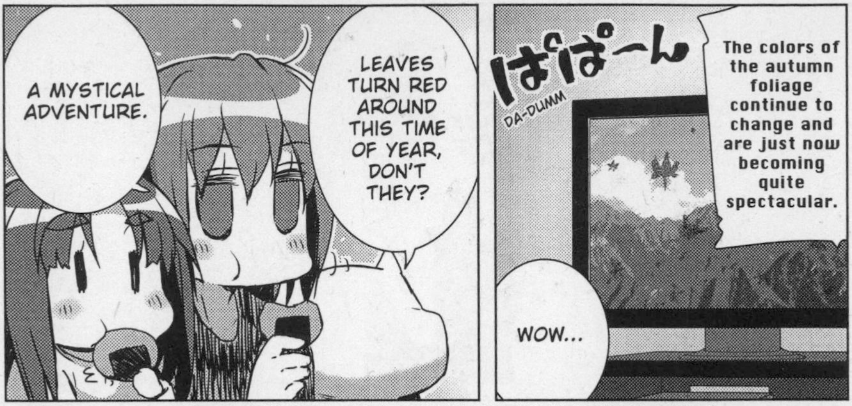

The colors of the autumn foliage continue to change and are just now becoming quite spectacular.
ぱぱーん
DA-DUMM
WOW...
LEAVES TURN RED AROUND THIS TIME OF YEAR, DON'T THEY?
A MYSTICAL ADVENTURE.


NOTE: A REFERENCE TO THE DRAGON BALL OPENING THEME SONG, "MAKAFUSHIGI ADVENTURE"

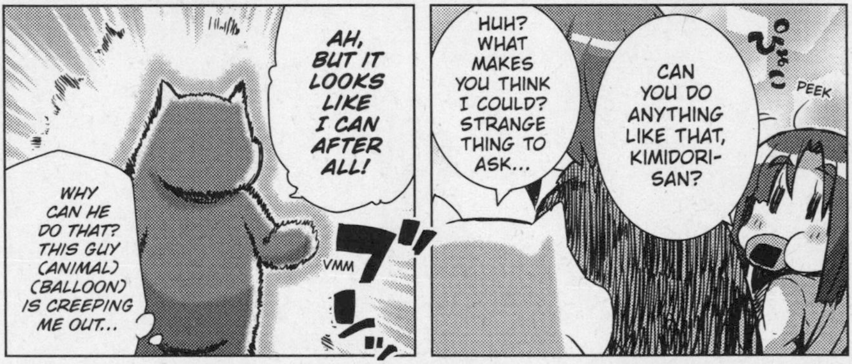

ぴょこ
PEEK
CAN YOU DO ANYTHING LIKE THAT, KIMIDORI-SAN?
HUH? WHAT MAKES YOU THINK I COULD? STRANGE THING TO ASK...
AH, BUT IT LOOKS LIKE I CAN AFTER ALL!
ブーン
VMM
WHY CAN HE DO THAT? THIS GUY (ANIMAL) (BALLOON) IS CREEPING ME OUT...


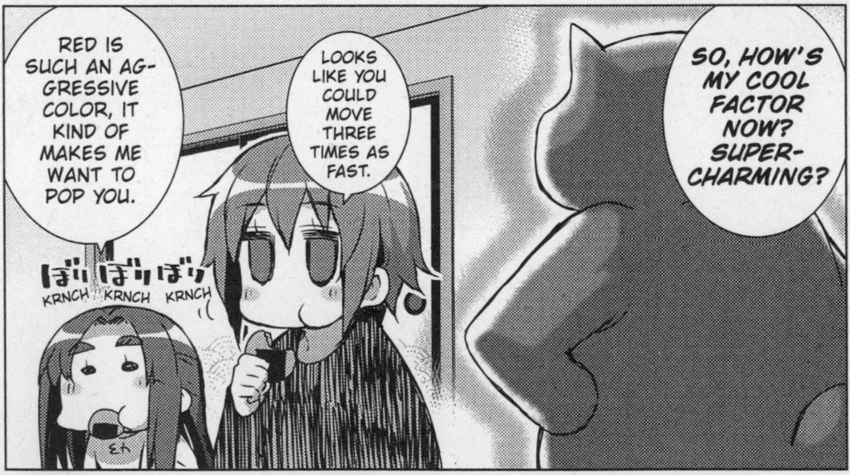

SO, HOW'S MY COOL FACTOR NOW? SUPER-CHARMING?
LOOKS LIKE YOU COULD MOVE THREE TIMES AS FAST.
RED IS SUCH AN AG-GRESSIVE COLOR, IT KIND OF MAKES ME WANT TO POP YOU.
ぼりぼりぼり
KRNCH KRNCH KRNCH


NOTE: A REFERENCE TO THE ZAKU MOBILE SUIT PILOTED BY CHAR IN THE SERIES MOBILE SUIT GUNDAM. CHAR WAS KNOWN FOR UPGRADING AND REPAINTING HIS MOBILE SUITS—TYPICALLY PAINTED RED—AND BOASTED THAT HIS RED ZAKU COULD GO THREE TIMES AS FAST AS THE ORIGINAL.

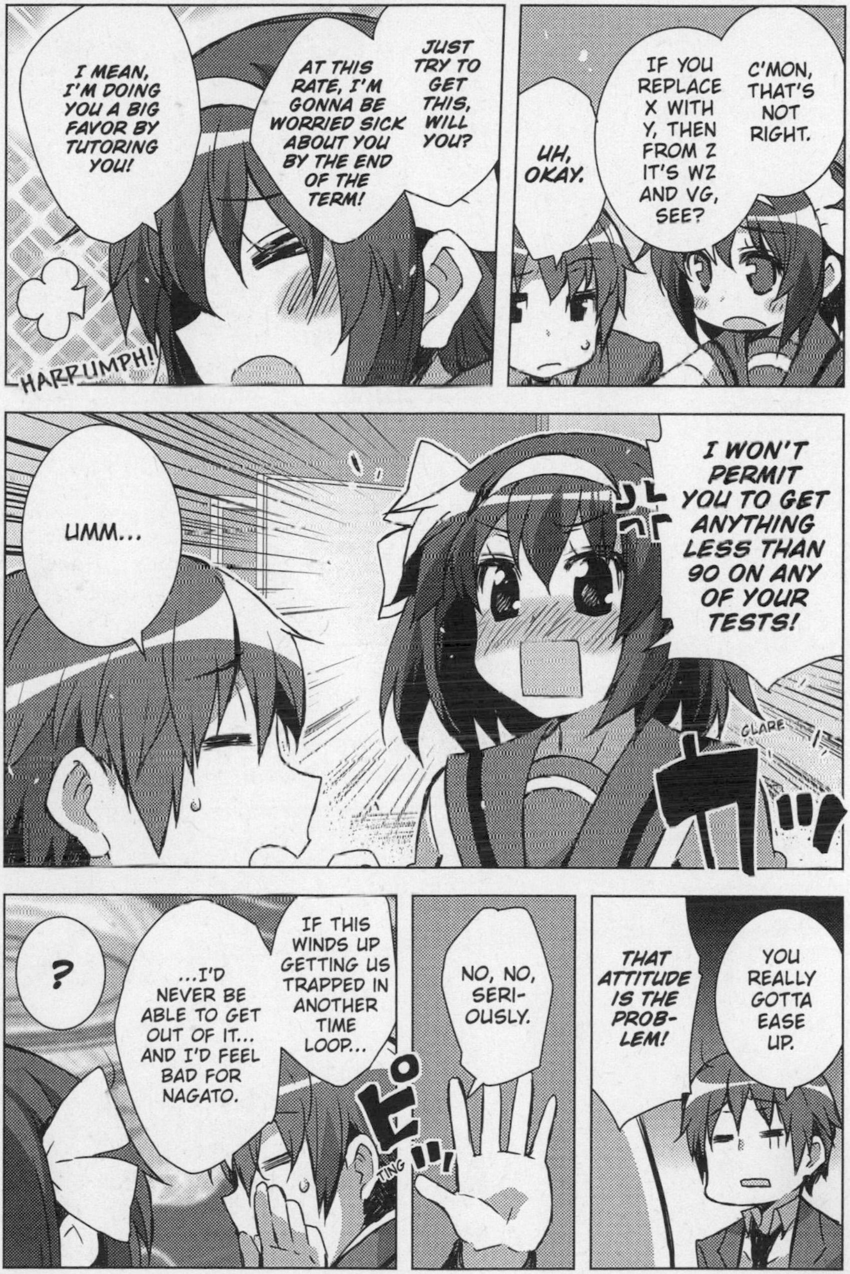
C'MON, THAT'S NOT RIGHT.
IF YOU REPLACE X WITH Y, THEN FROM Z IT'S WZ AND VG, SEE?
UH, OKAY.
JUST TRY TO GET THIS, WILL YOU?
AT THIS RATE, I'M GONNA BE WORRIED SICK ABOUT YOU BY THE END OF THE TERM!
I MEAN, I'M DOING YOU A BIG FAVOR BY TUTORING YOU!
HARRUMPH!
I WON'T PERMIT YOU TO GET ANYTHING LESS THAN 90 ON ANY OF YOUR TESTS!
GLARE
UMM...
YOU REALLY GOTTA EASE UP.
THAT ATTITUDE IS THE PROB-LEM!
NO, NO, SERI-OUSLY.
TING
IF THIS WINDS UP GETTING US TRAPPED IN ANOTHER TIME LOOP...
...I'D NEVER BE ABLE TO GET OUT OF IT... AND I'D FEEL BAD FOR NAGATO.
?

## AUTUMN OF EXERCISE ②

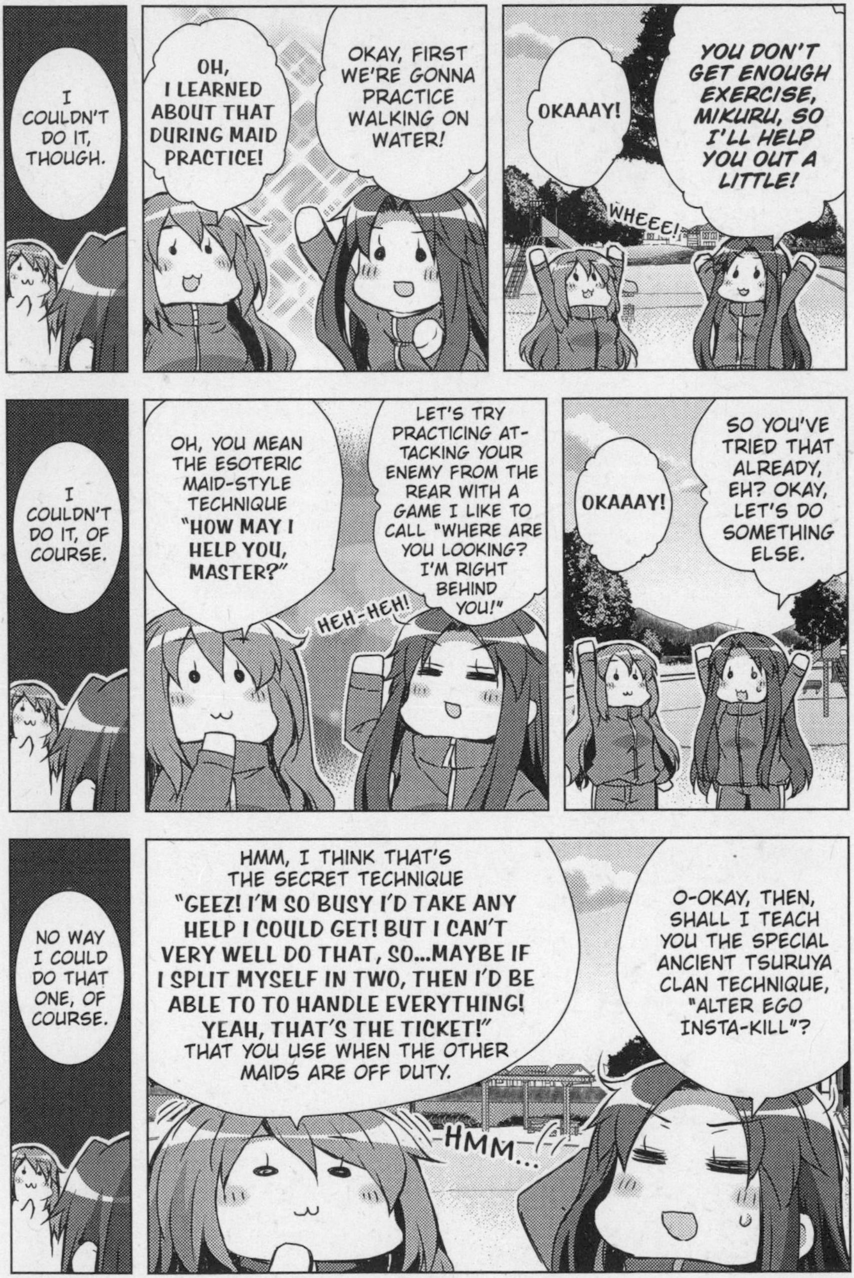
YOU DON'T GET ENOUGH EXERCISE, MIKURU, SO I'LL HELP YOU OUT A LITTLE!
OKAAAY!
WHEEE!
OKAY, FIRST WE'RE GONNA PRACTICE WALKING ON WATER!
OH, I LEARNED ABOUT THAT DURING MAID PRACTICE!
I COULDN'T DO IT, THOUGH.
SO YOU'VE TRIED THAT ALREADY, EH? OKAY, LET'S DO SOMETHING ELSE.
OKAAAY!
LET'S TRY PRACTICING AT-TACKING YOUR ENEMY FROM THE REAR WITH A GAME I LIKE TO CALL "WHERE ARE YOU LOOKING? I'M RIGHT BEHIND YOU!"
HEH-HEH!
OH, YOU MEAN THE ESOTERIC MAID-STYLE TECHNIQUE "HOW MAY I HELP YOU, MASTER?"
I COULDN'T DO IT, OF COURSE.
O-OKAY, THEN, SHALL I TEACH YOU THE SPECIAL ANCIENT TSURUYA CLAN TECHNIQUE, "ALTER EGO INSTA-KILL"?
HMM...
HMM, I THINK THAT'S THE SECRET TECHNIQUE "GEEZ! I'M SO BUSY I'D TAKE ANY HELP I COULD GET! BUT I CAN'T VERY WELL DO THAT, SO...MAYBE IF I SPLIT MYSELF IN TWO, THEN I'D BE ABLE TO TO HANDLE EVERYTHING! YEAH, THAT'S THE TICKET!" THAT YOU USE WHEN THE OTHER MAIDS ARE OFF DUTY.
NO WAY I COULD DO THAT ONE, OF COURSE.

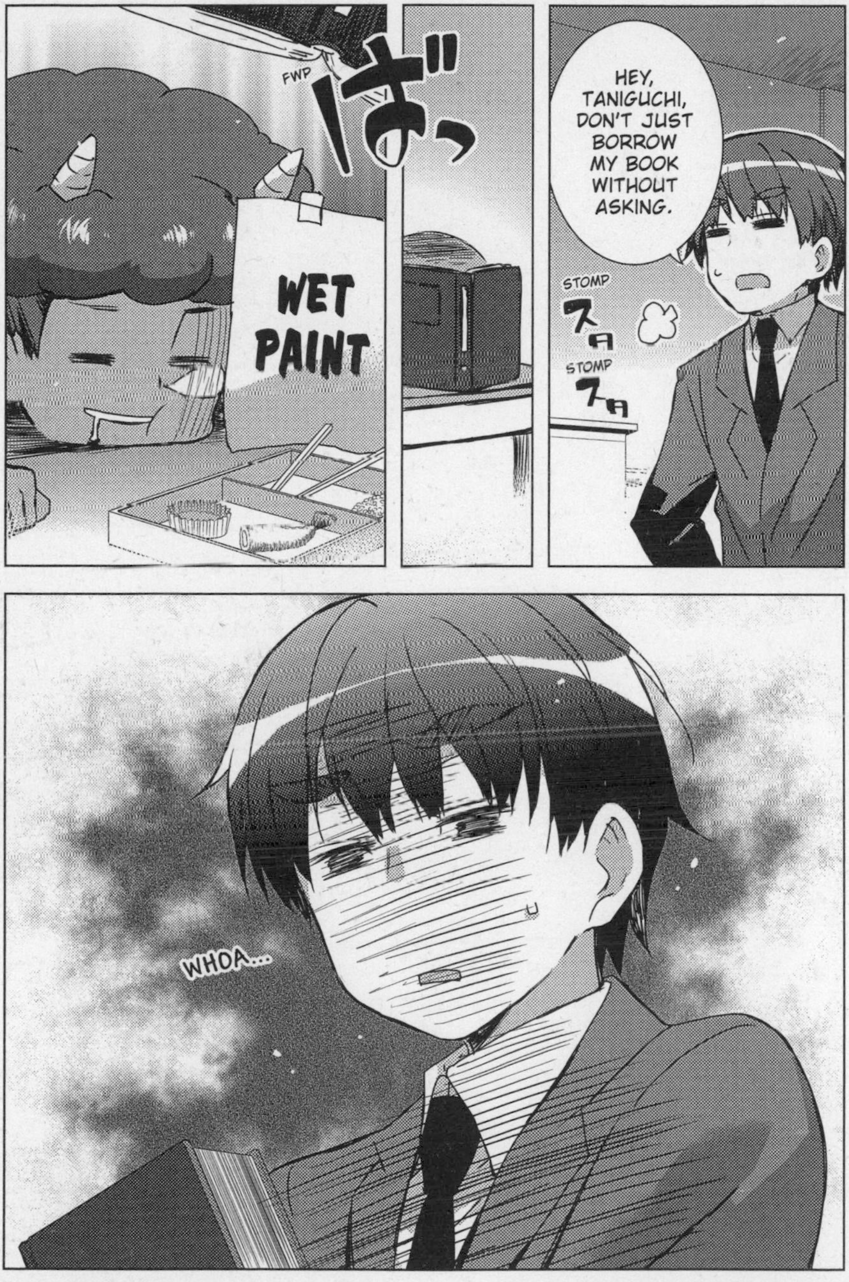
HEY, TANIGUCHI, DON'T JUST BORROW MY BOOK WITHOUT ASKING.
STOMP
スタ
STOMP
スタ
FWP
ばっ
WET PAINT
WHOA...

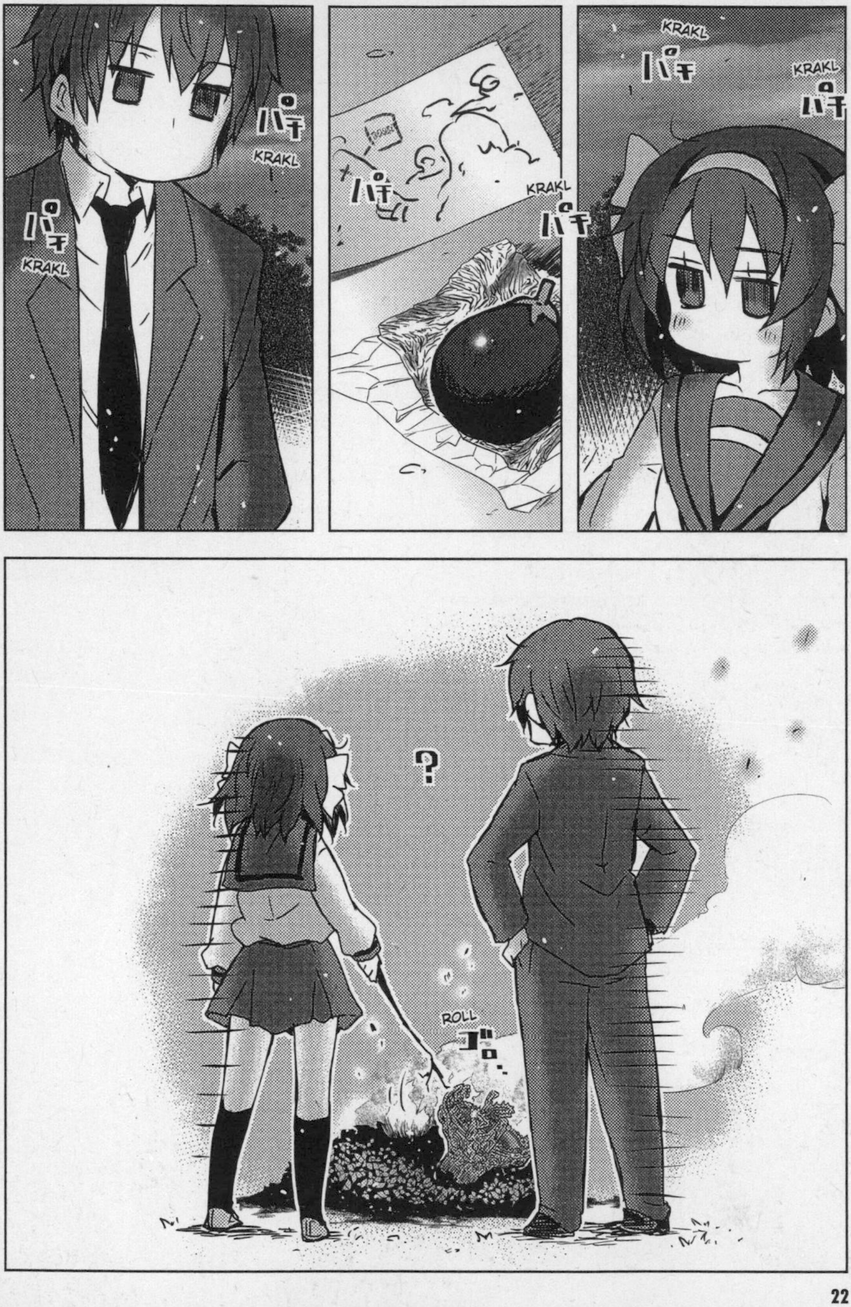
KRAKL
パチ
KRAKL
パチ
KRAKL
パチ
パチ
パチ
KRAKL
パチ
KRAKL
?
ROLL
ゴロ..

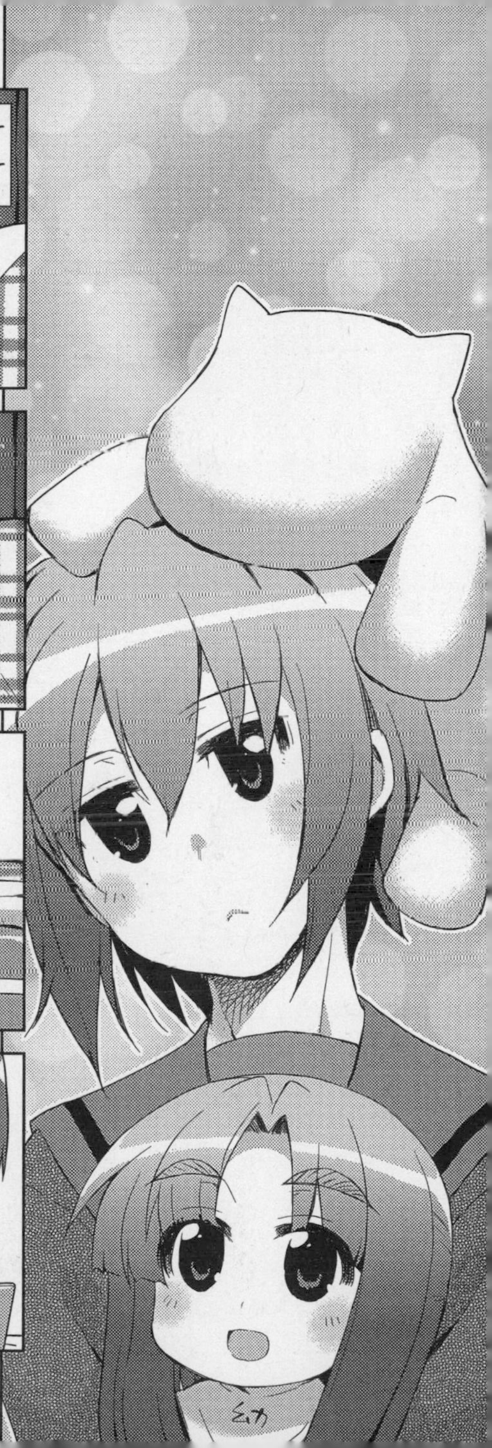

## WAKING UP

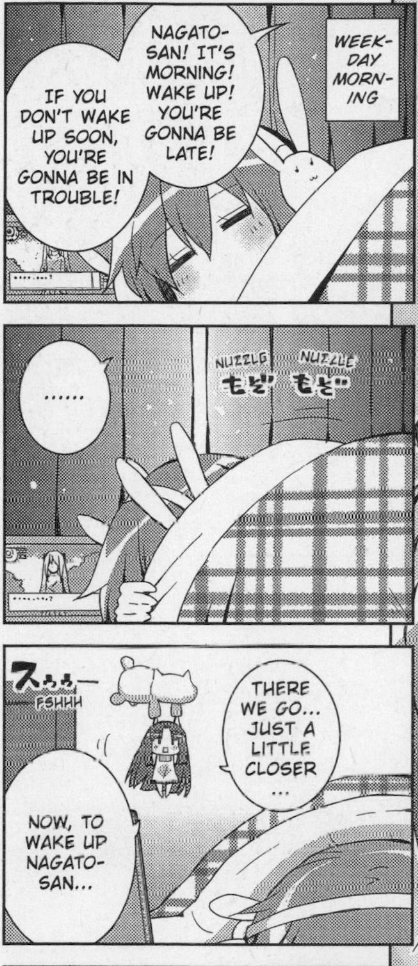

WEEK-DAY MORNING
NAGATO-SAN! IT'S MORNING! WAKE UP! YOU'RE GONNA BE LATE!
IF YOU DON'T WAKE UP SOON, YOU'RE GONNA BE IN TROUBLE!
NUZZLE NUZZLE
もぞ もぞ
......
THERE WE GO... JUST A LITTLE CLOSER ...
FSHHH
NOW, TO WAKE UP NAGATO-SAN...
...I'LL JUST DROP DOWN ON HER COMPUTER, GOOD AND HARD.
I'M AWAKE.
BOLT

SEEING OFF

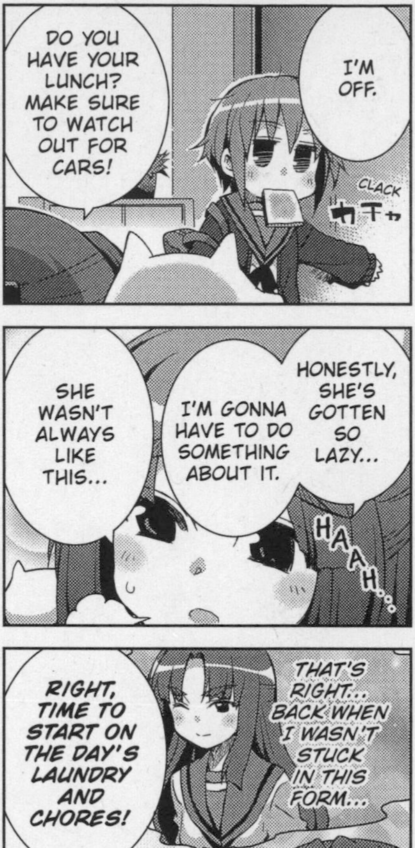
I'M OFF.
DO YOU HAVE YOUR LUNCH? MAKE SURE TO WATCH OUT FOR CARS!
CLACK
HONESTLY, SHE'S GOTTEN SO LAZY...
I'M GONNA HAVE TO DO SOMETHING ABOUT IT.
SHE WASN'T ALWAYS LIKE THIS...
HAAAH...
THAT'S RIGHT... BACK WHEN I WASN'T STUCK IN THIS FORM...
RIGHT, TIME TO START ON THE DAY'S LAUNDRY AND CHORES!
......
AND I NEVER EVEN CONSIDERED I'D BE DOING STUFF LIKE THIS BACK THEN EITHER...
OKAY, LET'S DO OUR BEST!

CONVENIENT PERVERT

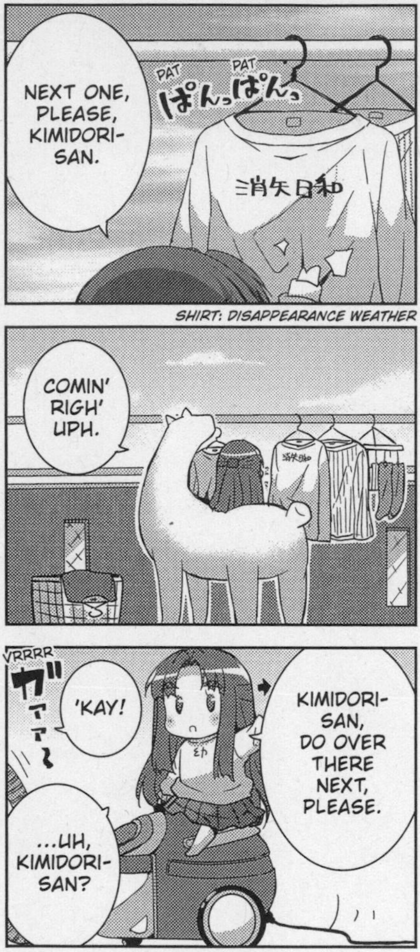
PAT PAT
NEXT ONE, PLEASE, KIMIDORI-SAN.
消失日和
SHIRT: DISAPPEARANCE WEATHER
COMIN' RIGH' UPH.
KIMIDORI-SAN, DO OVER THERE NEXT, PLEASE.
'KAY!
VRRRR
...UH, KIMIDORI-SAN?
THAT'S GOING TOO FAR.
NO GOOD, HUH?

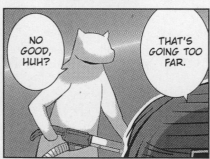

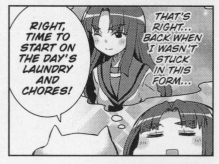

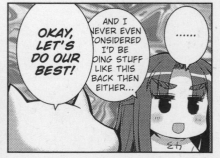

## LUNCH

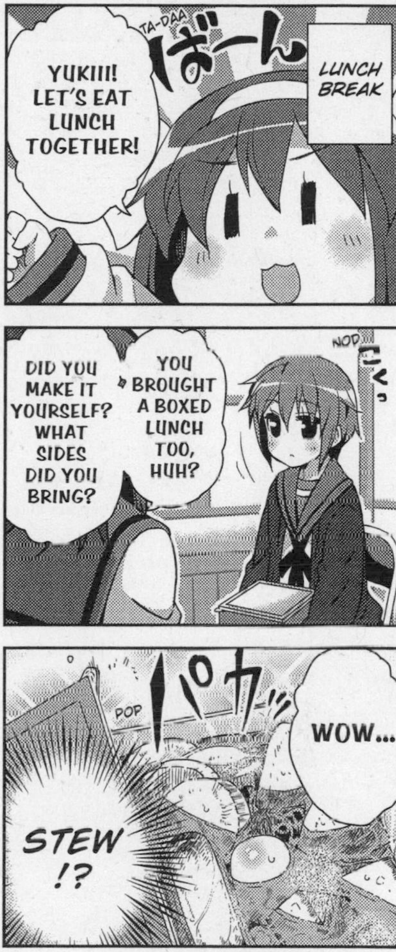
LUNCH BREAK
TA-DAA
ばーん
YUKIII! LET'S EAT LUNCH TOGETHER!
NOD
YOU BROUGHT A BOXED LUNCH TOO, HUH?
DID YOU MAKE IT YOURSELF? WHAT SIDES DID YOU BRING?
WOW...
POP
パカッ
STEW !?
LUNCH-TIME! LUNCH-TIME!
STEW AGAIN, HUH? YOU SURE LIKE THAT STUFF.

## FIFTH PERIOD P.E.

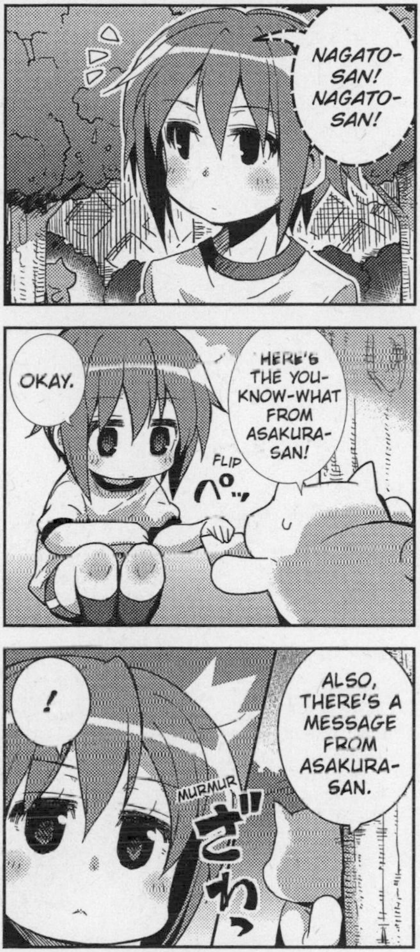
NAGATO-SAN! NAGATO-SAN!
HERE'S THE YOU-KNOW-WHAT FROM ASAKURA-SAN!
FLIP
OKAY.
ALSO, THERE'S A MESSAGE FROM ASAKURA-SAN.
MURMUR
ざわっ
!
"YOU CAN HAVE ¥500 WORTH OF SNACKS, BUT NO MORE."
UNDER-STOOD.
SHOPPING LIST

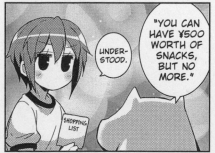

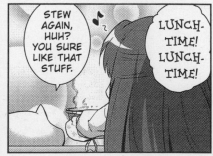

## BRINGING IN THE LAUNDRY

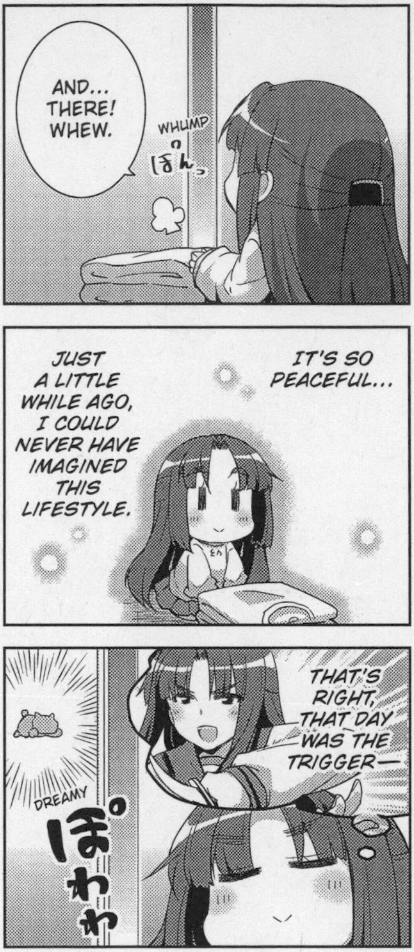
AND... THERE! WHEW.
WHUMP
ぽんっ
IT'S SO PEACEFUL...
JUST A LITTLE WHILE AGO, I COULD NEVER HAVE IMAGINED THIS LIFESTYLE.
THAT'S RIGHT, THAT DAY WAS THE TRIGGER—
DREAMY
ぽわわ
I WON'T ALLOW IT!
KABOOM
WHY ARE YOU SO DETERMINED TO STOP ME FROM DOING ANY REMINISCING!?

## EXPLANATION

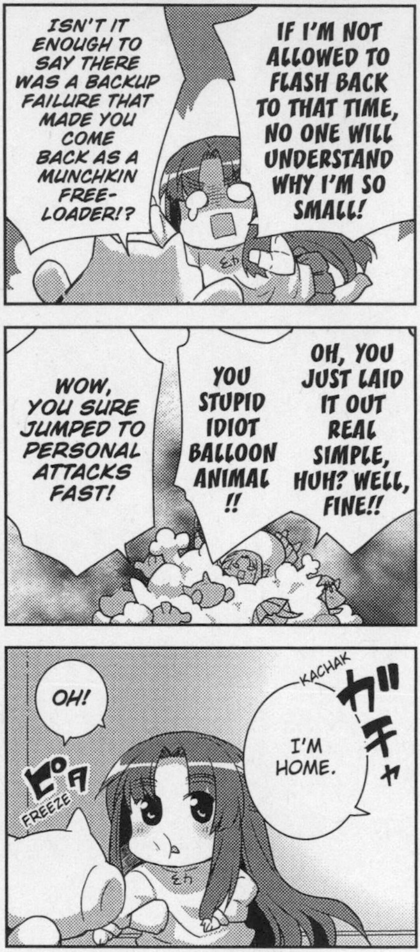
IF I'M NOT ALLOWED TO FLASH BACK TO THAT TIME, NO ONE WILL UNDERSTAND WHY I'M SO SMALL!
ISN'T IT ENOUGH TO SAY THERE WAS A BACKUP FAILURE THAT MADE YOU COME BACK AS A MUNCHKIN FREE-LOADER!?
OH, YOU JUST LAID IT OUT REAL SIMPLE, HUH? WELL, FINE!!
YOU STUPID IDIOT BALLOON ANIMAL!!
WOW, YOU SURE JUMPED TO PERSONAL ATTACKS FAST!
ガチャ
KACHAK
I'M HOME.
OH!
ピタ
FREEZE
WEL-COME HOME!
ALL IS WELL AT THE NAGATO RESI-DENCE.
すてててー
PATTER

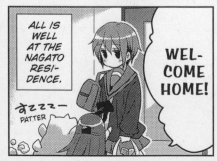

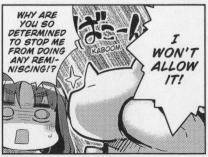

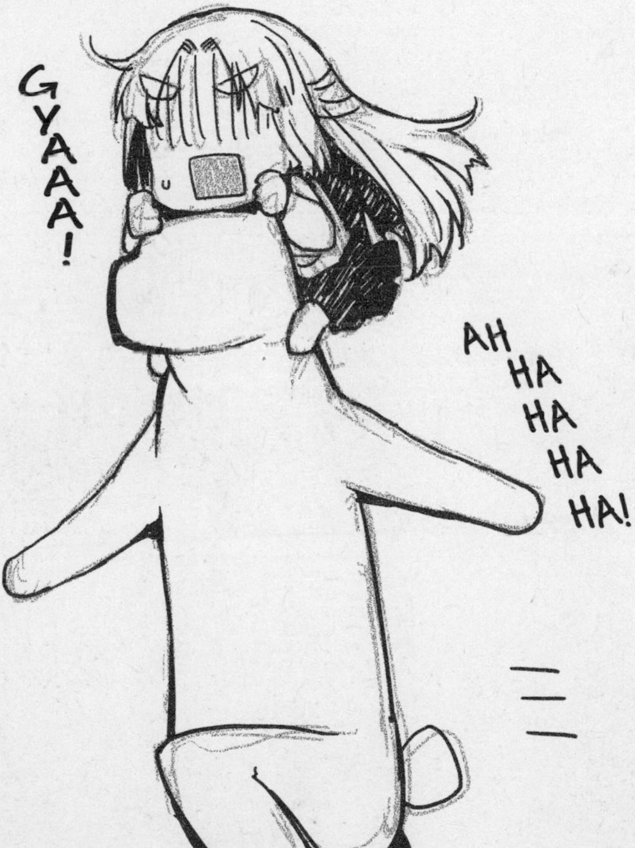
GYAAAA!
AH HA HA HA HA!

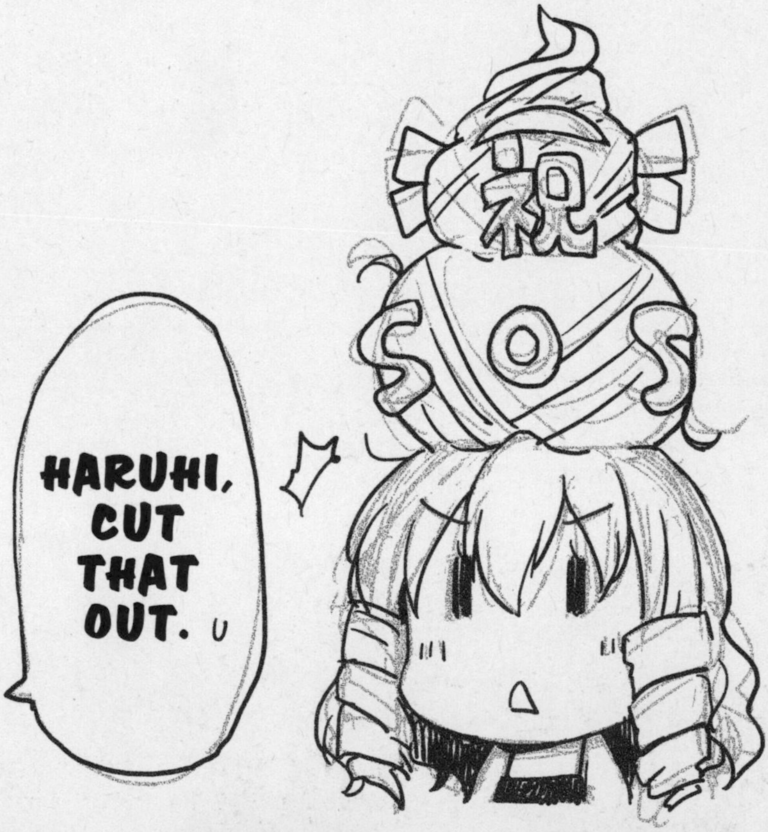
祝
SOS
HARUHI, CUT THAT OUT.

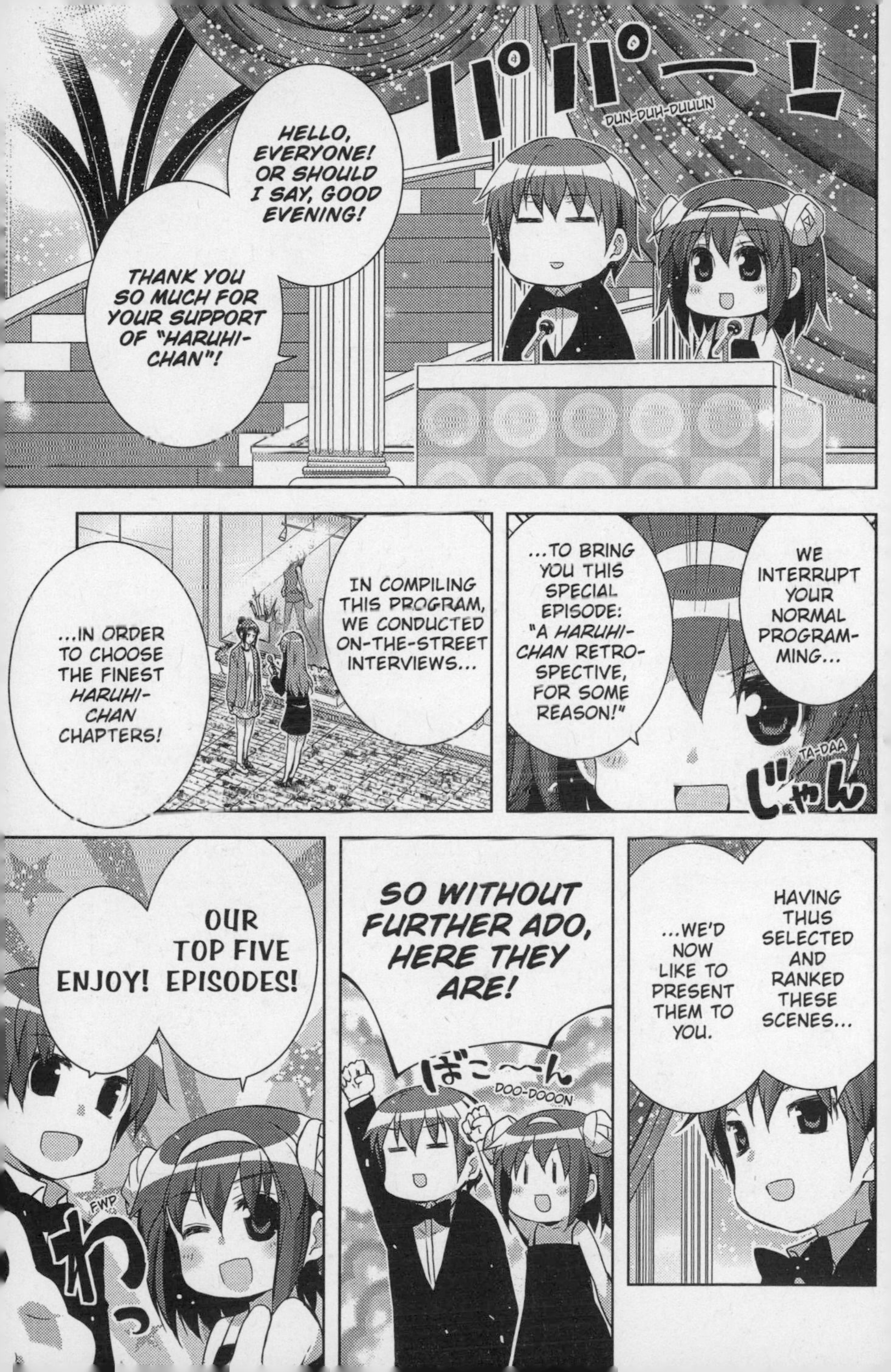
パパーー！
DUN-DUH-DUUUN
HELLO, EVERYONE! OR SHOULD I SAY, GOOD EVENING!
THANK YOU SO MUCH FOR YOUR SUPPORT OF "HARUHI-CHAN"!
WE INTERRUPT YOUR NORMAL PROGRAMMING...
...TO BRING YOU THIS SPECIAL EPISODE: "A HARUHI-CHAN RETROSPECTIVE, FOR SOME REASON!"
じゃん
TA-DAA
IN COMPILING THIS PROGRAM, WE CONDUCTED ON-THE-STREET INTERVIEWS...
...IN ORDER TO CHOOSE THE FINEST HARUHI-CHAN CHAPTERS!
HAVING THUS SELECTED AND RANKED THESE SCENES...
...WE'D NOW LIKE TO PRESENT THEM TO YOU.
SO WITHOUT FURTHER ADO, HERE THEY ARE!
ぼこ～ん
DOO-DOOON
OUR TOP FIVE EPISODES!
ENJOY!
わっ
FWP

## 5TH PLACE: *HARUHI-CHAN* CHAPTER 1, "THE BREAD PARTY OF HARUHI-CHAN"

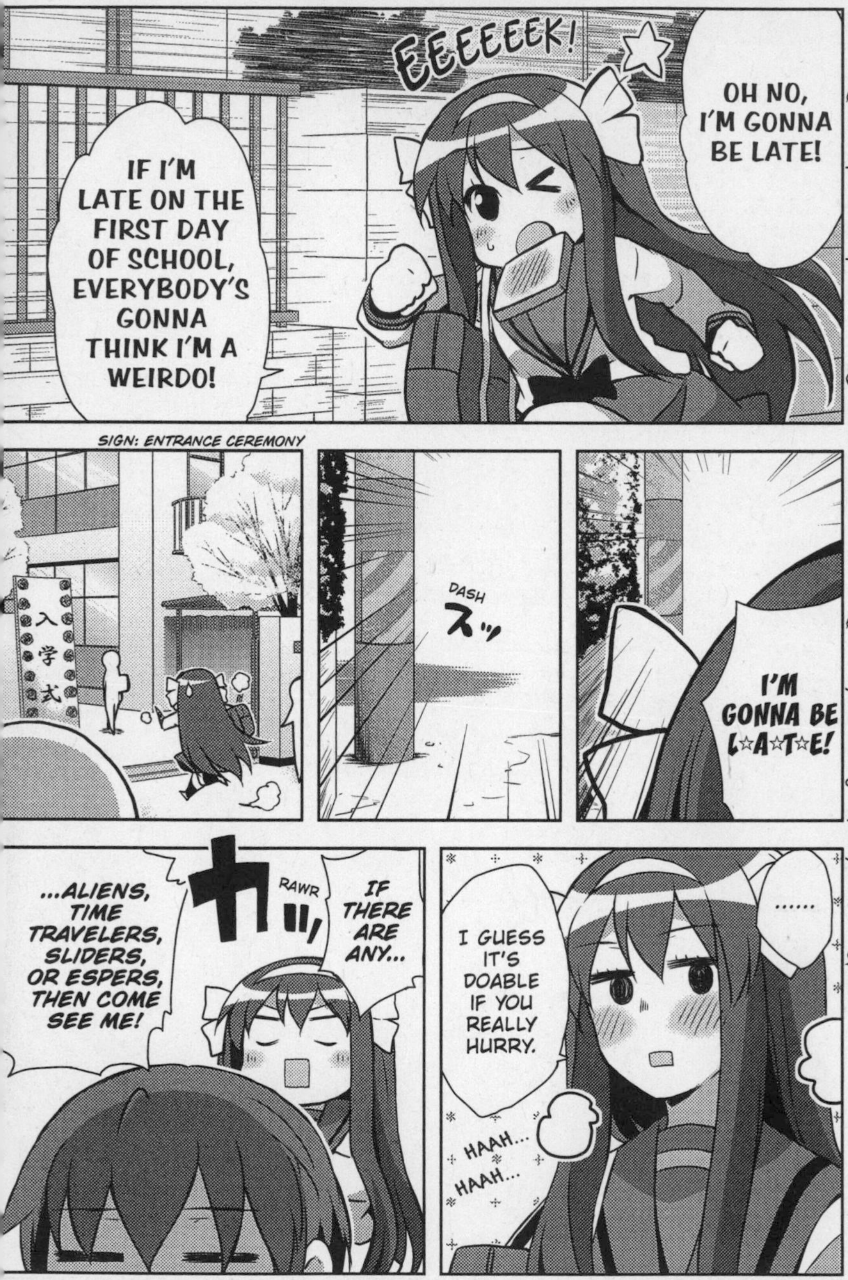
OH NO, I'M GONNA BE LATE!
EEEEEEK!
IF I'M LATE ON THE FIRST DAY OF SCHOOL, EVERYBODY'S GONNA THINK I'M A WEIRDO!
I'M GONNA BE L☆A☆T☆E!
DASH
スッ
SIGN: ENTRANCE CEREMONY
入学式
......
I GUESS IT'S DOABLE IF YOU REALLY HURRY.
HAAH... HAAH...
IF THERE ARE ANY...
RAWR
カッ
...ALIENS, TIME TRAVELERS, SLIDERS, OR ESPERS, THEN COME SEE ME!

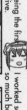

Pretty nostalgic, seeing the first chapter in the top five.

I worked so hard on so much back then!

You didn't wind up crashing into anyone or being late, did you?

I did not!

## 4TH PLACE: *HARUHI-CHAN* CHAPTER 24, "GROWING FEELINGS AFTER SCHOOL"

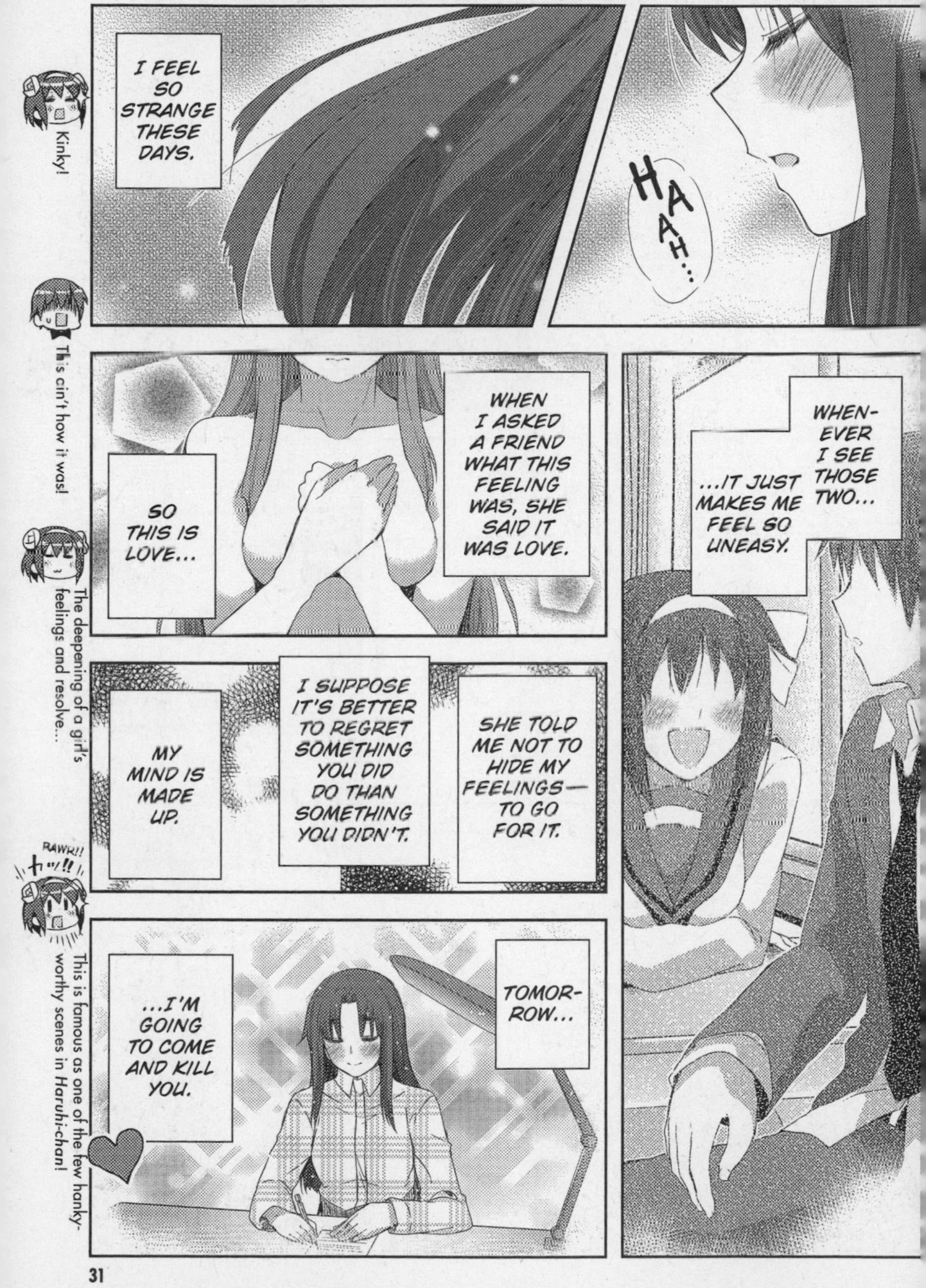
HAAH...
I FEEL SO STRANGE THESE DAYS.
WHENEVER I SEE THOSE TWO...
...IT JUST MAKES ME FEEL SO UNEASY.
WHEN I ASKED A FRIEND WHAT THIS FEELING WAS, SHE SAID IT WAS LOVE.
SO THIS IS LOVE...
SHE TOLD ME NOT TO HIDE MY FEELINGS—TO GO FOR IT.
I SUPPOSE IT'S BETTER TO REGRET SOMETHING YOU DID DO THAN SOMETHING YOU DIDN'T.
MY MIND IS MADE UP.
TOMORROW...
...I'M GOING TO COME AND KILL YOU.

Kinky!

This ain't how it was!

The deepening of a girl's feelings and resolve...

RAWR!! カッ!!

This is famous as one of the few hanky-worthy scenes in *Haruhi-chan*!

3RD PLACE: *HARUHI-CHAN* (DUBBED VERSION) NO. 7, "I AM A HERO!"

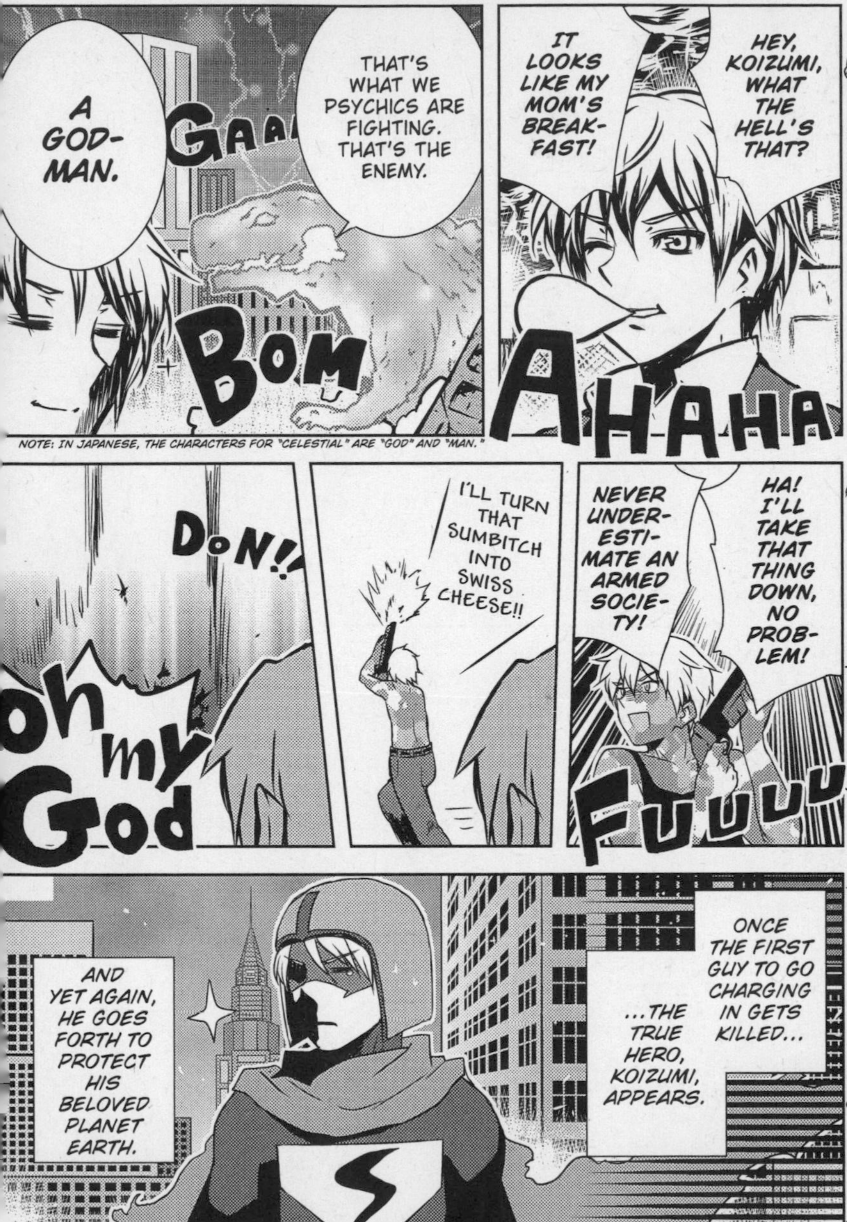
HEY, KOIZUMI, WHAT THE HELL'S THAT?
IT LOOKS LIKE MY MOM'S BREAK-FAST!
AHAHA
THAT'S WHAT WE PSYCHICS ARE FIGHTING. THAT'S THE ENEMY.
A GOD-MAN.
GAAA
BOM
NOTE: IN JAPANESE, THE CHARACTERS FOR "CELESTIAL" ARE "GOD" AND "MAN."
HA! I'LL TAKE THAT THING DOWN, NO PROB-LEM!
NEVER UNDER-ESTI-MATE AN ARMED SOCIE-TY!
FUUUU
I'LL TURN THAT SUMBITCH INTO SWISS CHEESE!!
DON!!
Oh my God
ONCE THE FIRST GUY TO GO CHARGING IN GETS KILLED...
...THE TRUE HERO, KOIZUMI, APPEARS.
AND YET AGAIN, HE GOES FORTH TO PROTECT HIS BELOVED PLANET EARTH.
TO BE CONTINUED!!

This is the foreign version of *Haruhi-chan* that was inserted while *Haruhi-chan* was on hiatus.

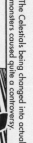

The Celestials being changed into actual monsters caused quite a controversy.

Since Koizumi's the hero, they used a muscle-bound actor for his role, which got a mixed reception.

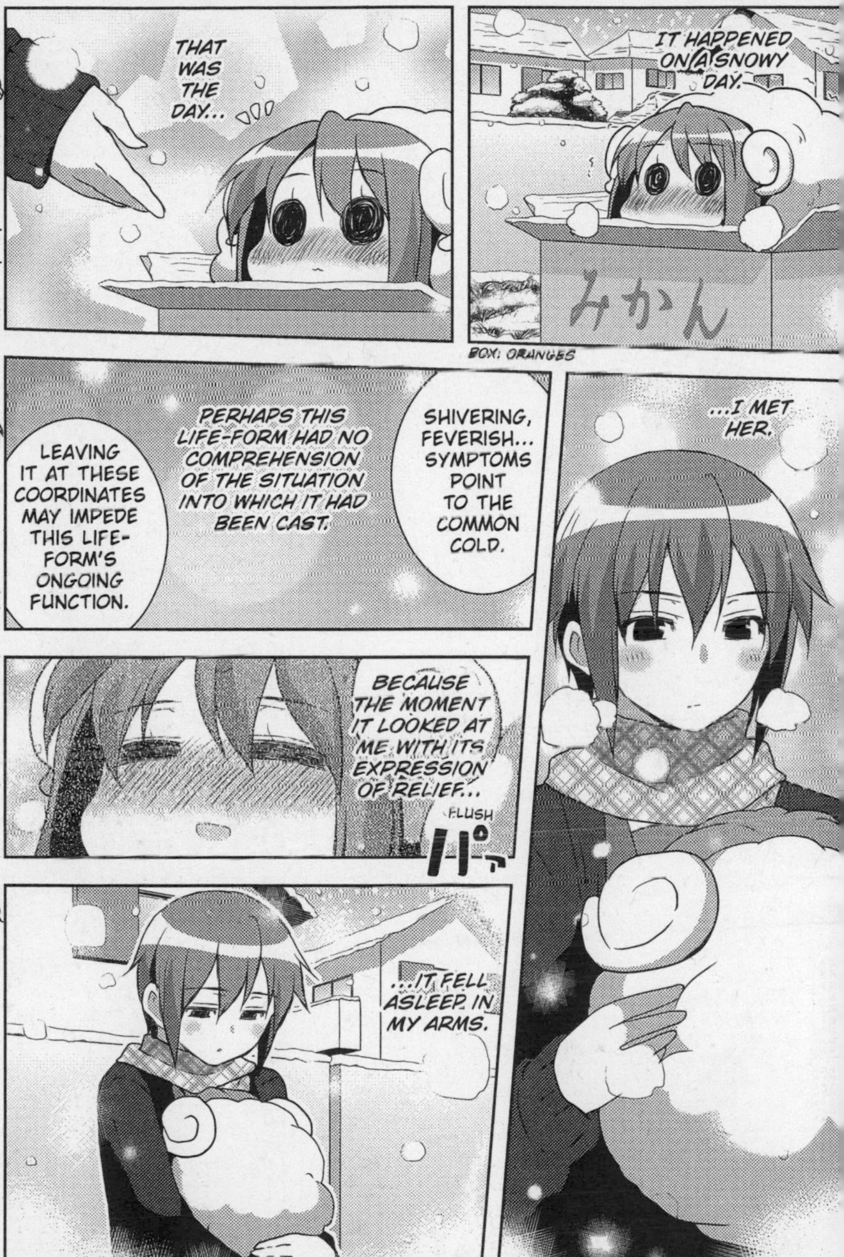
IT HAPPENED ON A SNOWY DAY.
みかん
BOX: ORANGES
THAT WAS THE DAY...
...I MET HER.
SHIVERING, FEVERISH... SYMPTOMS POINT TO THE COMMON COLD.
PERHAPS THIS LIFE-FORM HAD NO COMPREHENSION OF THE SITUATION INTO WHICH IT HAD BEEN CAST.
LEAVING IT AT THESE COORDINATES MAY IMPEDE THIS LIFE-FORM'S ONGOING FUNCTION.
BECAUSE THE MOMENT IT LOOKED AT ME WITH ITS EXPRESSION OF RELIEF...
FLUSH
...IT FELL ASLEEP IN MY ARMS.

No surprise this chapter's so high in the ranks.

Nagato's sort of clumsy, but you gotta shed a tear at how she communicates with the sheep.

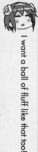

I want a ball of fluff like that too!

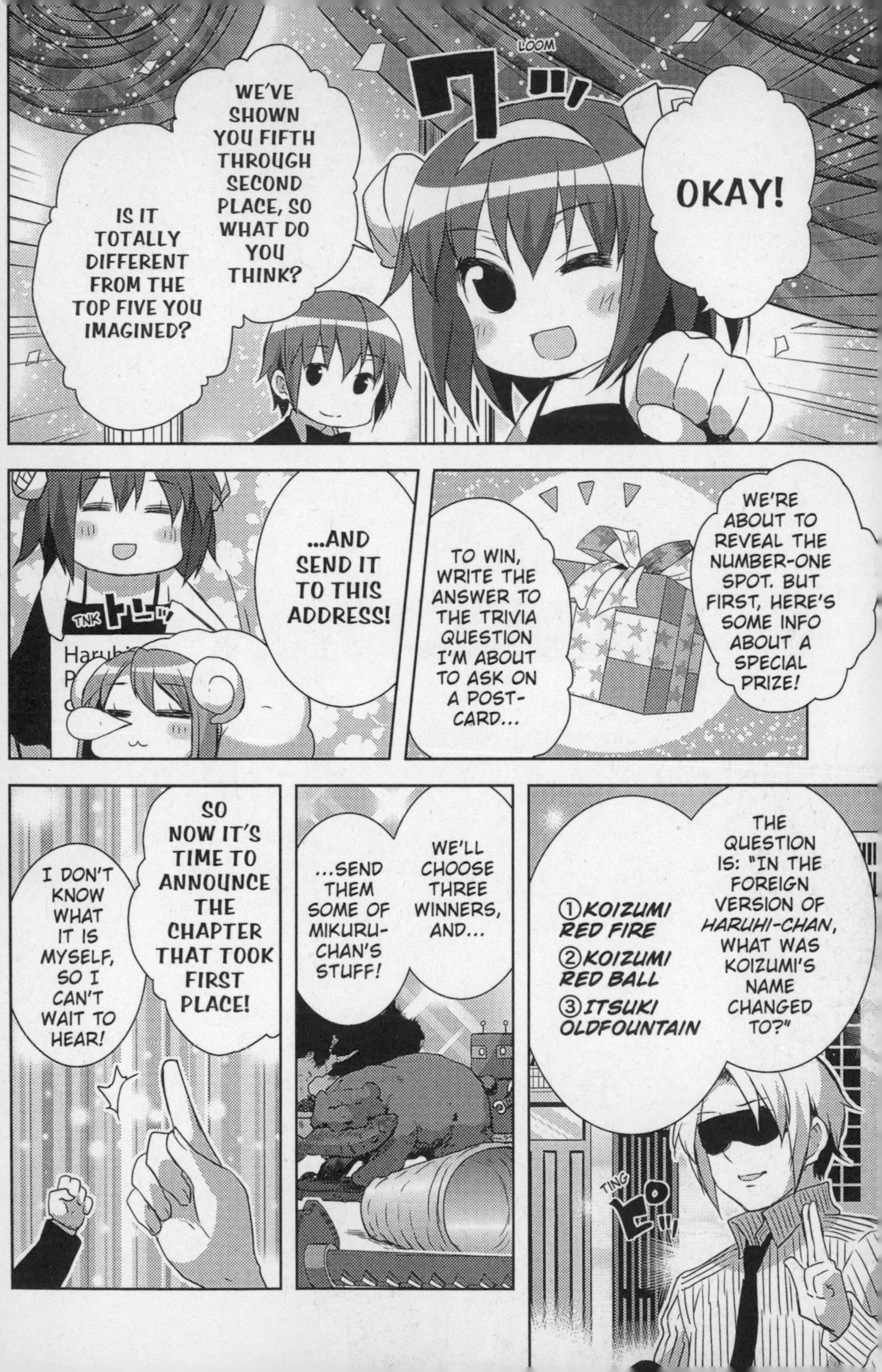
LOOM
OKAY!
WE'VE SHOWN YOU FIFTH THROUGH SECOND PLACE, SO WHAT DO YOU THINK?
IS IT TOTALLY DIFFERENT FROM THE TOP FIVE YOU IMAGINED?
WE'RE ABOUT TO REVEAL THE NUMBER-ONE SPOT. BUT FIRST, HERE'S SOME INFO ABOUT A SPECIAL PRIZE!
TO WIN, WRITE THE ANSWER TO THE TRIVIA QUESTION I'M ABOUT TO ASK ON A POST-CARD...
...AND SEND IT TO THIS ADDRESS!
TNK
THE QUESTION IS: "IN THE FOREIGN VERSION OF *HARUHI-CHAN*, WHAT WAS KOIZUMI'S NAME CHANGED TO?"
①*KOIZUMI RED FIRE*
②*KOIZUMI RED BALL*
③*ITSUKI OLDFOUNTAIN*
TING
WE'LL CHOOSE THREE WINNERS, AND...
...SEND THEM SOME OF MIKURU-CHAN'S STUFF!
SO NOW IT'S TIME TO ANNOUNCE THE CHAPTER THAT TOOK FIRST PLACE!
I DON'T KNOW WHAT IT IS MYSELF, SO I CAN'T WAIT TO HEAR!

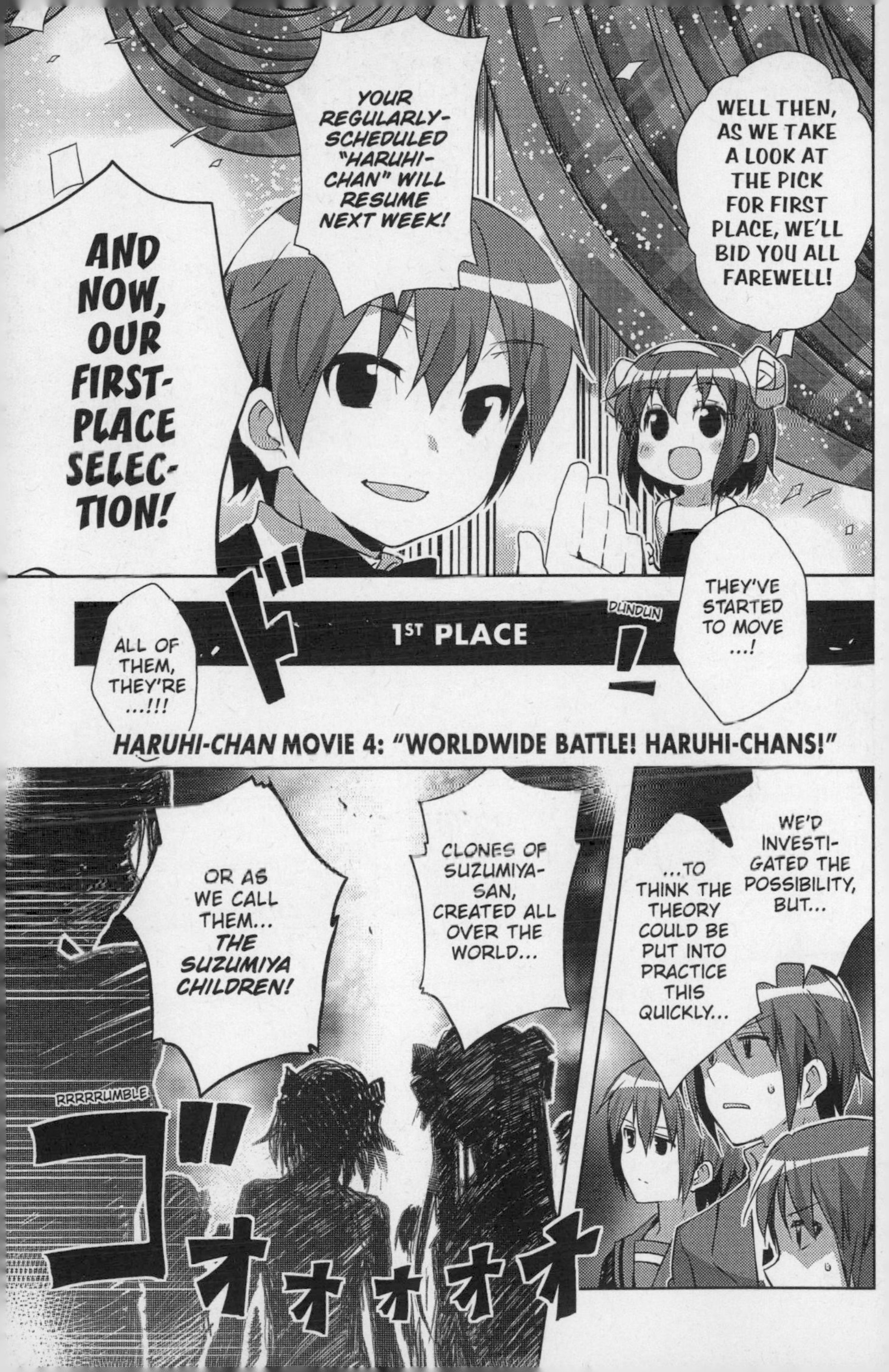
WELL THEN, AS WE TAKE A LOOK AT THE PICK FOR FIRST PLACE, WE'LL BID YOU ALL FAREWELL!
YOUR REGULARLY-SCHEDULED "HARUHI-CHAN" WILL RESUME NEXT WEEK!
AND NOW, OUR FIRST-PLACE SELECTION!
DUNDUN
1ST PLACE
THEY'VE STARTED TO MOVE ...!
ALL OF THEM, THEY'RE ...!!!
HARUHI-CHAN MOVIE 4: "WORLDWIDE BATTLE! HARUHI-CHANS!"
WE'D INVESTIGATED THE POSSIBILITY, BUT...
...TO THINK THE THEORY COULD BE PUT INTO PRACTICE THIS QUICKLY...
CLONES OF SUZUMIYA-SAN, CREATED ALL OVER THE WORLD...
OR AS WE CALL THEM... THE SUZUMIYA CHILDREN!
RRRRRUMBLE

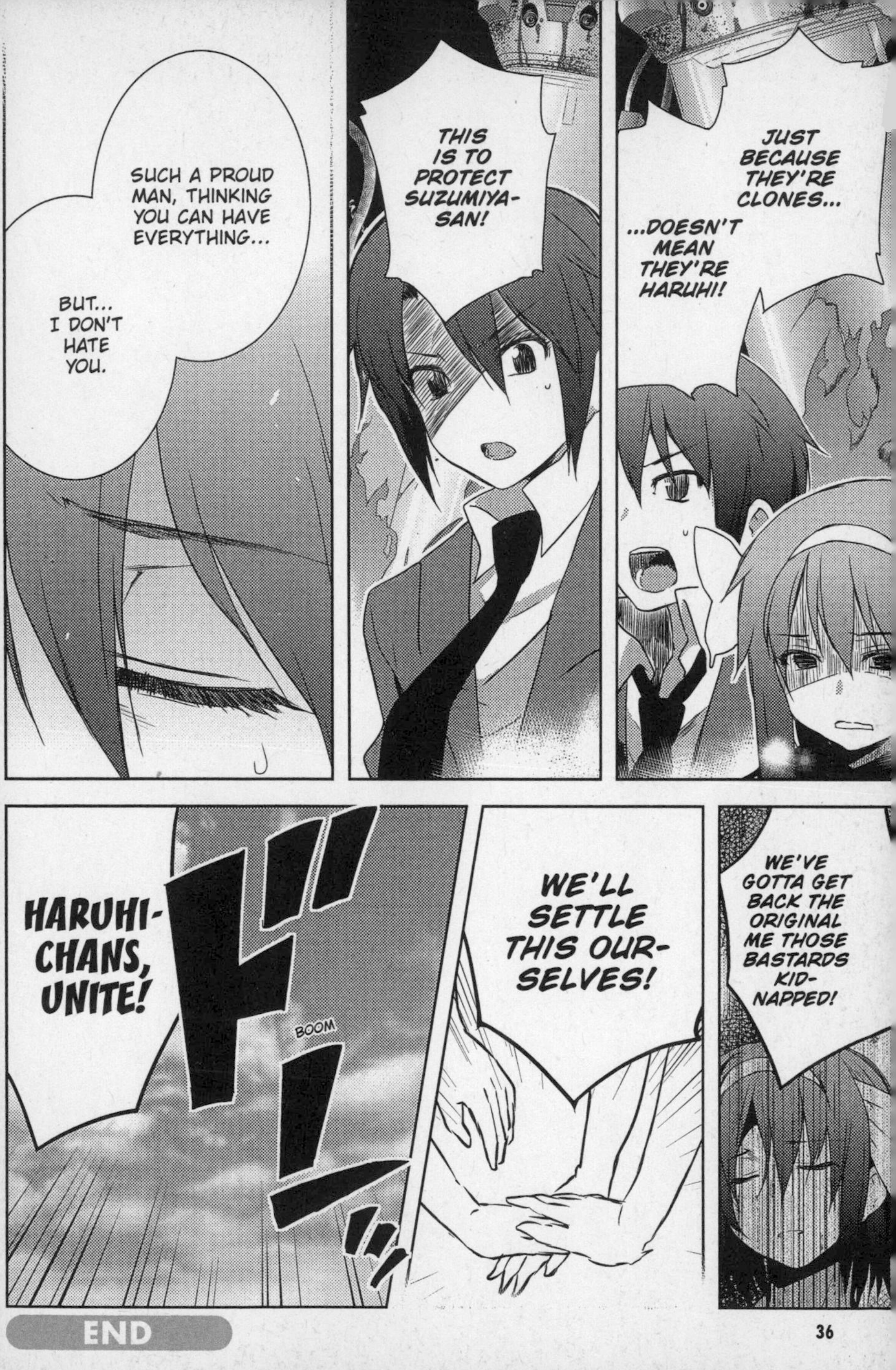
JUST BECAUSE THEY'RE CLONES...
...DOESN'T MEAN THEY'RE HARUHI!
THIS IS TO PROTECT SUZUMIYA-SAN!
SUCH A PROUD MAN, THINKING YOU CAN HAVE EVERYTHING...
BUT... I DON'T HATE YOU.
WE'VE GOTTA GET BACK THE ORIGINAL ME THOSE BASTARDS KID-NAPPED!
WE'LL SETTLE THIS OUR-SELVES!
HARUHI-CHANS, UNITE!
BOOM

END

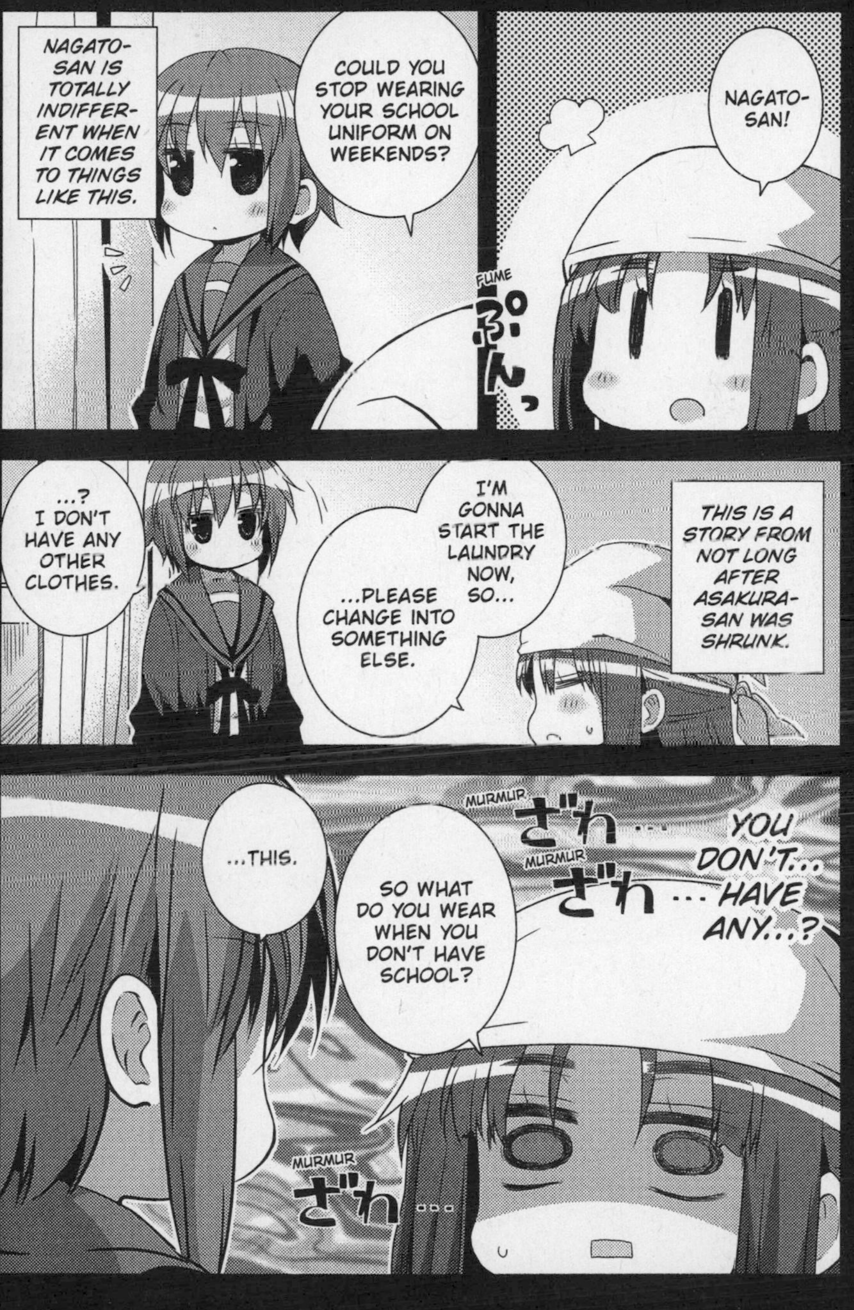
NAGATO-SAN!
FUME
ぷんっ
COULD YOU STOP WEARING YOUR SCHOOL UNIFORM ON WEEKENDS?
NAGATO-SAN IS TOTALLY INDIFFERENT WHEN IT COMES TO THINGS LIKE THIS.
THIS IS A STORY FROM NOT LONG AFTER ASAKURA-SAN WAS SHRUNK.
I'M GONNA START THE LAUNDRY NOW, SO...
...PLEASE CHANGE INTO SOMETHING ELSE.
...? I DON'T HAVE ANY OTHER CLOTHES.
YOU DON'T... HAVE ANY...?
MURMUR
ざわ...
MURMUR
ざわ...
SO WHAT DO YOU WEAR WHEN YOU DON'T HAVE SCHOOL?
...THIS.
MURMUR
ざわ...

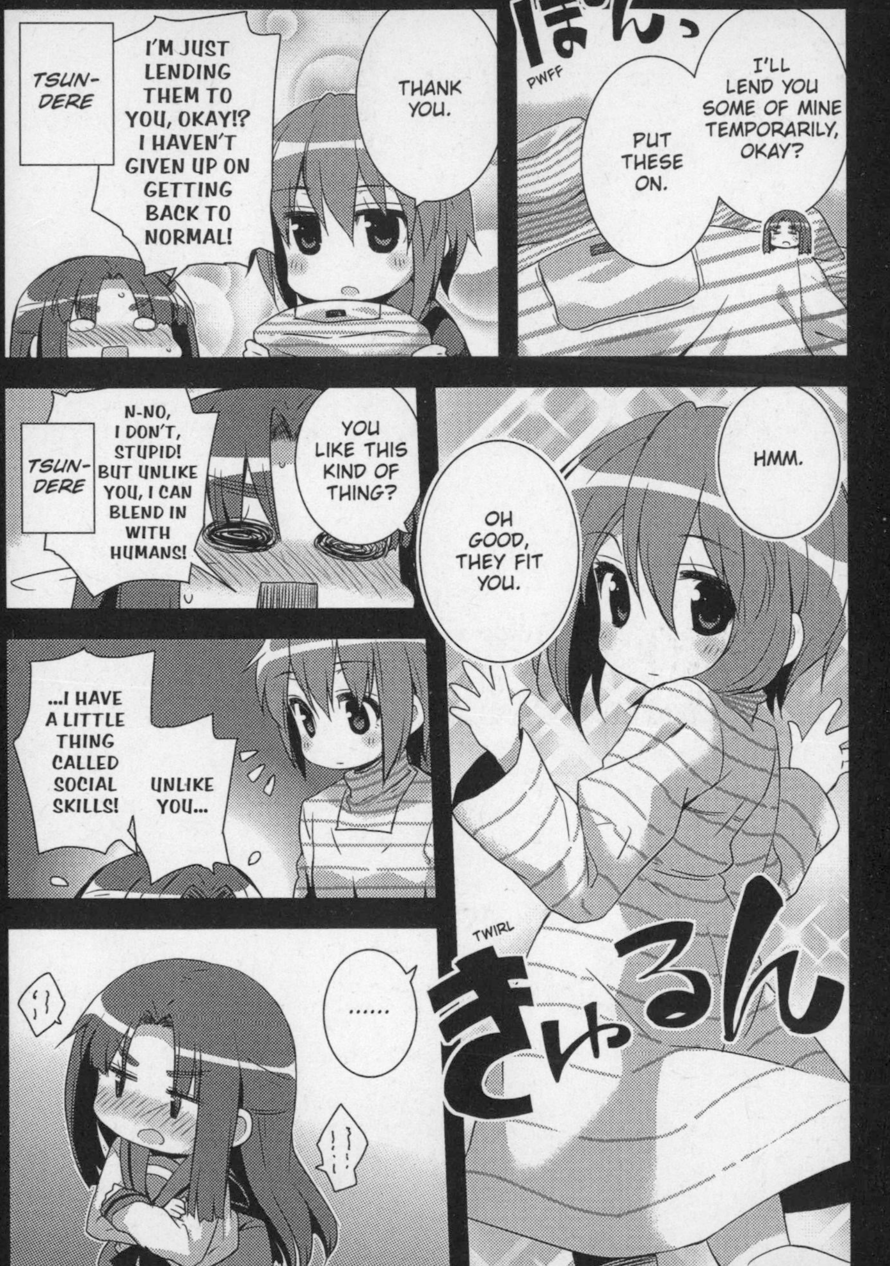

ぽんっ
PWFF
I'LL LEND YOU SOME OF MINE TEMPORARILY, OKAY?
PUT THESE ON.
THANK YOU.
I'M JUST LENDING THEM TO YOU, OKAY!? I HAVEN'T GIVEN UP ON GETTING BACK TO NORMAL!
TSUN-DERE
HMM.
OH GOOD, THEY FIT YOU.
TWIRL
きゅるん
YOU LIKE THIS KIND OF THING?
N-NO, I DON'T, STUPID! BUT UNLIKE YOU, I CAN BLEND IN WITH HUMANS!
TSUN-DERE
UNLIKE YOU...
...I HAVE A LITTLE THING CALLED SOCIAL SKILLS!
......

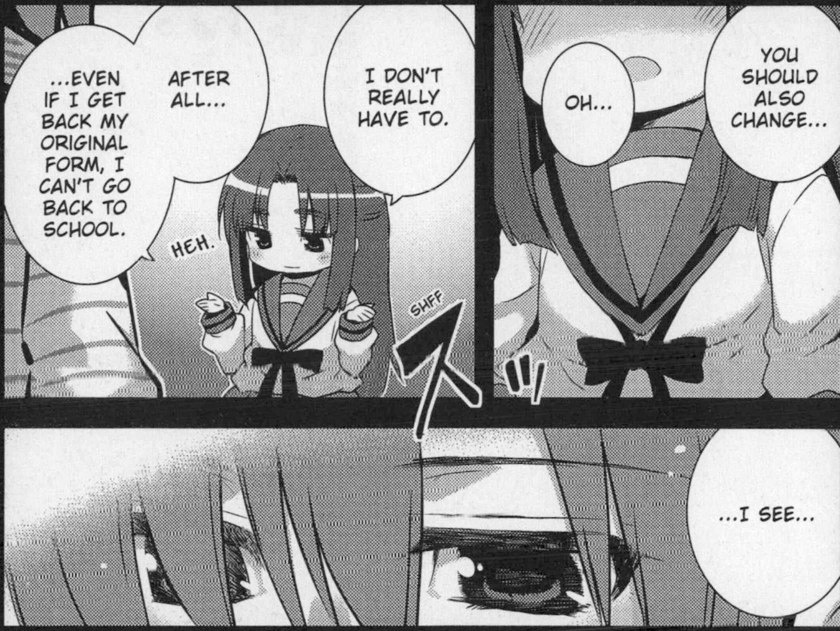
YOU SHOULD ALSO CHANGE...
OH...
I DON'T REALLY HAVE TO.
AFTER ALL...
...EVEN IF I GET BACK MY ORIGINAL FORM, I CAN'T GO BACK TO SCHOOL.
HEH.
SHFF
...I SEE...

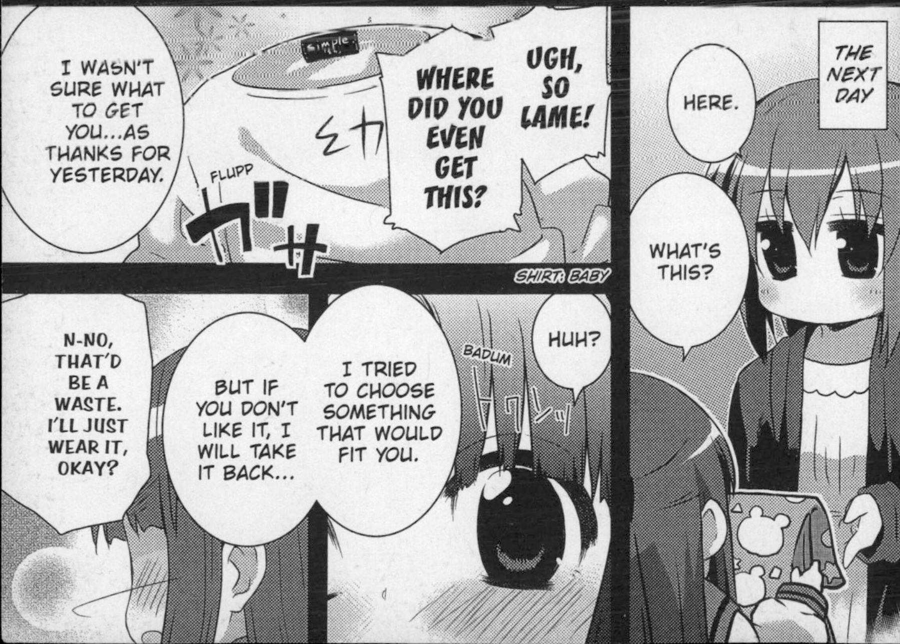
THE NEXT DAY
HERE.
WHAT'S THIS?
UGH, SO LAME!
WHERE DID YOU EVEN GET THIS?
simple
I WASN'T SURE WHAT TO GET YOU...AS THANKS FOR YESTERDAY.
FLUPP
SHIRT: BABY
HUH?
BADUM
I TRIED TO CHOOSE SOMETHING THAT WOULD FIT YOU.
BUT IF YOU DON'T LIKE IT, I WILL TAKE IT BACK...
N-NO, THAT'D BE A WASTE. I'LL JUST WEAR IT, OKAY?

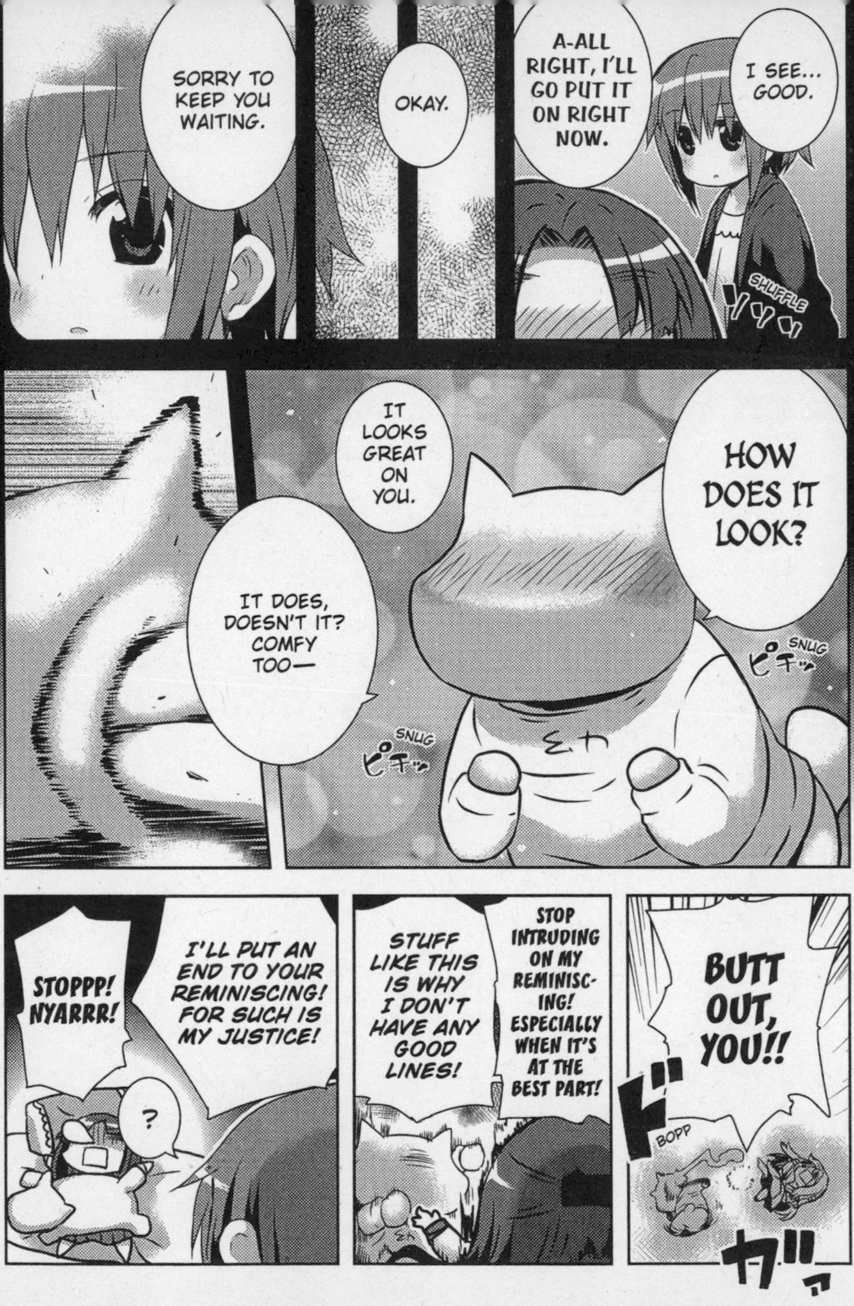
I SEE... GOOD.
A-ALL RIGHT, I'LL GO PUT IT ON RIGHT NOW.
SHUFFLE
OKAY.
SORRY TO KEEP YOU WAITING.
HOW DOES IT LOOK?
IT LOOKS GREAT ON YOU.
SNUG
IT DOES, DOESN'T IT? COMFY TOO—
SNUG
BUTT OUT, YOU!!
BOPP
STOP INTRUDING ON MY REMINISC-ING! ESPECIALLY WHEN IT'S AT THE BEST PART!
STUFF LIKE THIS IS WHY I DON'T HAVE ANY GOOD LINES!
I'LL PUT AN END TO YOUR REMINISCING! FOR SUCH IS MY JUSTICE!
STOPPP! NYARRR!
?

TALL
MEDIUM
SMALL
BABY

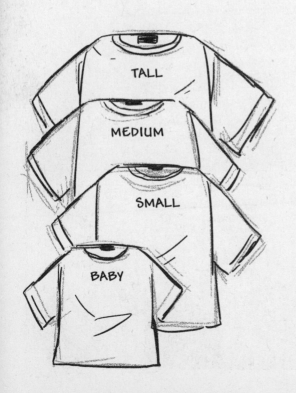

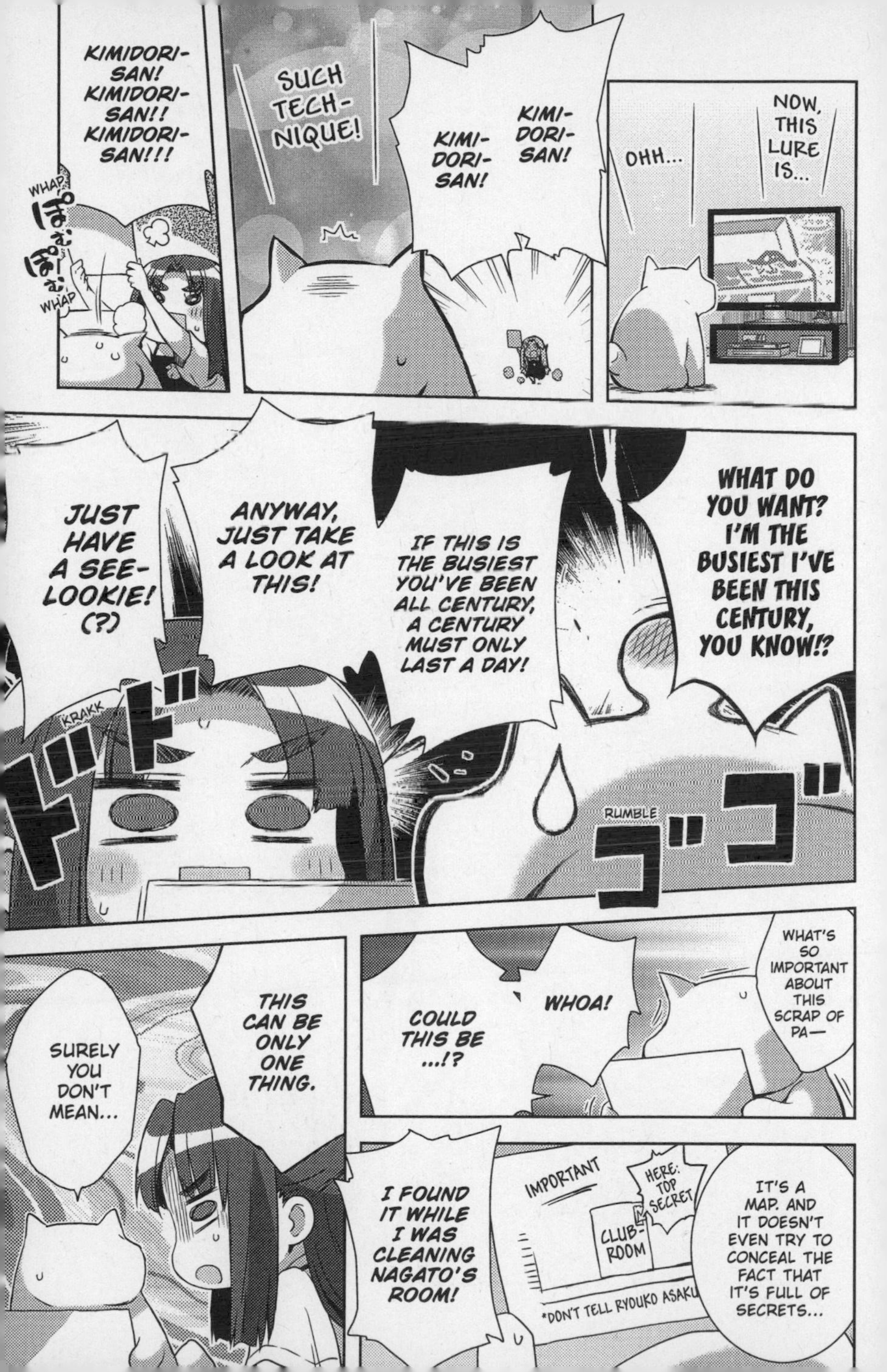
NOW, THIS LURE IS...
OHH...
KIMI-DORI-SAN!
KIMI-DORI-SAN!
SUCH TECH-NIQUE!
KIMIDORI-SAN! KIMIDORI-SAN!! KIMIDORI-SAN!!!
WHAP
WHAP
WHAT DO YOU WANT? I'M THE BUSIEST I'VE BEEN THIS CENTURY, YOU KNOW!?
RUMBLE
ゴゴ
IF THIS IS THE BUSIEST YOU'VE BEEN ALL CENTURY, A CENTURY MUST ONLY LAST A DAY!
ANYWAY, JUST TAKE A LOOK AT THIS!
JUST HAVE A SEE-LOOKIE! (?)
KRAKK
ドド
WHAT'S SO IMPORTANT ABOUT THIS SCRAP OF PA—
WHOA!
COULD THIS BE ...!?
IT'S A MAP. AND IT DOESN'T EVEN TRY TO CONCEAL THE FACT THAT IT'S FULL OF SECRETS...
HERE: TOP SECRET
IMPORTANT
CLUB-ROOM
*DON'T TELL RYOUKO ASAKU
I FOUND IT WHILE I WAS CLEANING NAGATO'S ROOM!
THIS CAN BE ONLY ONE THING.
SURELY YOU DON'T MEAN...

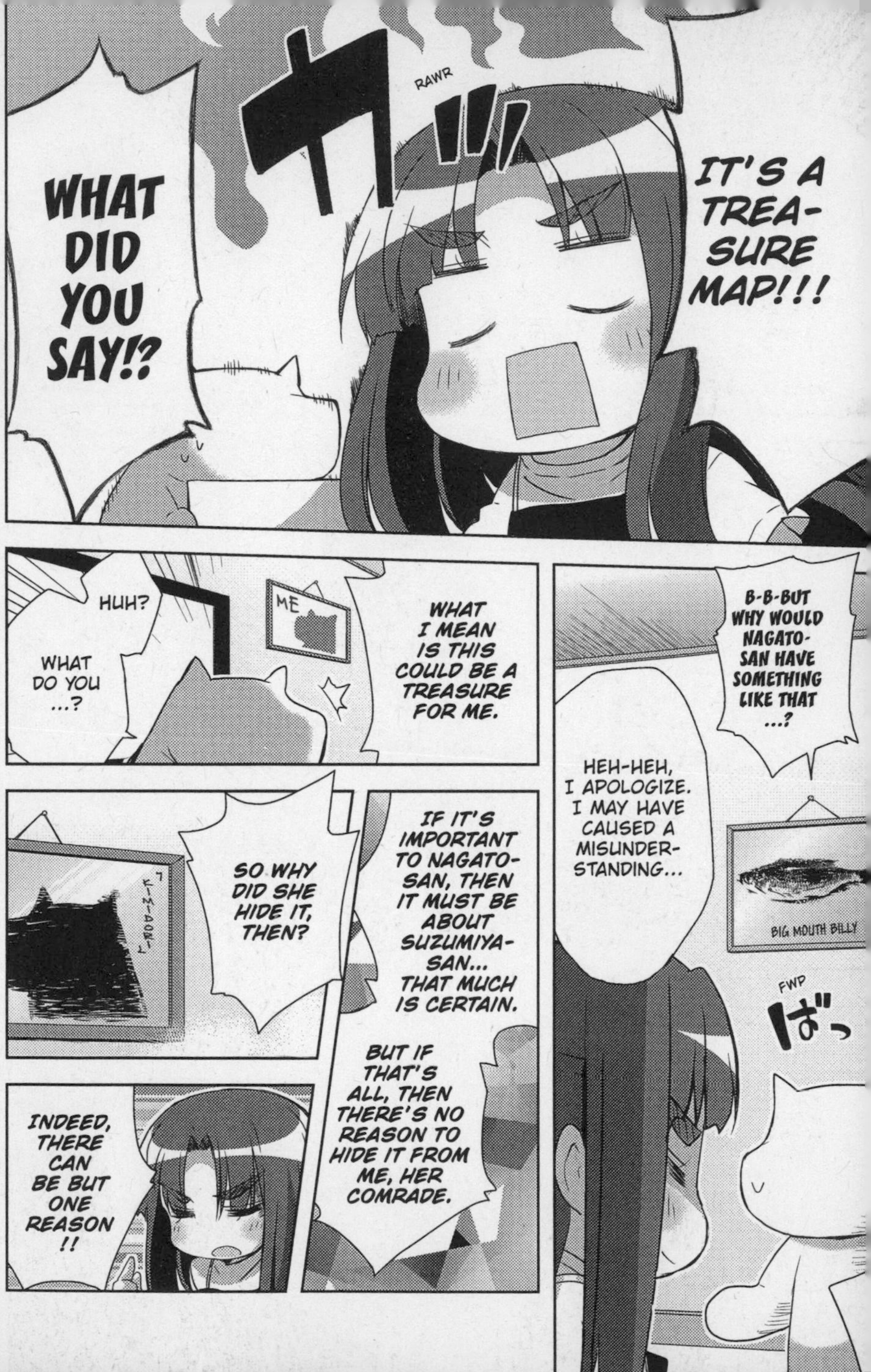
RAWR
IT'S A TREA-SURE MAP!!!
WHAT DID YOU SAY!?
B-B-BUT WHY WOULD NAGATO-SAN HAVE SOMETHING LIKE THAT ...?
HEH-HEH, I APOLOGIZE. I MAY HAVE CAUSED A MISUNDERSTANDING...
BIG MOUTH BILLY
FWP
ばっ
WHAT I MEAN IS THIS COULD BE A TREASURE FOR ME.
ME
HUH?
WHAT DO YOU ...?
IF IT'S IMPORTANT TO NAGATO-SAN, THEN IT MUST BE ABOUT SUZUMIYA-SAN... THAT MUCH IS CERTAIN.
SO WHY DID SHE HIDE IT, THEN?
KIMIDORI
BUT IF THAT'S ALL, THEN THERE'S NO REASON TO HIDE IT FROM ME, HER COMRADE.
INDEED, THERE CAN BE BUT ONE REASON !!

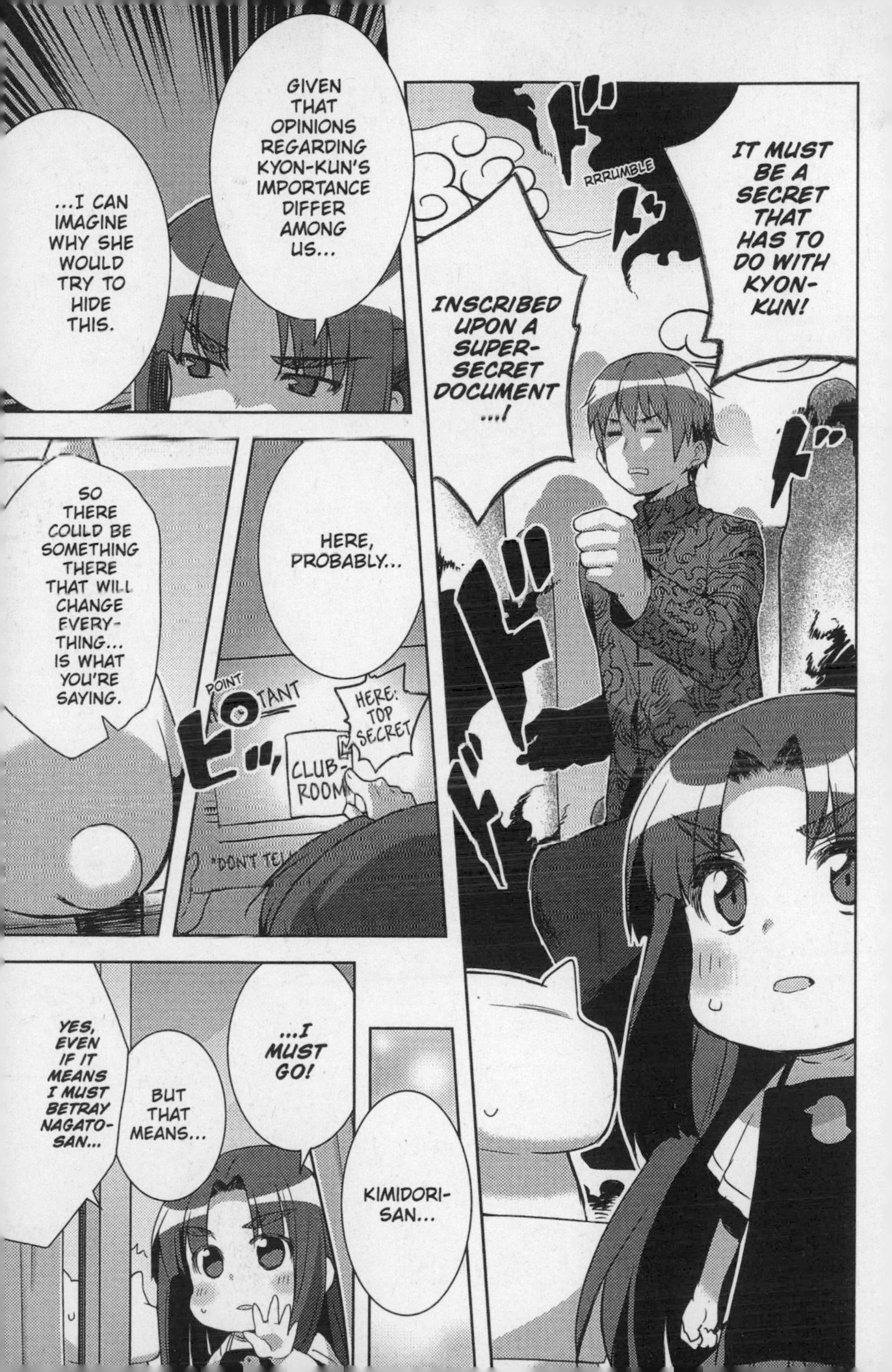
IT MUST BE A SECRET THAT HAS TO DO WITH KYON-KUN!
RRRUMBLE
INSCRIBED UPON A SUPER-SECRET DOCUMENT ...!
GIVEN THAT OPINIONS REGARDING KYON-KUN'S IMPORTANCE DIFFER AMONG US...
...I CAN IMAGINE WHY SHE WOULD TRY TO HIDE THIS.
HERE, PROBABLY...
HERE: TOP SECRET
CLUB-ROOM
POINT
SO THERE COULD BE SOMETHING THERE THAT WILL CHANGE EVERY-THING... IS WHAT YOU'RE SAYING.
KIMIDORI-SAN...
...I MUST GO!
BUT THAT MEANS...
YES, EVEN IF IT MEANS I MUST BETRAY NAGATO-SAN...

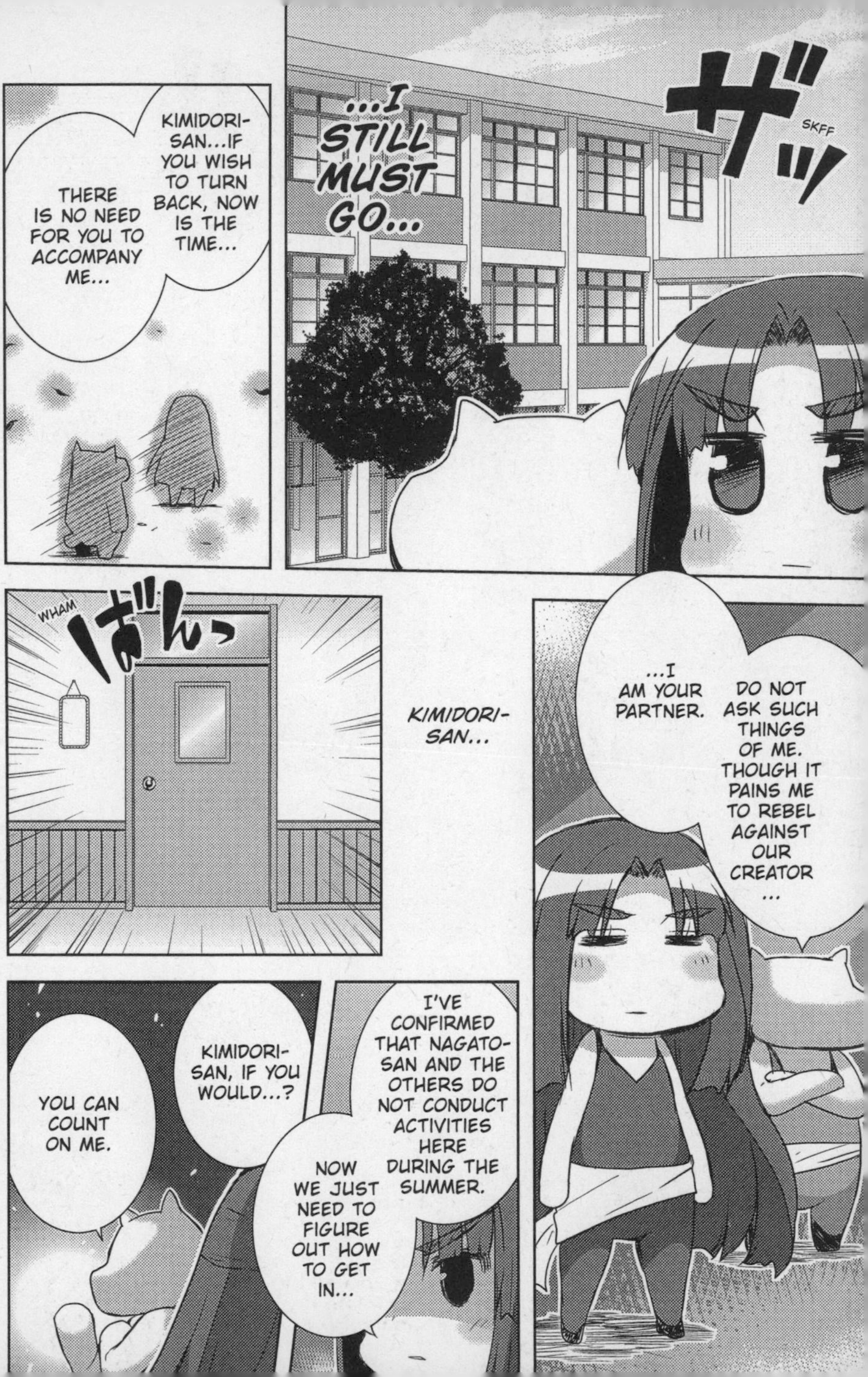
ザッ
SKFF
...I STILL MUST GO...
KIMIDORI-SAN...IF YOU WISH TO TURN BACK, NOW IS THE TIME...
THERE IS NO NEED FOR YOU TO ACCOMPANY ME...
KIMIDORI-SAN...
DO NOT ASK SUCH THINGS OF ME. THOUGH IT PAINS ME TO REBEL AGAINST OUR CREATOR...
...I AM YOUR PARTNER.
ばんっ
WHAM
I'VE CONFIRMED THAT NAGATO-SAN AND THE OTHERS DO NOT CONDUCT ACTIVITIES HERE DURING THE SUMMER.
NOW WE JUST NEED TO FIGURE OUT HOW TO GET IN...
KIMIDORI-SAN, IF YOU WOULD...?
YOU CAN COUNT ON ME.

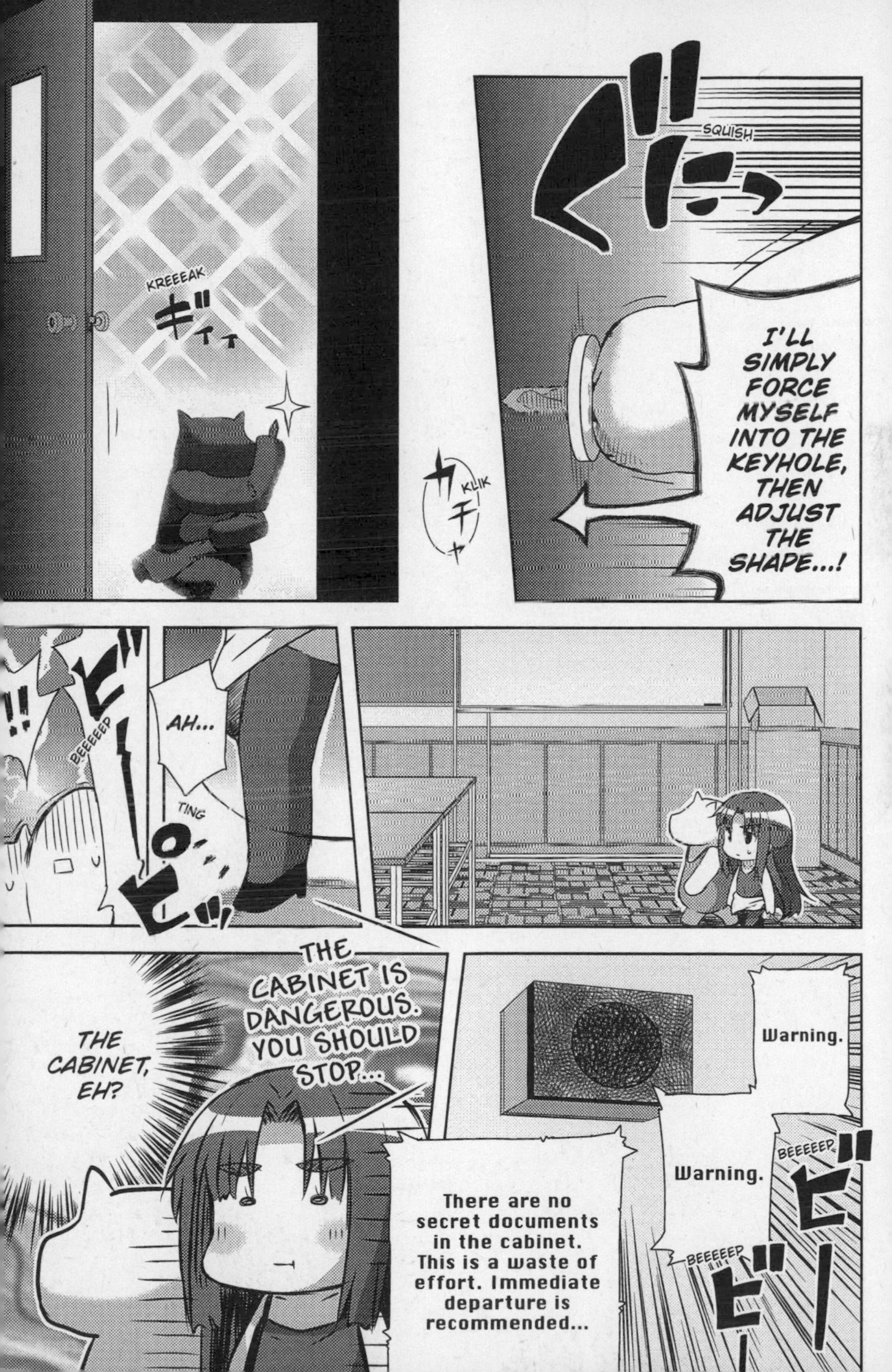
SQUISH
I'LL SIMPLY FORCE MYSELF INTO THE KEYHOLE, THEN ADJUST THE SHAPE...!
KLIK
KREEEAK
AH...
TING
!!
BEEEEEP
Warning.
Warning.
There are no secret documents in the cabinet. This is a waste of effort. Immediate departure is recommended...
BEEEEEP
BEEEEEP
THE CABINET IS DANGEROUS. YOU SHOULD STOP...
THE CABINET, EH?

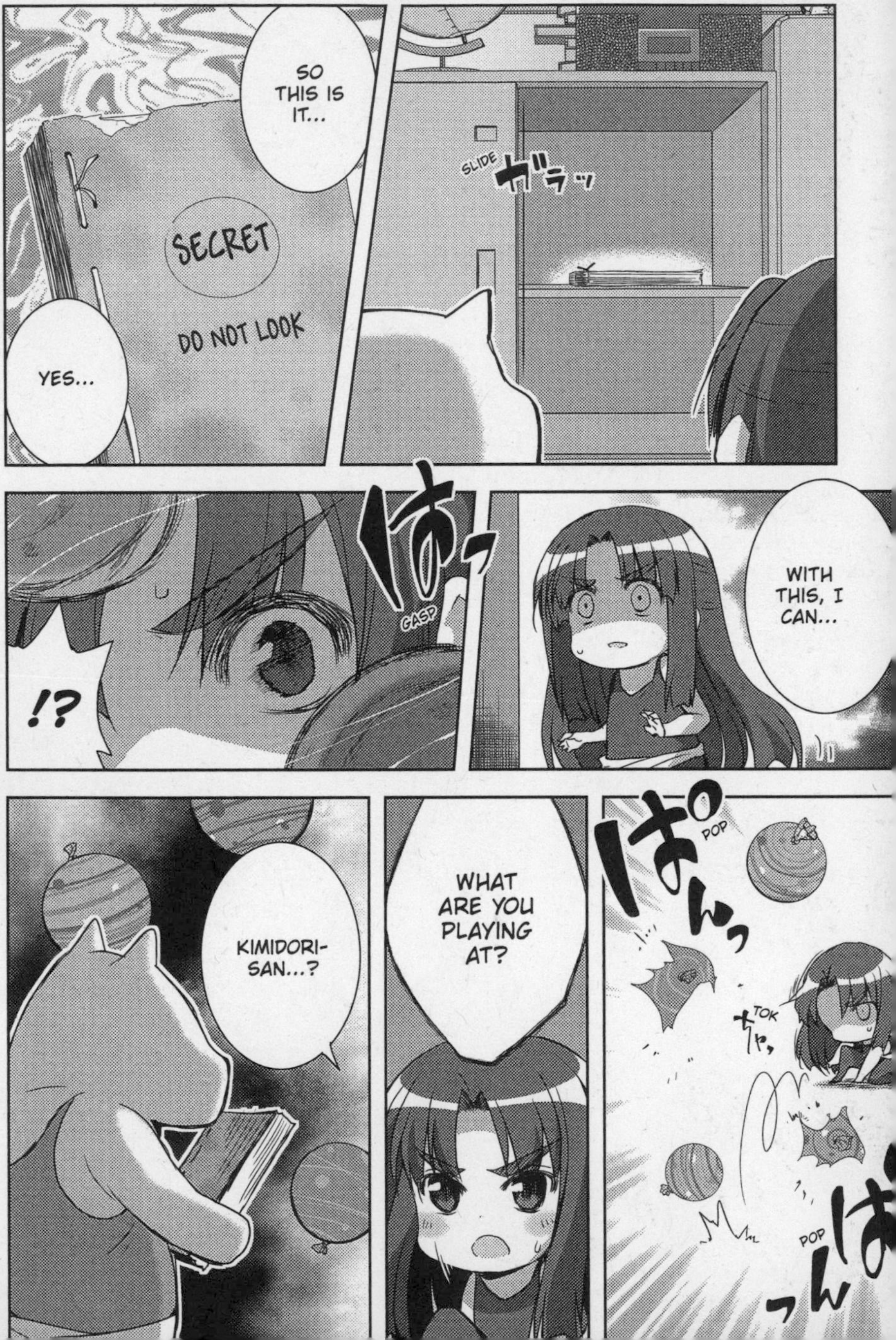
SLIDE
SO THIS IS IT...
SECRET
DO NOT LOOK
YES...
WITH THIS, I CAN...
GASP
!?
POP
TOK
POP
WHAT ARE YOU PLAYING AT?
KIMIDORI-SAN...?

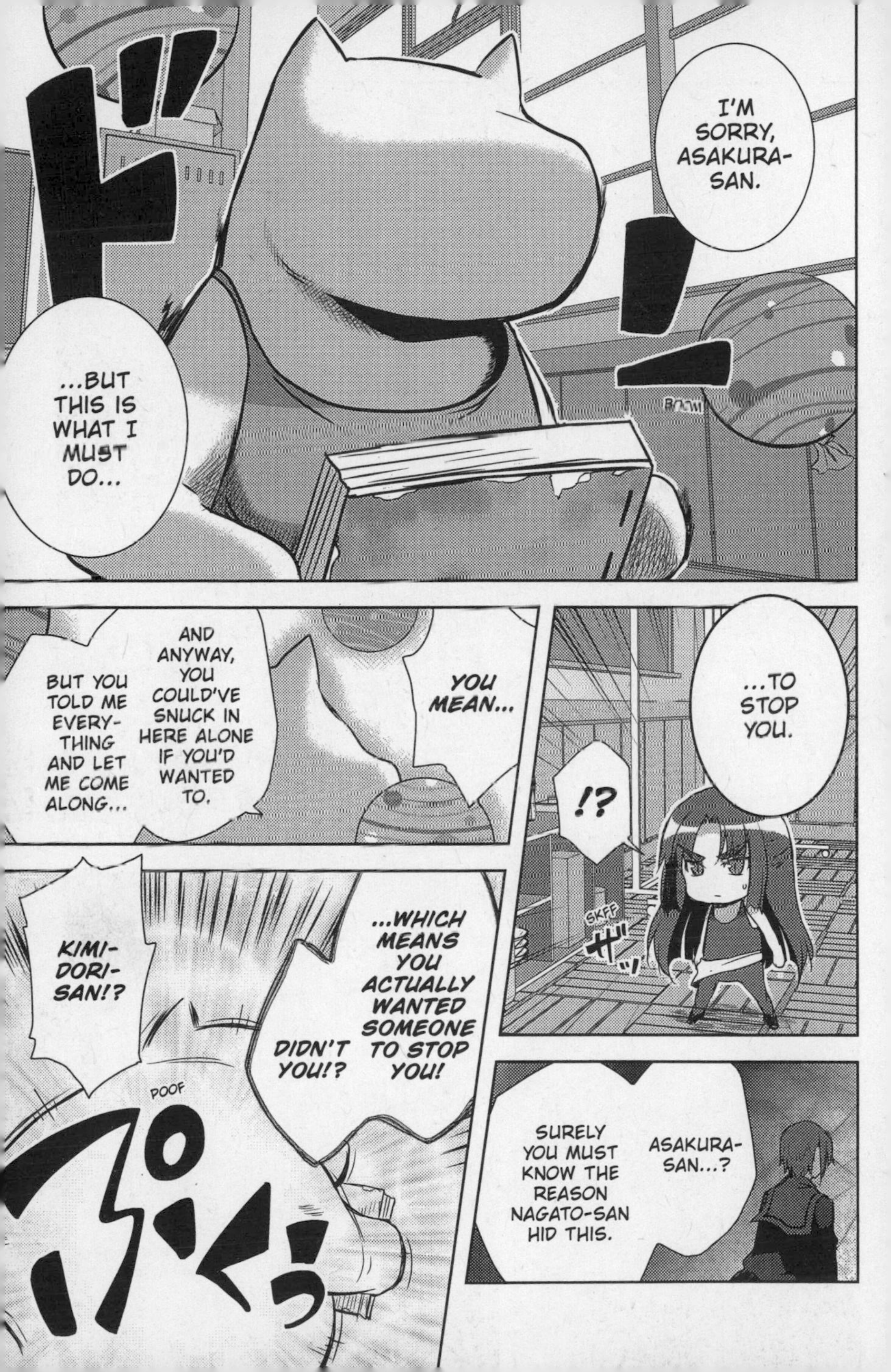
I'M SORRY, ASAKURA-SAN.
BAM
...BUT THIS IS WHAT I MUST DO...
...TO STOP YOU.
!?
SKFF
YOU MEAN...
AND ANYWAY, YOU COULD'VE SNUCK IN HERE ALONE IF YOU'D WANTED TO.
BUT YOU TOLD ME EVERYTHING AND LET ME COME ALONG...
ASAKURA-SAN...?
SURELY YOU MUST KNOW THE REASON NAGATO-SAN HID THIS.
...WHICH MEANS YOU ACTUALLY WANTED SOMEONE TO STOP YOU!
DIDN'T YOU!?
KIMI-DORI-SAN!?
POOF

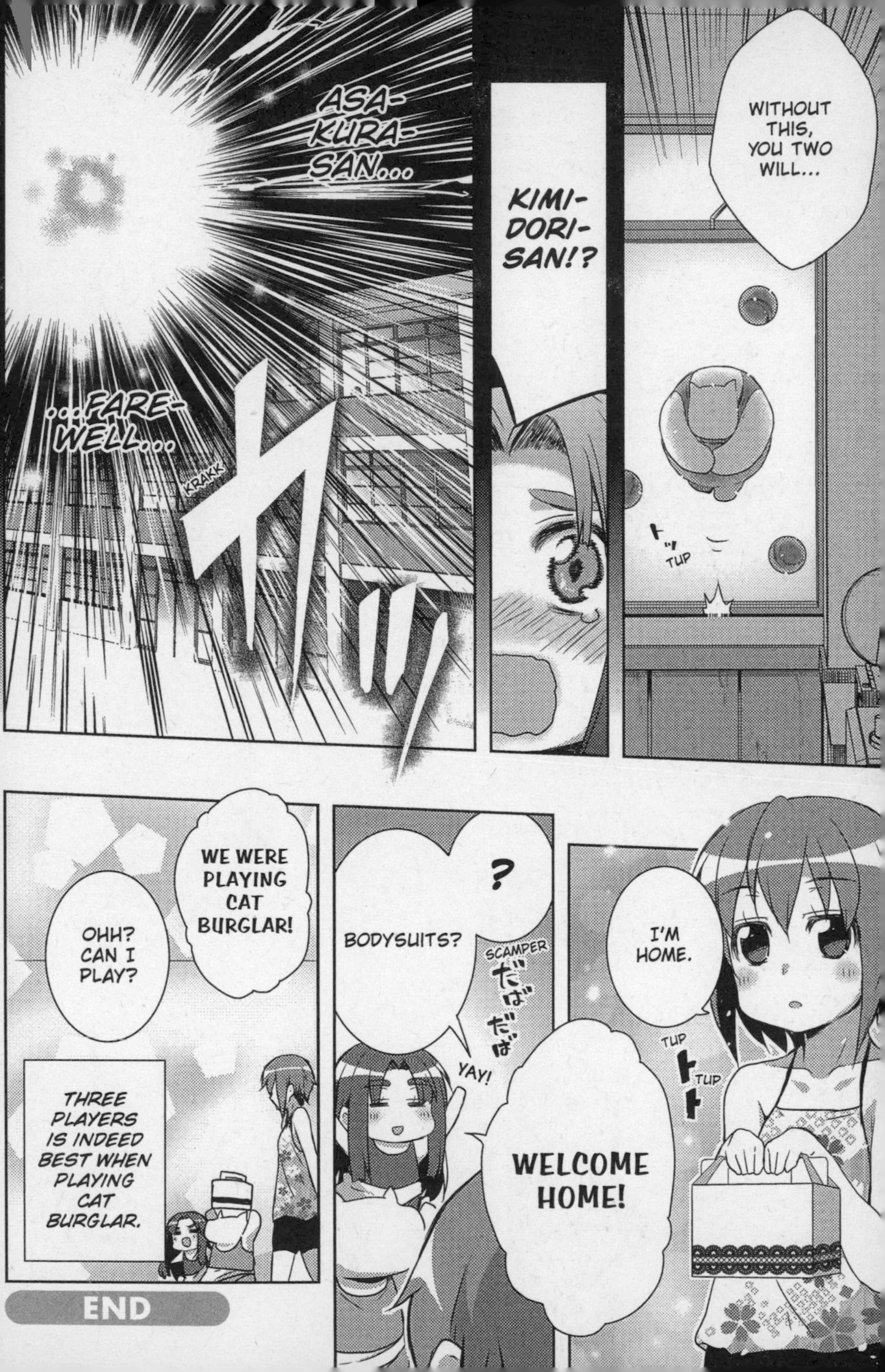

WITHOUT THIS, YOU TWO WILL...
KIMI-DORI-SAN!?
トッ
TUP
ASA-KURA-SAN...
...FARE-WELL...
KRAKK
I'M HOME.
トト
TUP
TUP
WELCOME HOME!
?
BODYSUITS?
だばだば
SCAMPER
YAY!
WE WERE PLAYING CAT BURGLAR!
OHH? CAN I PLAY?
THREE PLAYERS IS INDEED BEST WHEN PLAYING CAT BURGLAR.
END

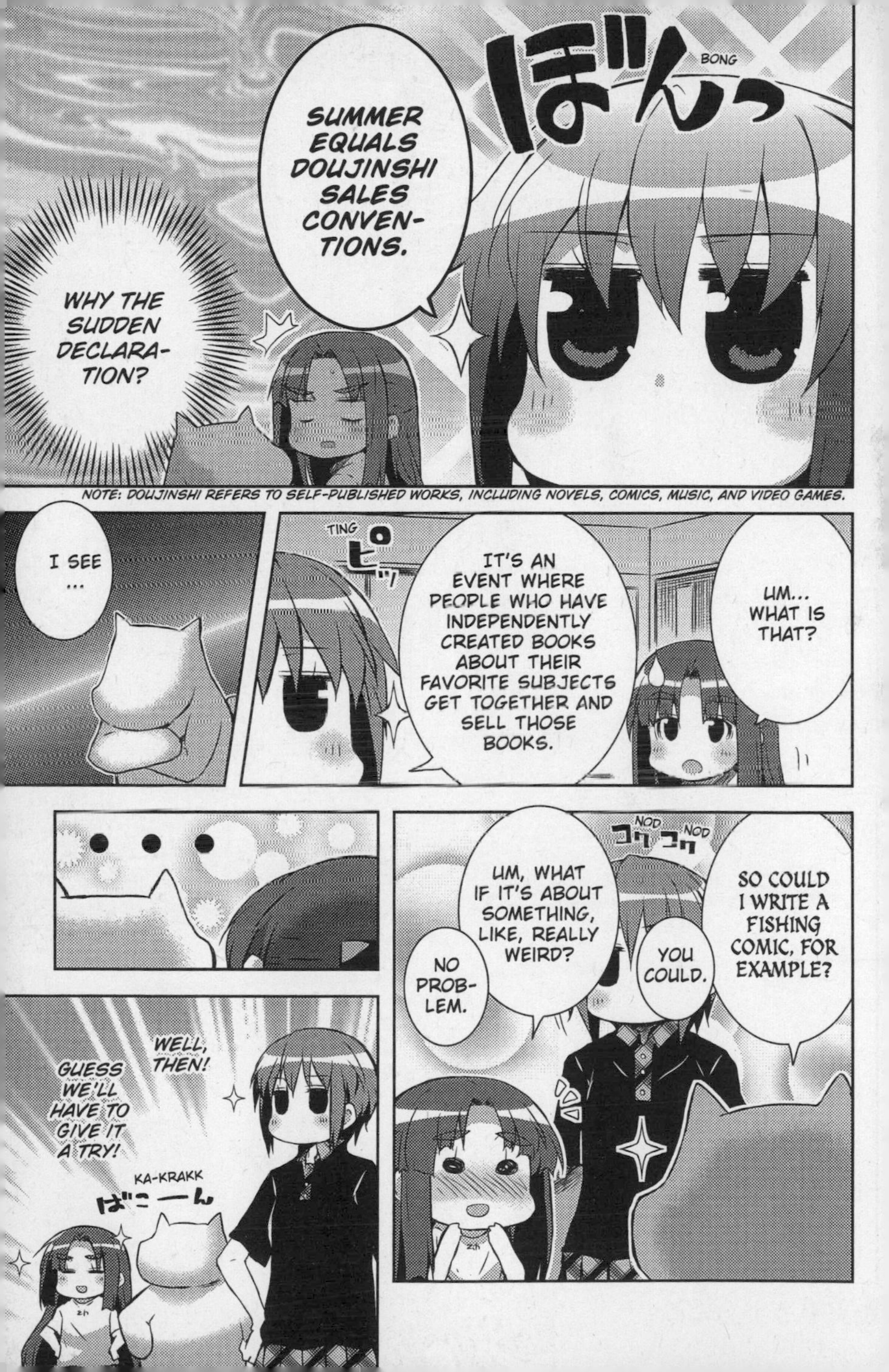
BONG
ぼんっ
SUMMER EQUALS DOUJINSHI SALES CONVEN-TIONS.
WHY THE SUDDEN DECLARA-TION?
NOTE: DOUJINSHI REFERS TO SELF-PUBLISHED WORKS, INCLUDING NOVELS, COMICS, MUSIC, AND VIDEO GAMES.
UM... WHAT IS THAT?
TING
ピッ
IT'S AN EVENT WHERE PEOPLE WHO HAVE INDEPENDENTLY CREATED BOOKS ABOUT THEIR FAVORITE SUBJECTS GET TOGETHER AND SELL THOSE BOOKS.
I SEE ...
SO COULD I WRITE A FISHING COMIC, FOR EXAMPLE?
YOU COULD.
NOD NOD
コクコク
UM, WHAT IF IT'S ABOUT SOMETHING, LIKE, REALLY WEIRD?
NO PROB-LEM.
● ● ●
WELL, THEN!
GUESS WE'LL HAVE TO GIVE IT A TRY!
KA-KRAKK
ばこーん

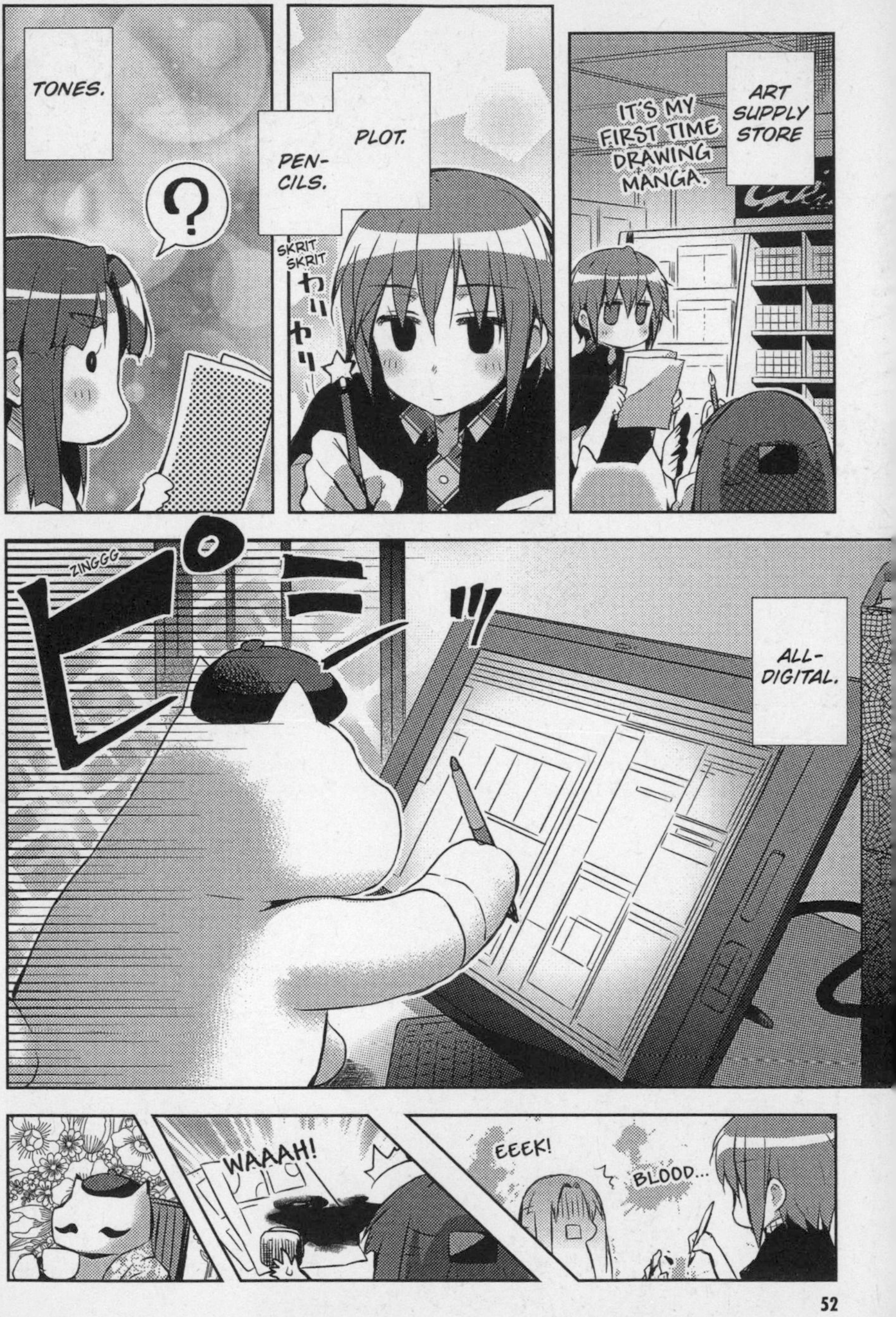

ART SUPPLY STORE
IT'S MY FIRST TIME DRAWING MANGA.
PLOT.
PEN-CILS.
SKRIT SKRIT
TONES.
?
ALL-DIGITAL.
ZINGGG
BLOOD...
EEEK!
WAAAH!

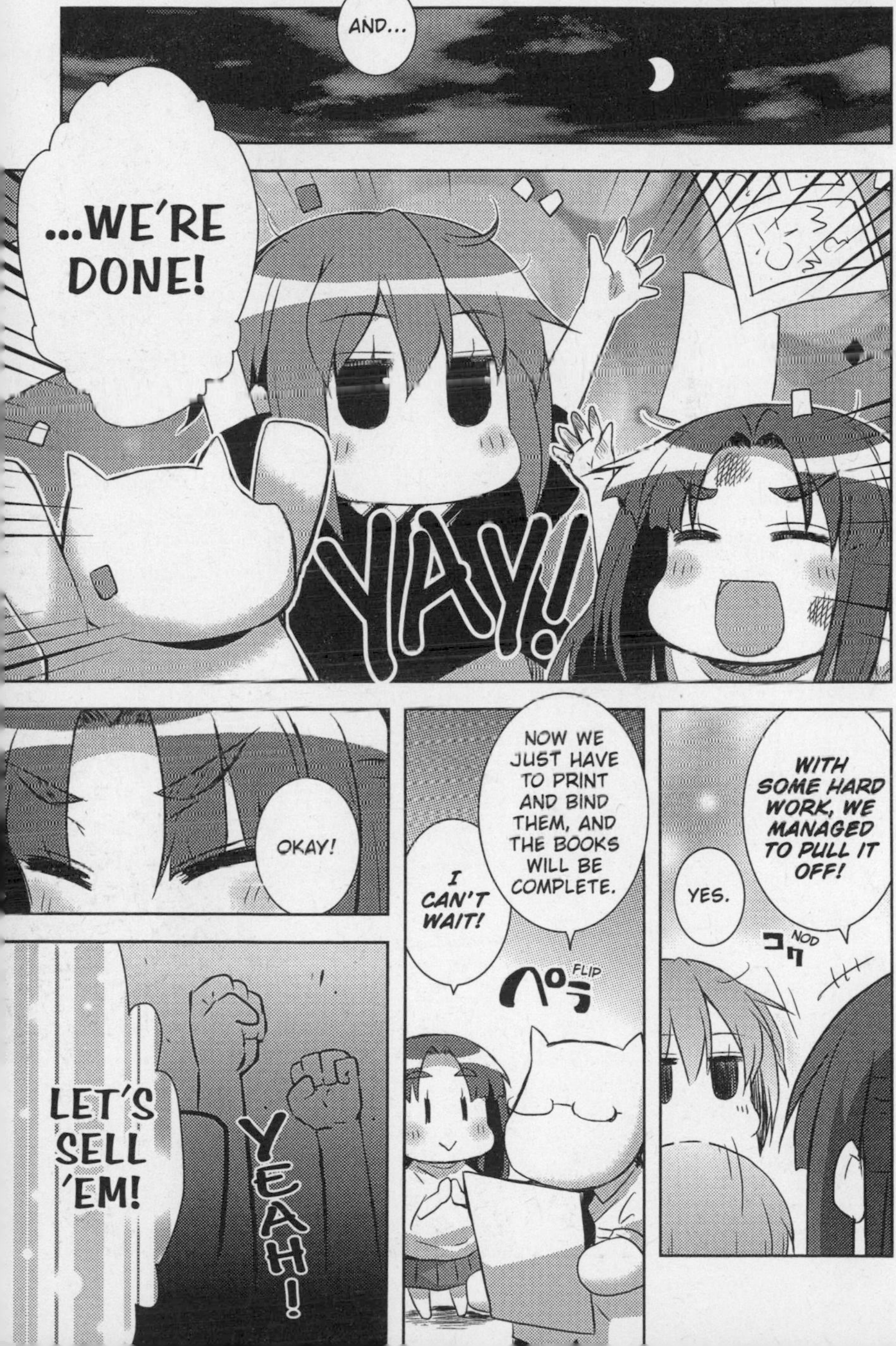
AND...
...WE'RE DONE!
YAY!
WITH SOME HARD WORK, WE MANAGED TO PULL IT OFF!
YES.
NOD
NOW WE JUST HAVE TO PRINT AND BIND THEM, AND THE BOOKS WILL BE COMPLETE.
I CAN'T WAIT!
FLIP
OKAY!
LET'S SELL 'EM!
YEAH!

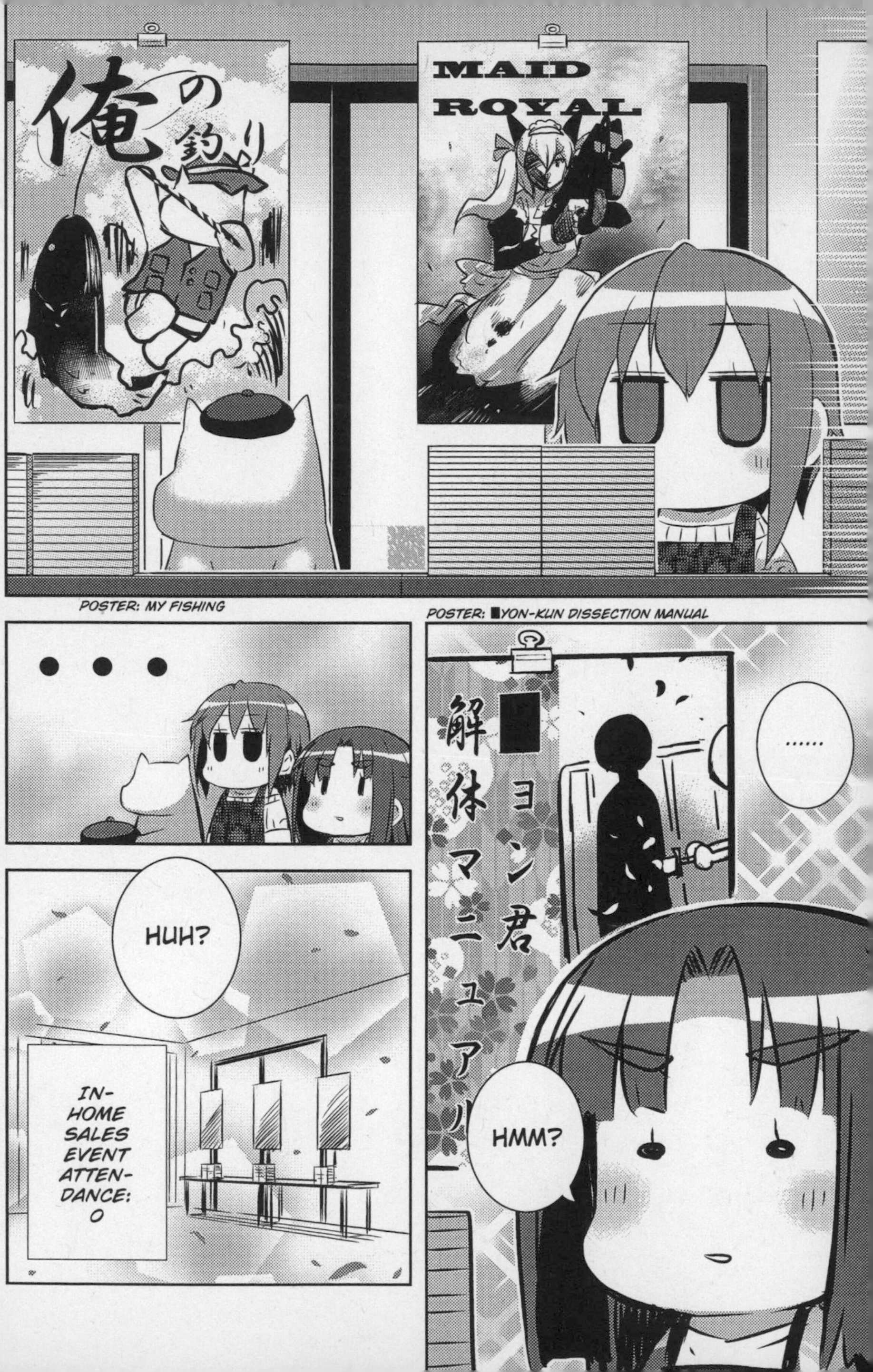
MAID ROYAL
俺の釣り
POSTER: [redacted]YON-KUN DISSECTION MANUAL
POSTER: MY FISHING
[redacted]ヨン君解体マニュアル
......
HMM?
• • •
HUH?
IN-HOME SALES EVENT ATTENDANCE: 0

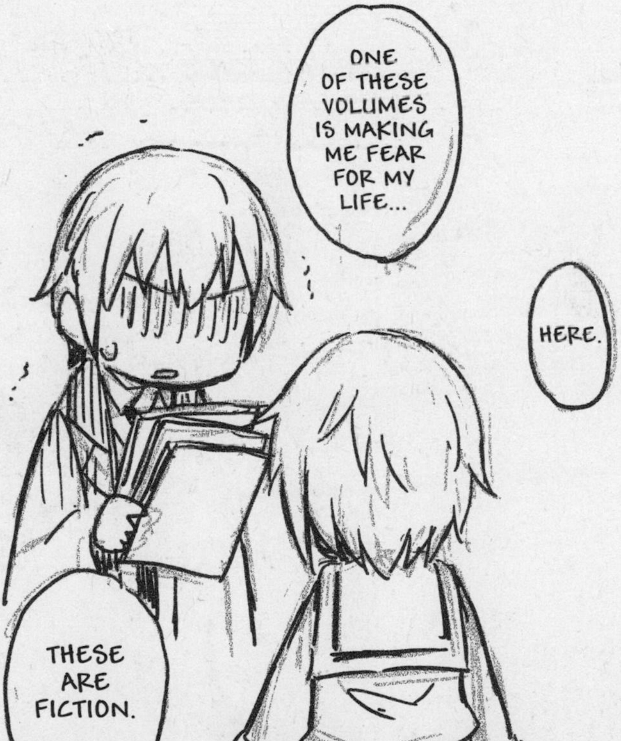
ONE OF THESE VOLUMES IS MAKING ME FEAR FOR MY LIFE...
HERE.
THESE ARE FICTION.

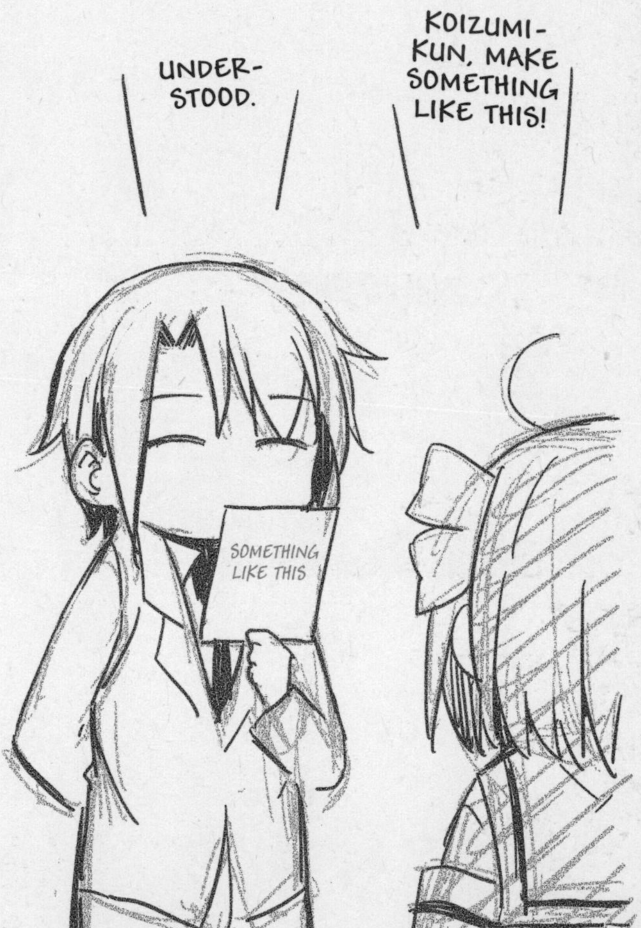
KOIZUMI-KUN, MAKE SOMETHING LIKE THIS!
UNDER-STOOD.
SOMETHING LIKE THIS

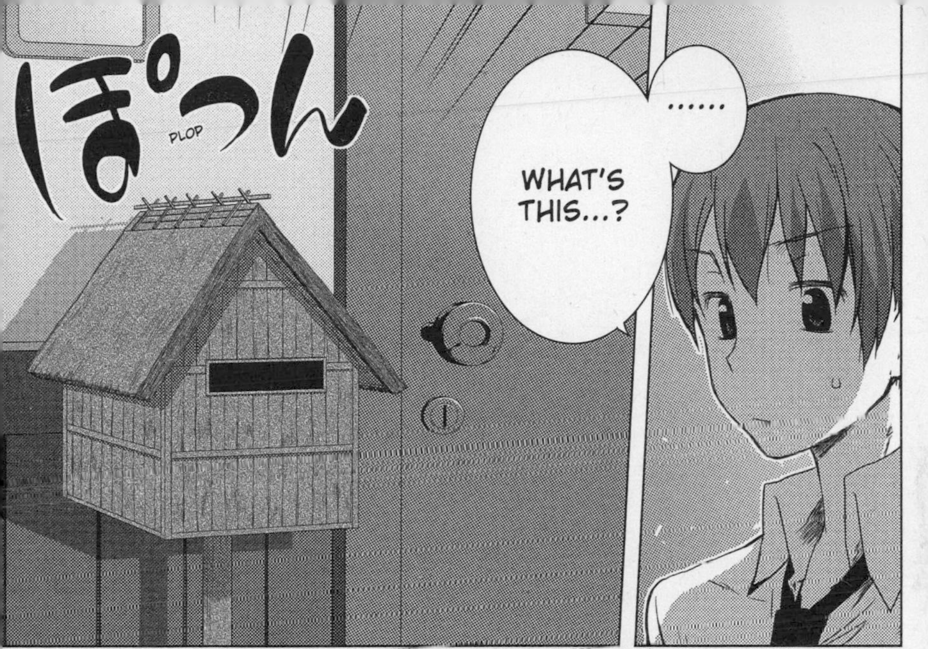
......
WHAT'S THIS...?
ぽつん
PLOP

NOTE: A REFERENCE TO THE MAIL SYSTEM USED BY YOUKAI (SUPERNATURAL CREATURES OF JAPANESE FOLKLORE) FROM THE FAMOUS MANGA GEGEGE NO KITARO.

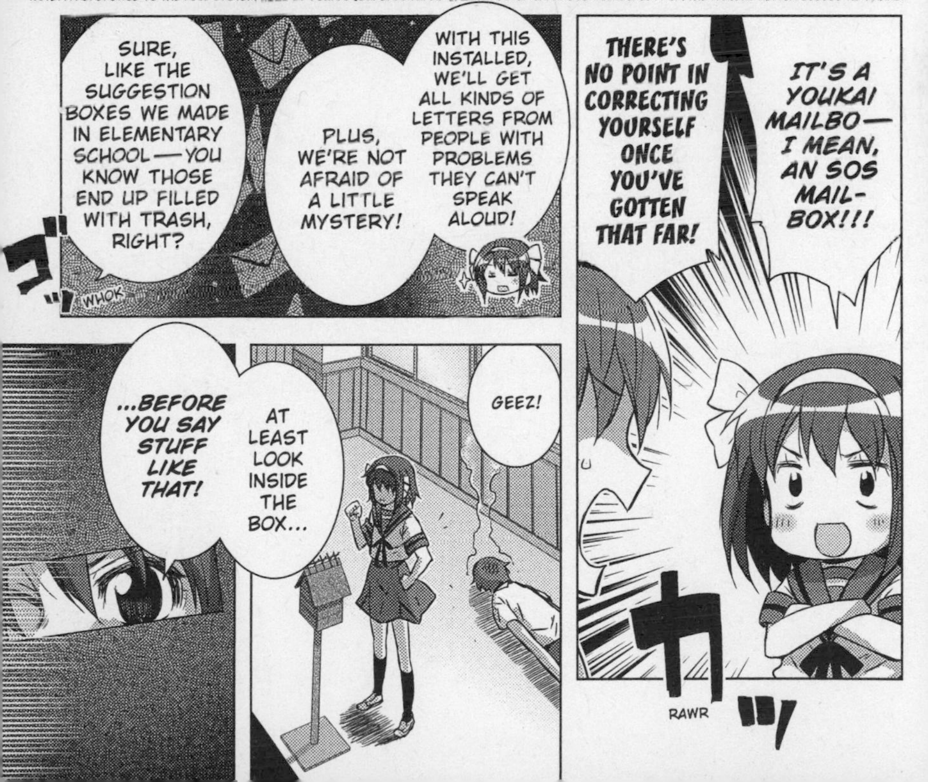
IT'S A YOUKAI MAILBO— I MEAN, AN SOS MAIL-BOX!!!
THERE'S NO POINT IN CORRECTING YOURSELF ONCE YOU'VE GOTTEN THAT FAR!
RAWR
WITH THIS INSTALLED, WE'LL GET ALL KINDS OF LETTERS FROM PEOPLE WITH PROBLEMS THEY CAN'T SPEAK ALOUD!
PLUS, WE'RE NOT AFRAID OF A LITTLE MYSTERY!
SURE, LIKE THE SUGGESTION BOXES WE MADE IN ELEMENTARY SCHOOL—YOU KNOW THOSE END UP FILLED WITH TRASH, RIGHT?
WHOK
GEEZ!
AT LEAST LOOK INSIDE THE BOX...
...BEFORE YOU SAY STUFF LIKE THAT!

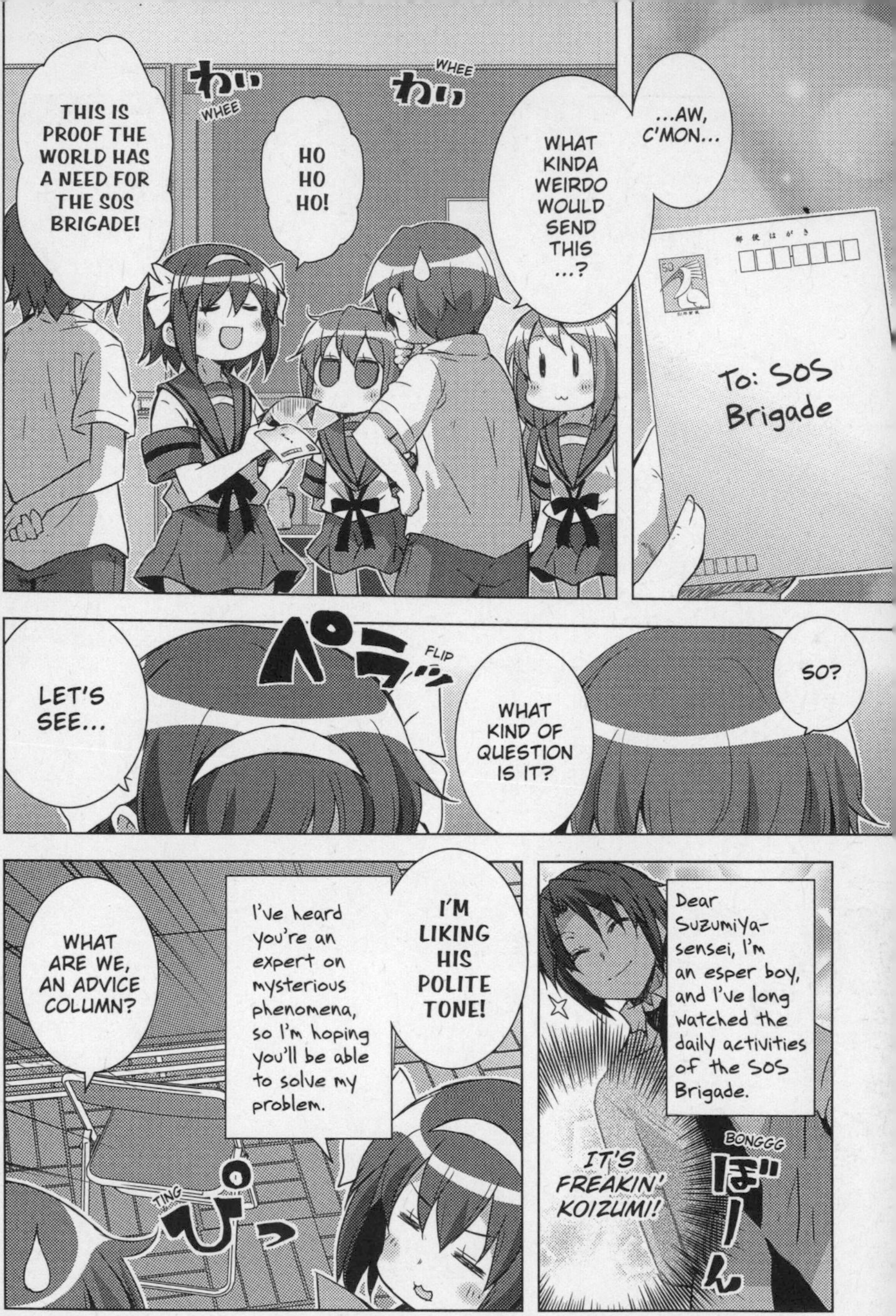

...AW, C'MON...
To: SOS Brigade
WHAT KINDA WEIRDO WOULD SEND THIS ...?
わい
WHEE
わい
WHEE
HO HO HO!
THIS IS PROOF THE WORLD HAS A NEED FOR THE SOS BRIGADE!
SO?
WHAT KIND OF QUESTION IS IT?
ペラッ
FLIP
LET'S SEE...
Dear Suzumiya-sensei, I'm an esper boy, and I've long watched the daily activities of the SOS Brigade.
ぼーん
BONGGG
IT'S FREAKIN' KOIZUMI!
I'M LIKING HIS POLITE TONE!
I've heard you're an expert on mysterious phenomena, so I'm hoping you'll be able to solve my problem.
WHAT ARE WE, AN ADVICE COLUMN?
ぴっ
TING

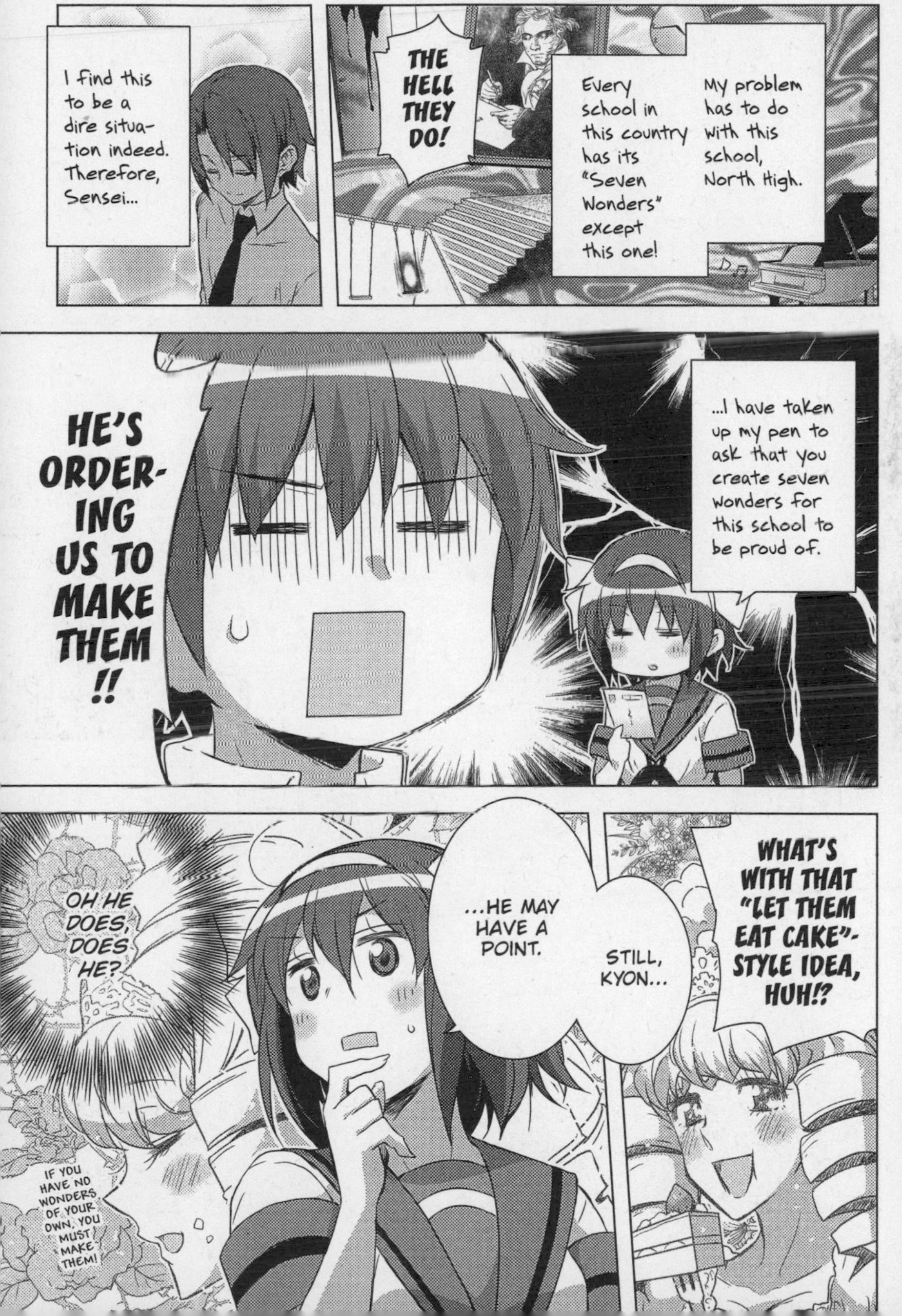

My problem has to do with this school, North High.
Every school in this country has its "Seven Wonders" except this one!
THE HELL THEY DO!
I find this to be a dire situation indeed. Therefore, Sensei...
...I have taken up my pen to ask that you create seven wonders for this school to be proud of.
HE'S ORDERING US TO MAKE THEM!!
STILL, KYON...
...HE MAY HAVE A POINT.
OH HE DOES, DOES HE?
IF YOU HAVE NO WONDERS OF YOUR OWN, YOU MUST MAKE THEM!
WHAT'S WITH THAT "LET THEM EAT CAKE"-STYLE IDEA, HUH!?

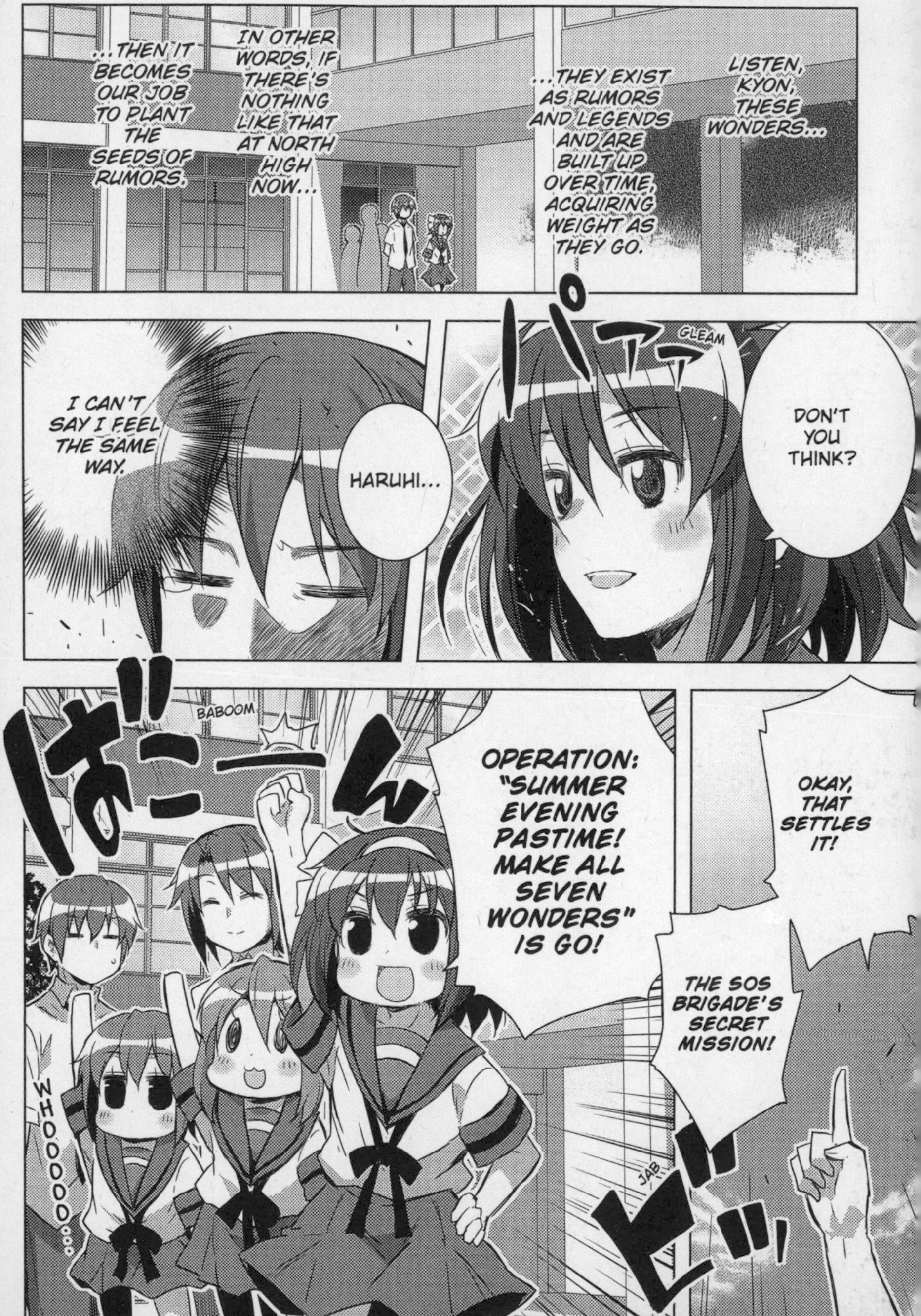
LISTEN, KYON, THESE WONDERS...
...THEY EXIST AS RUMORS AND LEGENDS AND ARE BUILT UP OVER TIME, ACQUIRING WEIGHT AS THEY GO.
IN OTHER WORDS, IF THERE'S NOTHING LIKE THAT AT NORTH HIGH NOW...
...THEN IT BECOMES OUR JOB TO PLANT THE SEEDS OF RUMORS.
パァァ
GLEAM
DON'T YOU THINK?
HARUHI...
I CAN'T SAY I FEEL THE SAME WAY.
OKAY, THAT SETTLES IT!
THE SOS BRIGADE'S SECRET MISSION!
ビッ
JAB
OPERATION: "SUMMER EVENING PASTIME! MAKE ALL SEVEN WONDERS" IS GO!
ばーん
BABOOM
WHOOOOOO...

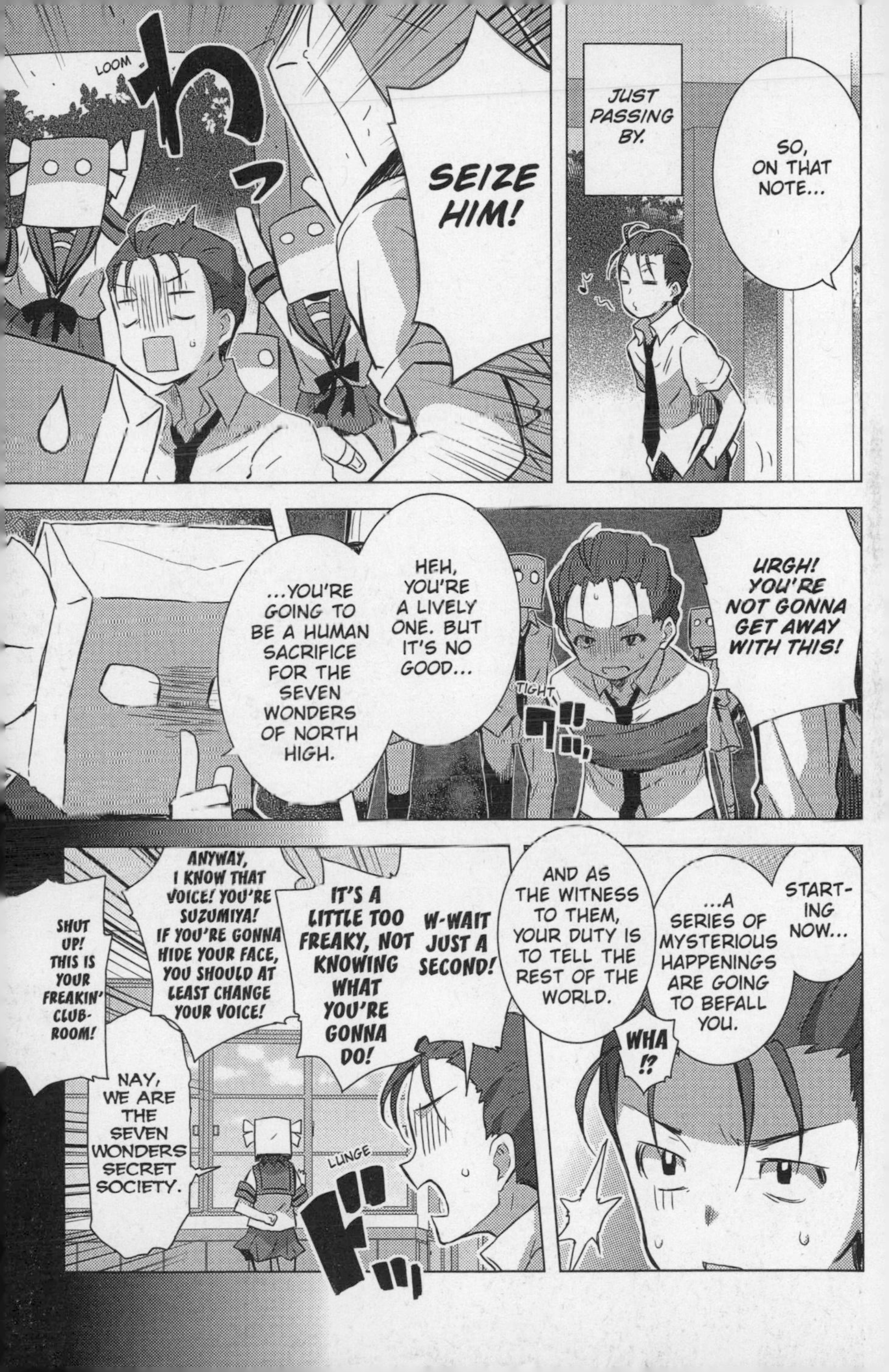
JUST PASSING BY.
SO, ON THAT NOTE...
LOOM
SEIZE HIM!
URGH! YOU'RE NOT GONNA GET AWAY WITH THIS!
TIGHT
HEH, YOU'RE A LIVELY ONE. BUT IT'S NO GOOD...
...YOU'RE GOING TO BE A HUMAN SACRIFICE FOR THE SEVEN WONDERS OF NORTH HIGH.
STARTING NOW...
...A SERIES OF MYSTERIOUS HAPPENINGS ARE GOING TO BEFALL YOU.
AND AS THE WITNESS TO THEM, YOUR DUTY IS TO TELL THE REST OF THE WORLD.
WHA!?
W-WAIT JUST A SECOND!
IT'S A LITTLE TOO FREAKY, NOT KNOWING WHAT YOU'RE GONNA DO!
ANYWAY, I KNOW THAT VOICE! YOU'RE SUZUMIYA! IF YOU'RE GONNA HIDE YOUR FACE, YOU SHOULD AT LEAST CHANGE YOUR VOICE!
SHUT UP! THIS IS YOUR FREAKIN' CLUB-ROOM!
NAY, WE ARE THE SEVEN WONDERS SECRET SOCIETY.
LUNGE

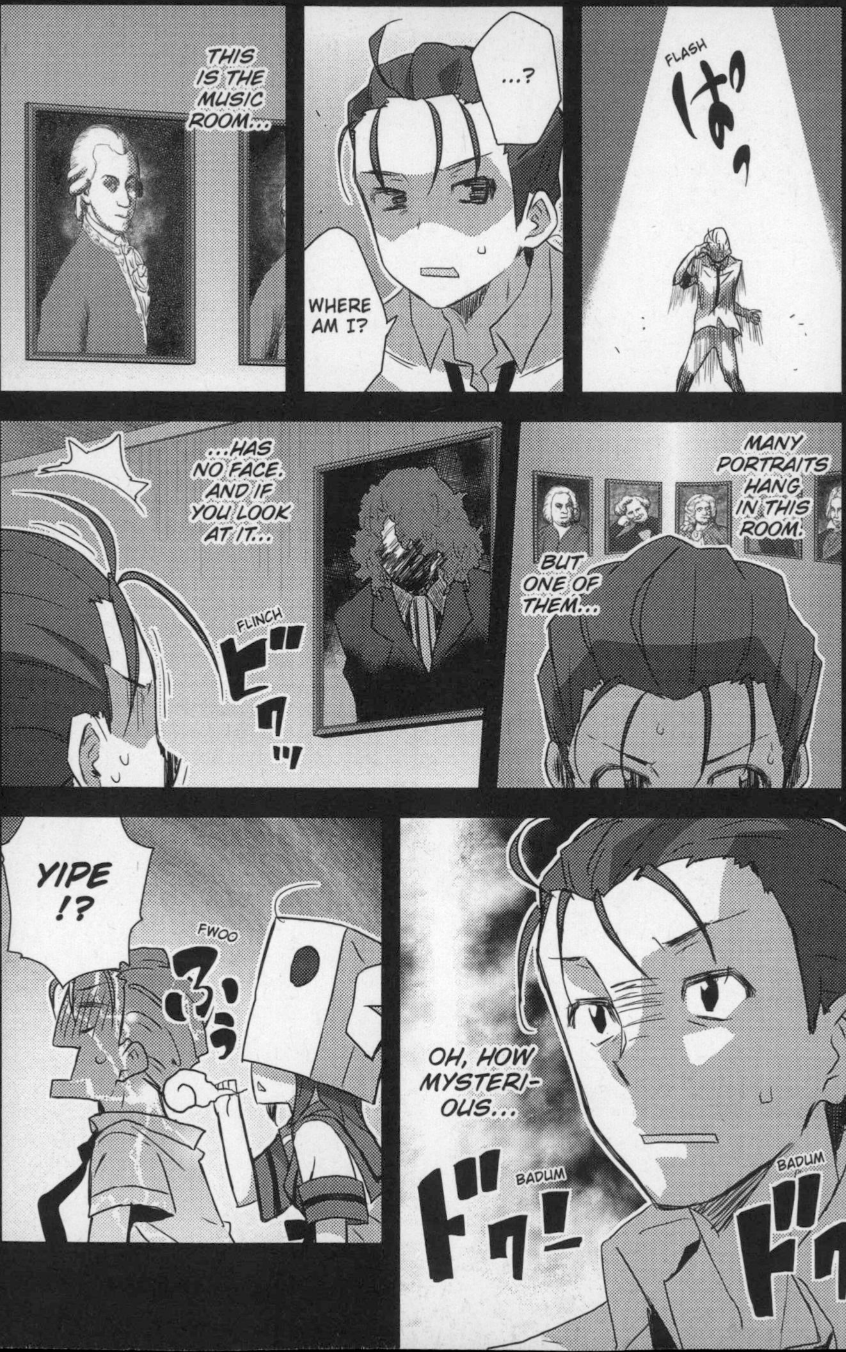
FLASH
...?
WHERE AM I?
THIS IS THE MUSIC ROOM...
MANY PORTRAITS HANG IN THIS ROOM.
BUT ONE OF THEM...
...HAS NO FACE. AND IF YOU LOOK AT IT...
FLINCH
OH, HOW MYSTERIOUS...
BADUM
BADUM
YIPE!?
FWOO

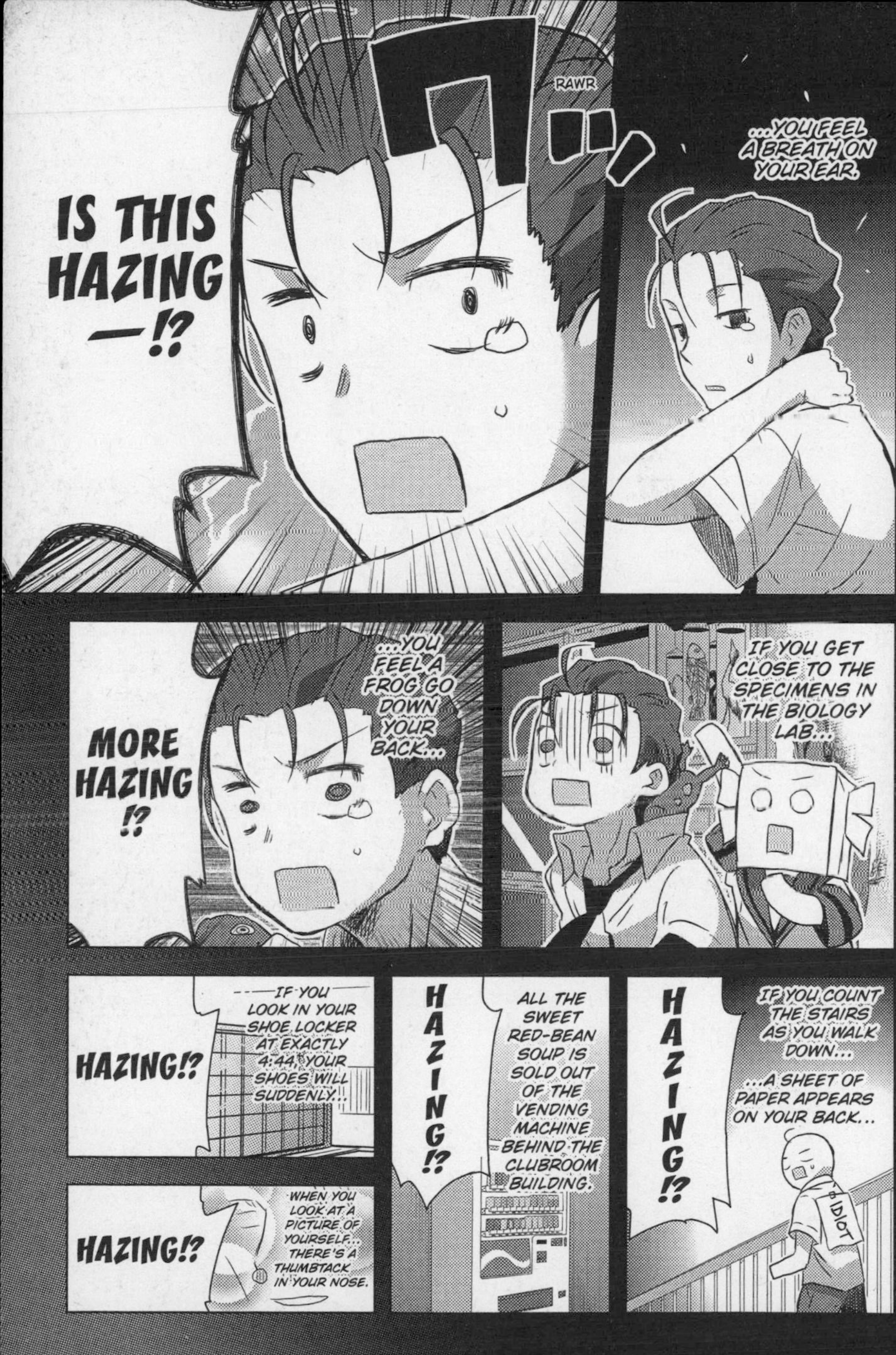
...YOU FEEL A BREATH ON YOUR EAR.
RAWR
IS THIS HAZING—!?
IF YOU GET CLOSE TO THE SPECIMENS IN THE BIOLOGY LAB...
...YOU FEEL A FROG GO DOWN YOUR BACK...
MORE HAZING!?
IF YOU COUNT THE STAIRS AS YOU WALK DOWN...
...A SHEET OF PAPER APPEARS ON YOUR BACK...
IDIOT
HAZING!?
ALL THE SWEET RED-BEAN SOUP IS SOLD OUT OF THE VENDING MACHINE BEHIND THE CLUBROOM BUILDING.
HAZING!?
—IF YOU LOOK IN YOUR SHOE LOCKER AT EXACTLY 4:44, YOUR SHOES WILL SUDDENLY...
HAZING!?
WHEN YOU LOOK AT A PICTURE OF YOURSELF... THERE'S A THUMBTACK IN YOUR NOSE.
HAZING!?

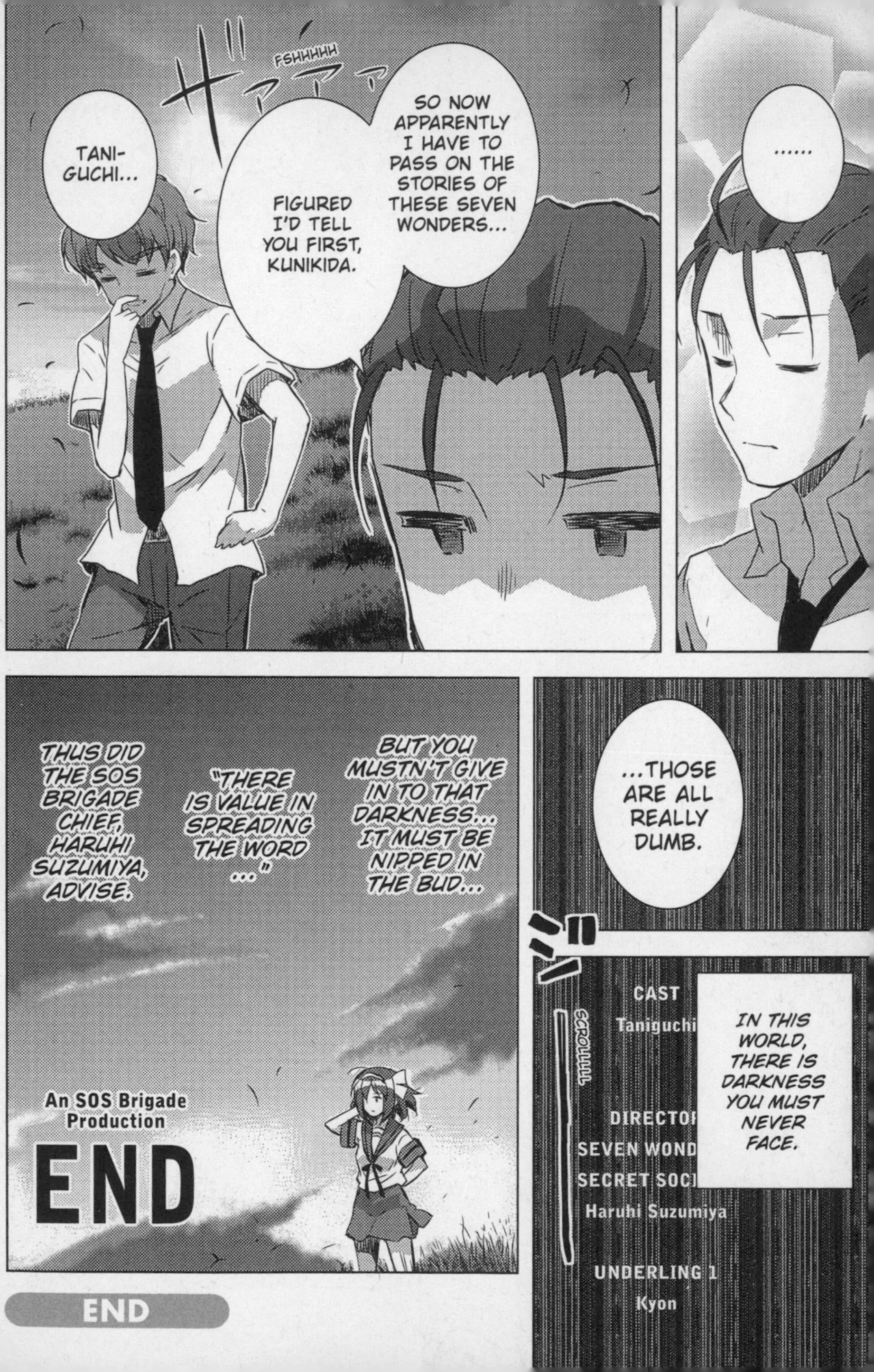
......
FSHHHHH
SO NOW APPARENTLY I HAVE TO PASS ON THE STORIES OF THESE SEVEN WONDERS...
FIGURED I'D TELL YOU FIRST, KUNIKIDA.
TANI-GUCHI...
...THOSE ARE ALL REALLY DUMB.
IN THIS WORLD, THERE IS DARKNESS YOU MUST NEVER FACE.
CAST
Taniguchi
DIRECTOR
SEVEN WOND
SECRET SOCI
Haruhi Suzumiya
UNDERLING 1
Kyon
SCROLLLL
BUT YOU MUSTN'T GIVE IN TO THAT DARKNESS... IT MUST BE NIPPED IN THE BUD...
"THERE IS VALUE IN SPREADING THE WORD ..."
THUS DID THE SOS BRIGADE CHIEF, HARUHI SUZUMIYA, ADVISE.
An SOS Brigade Production
END
END

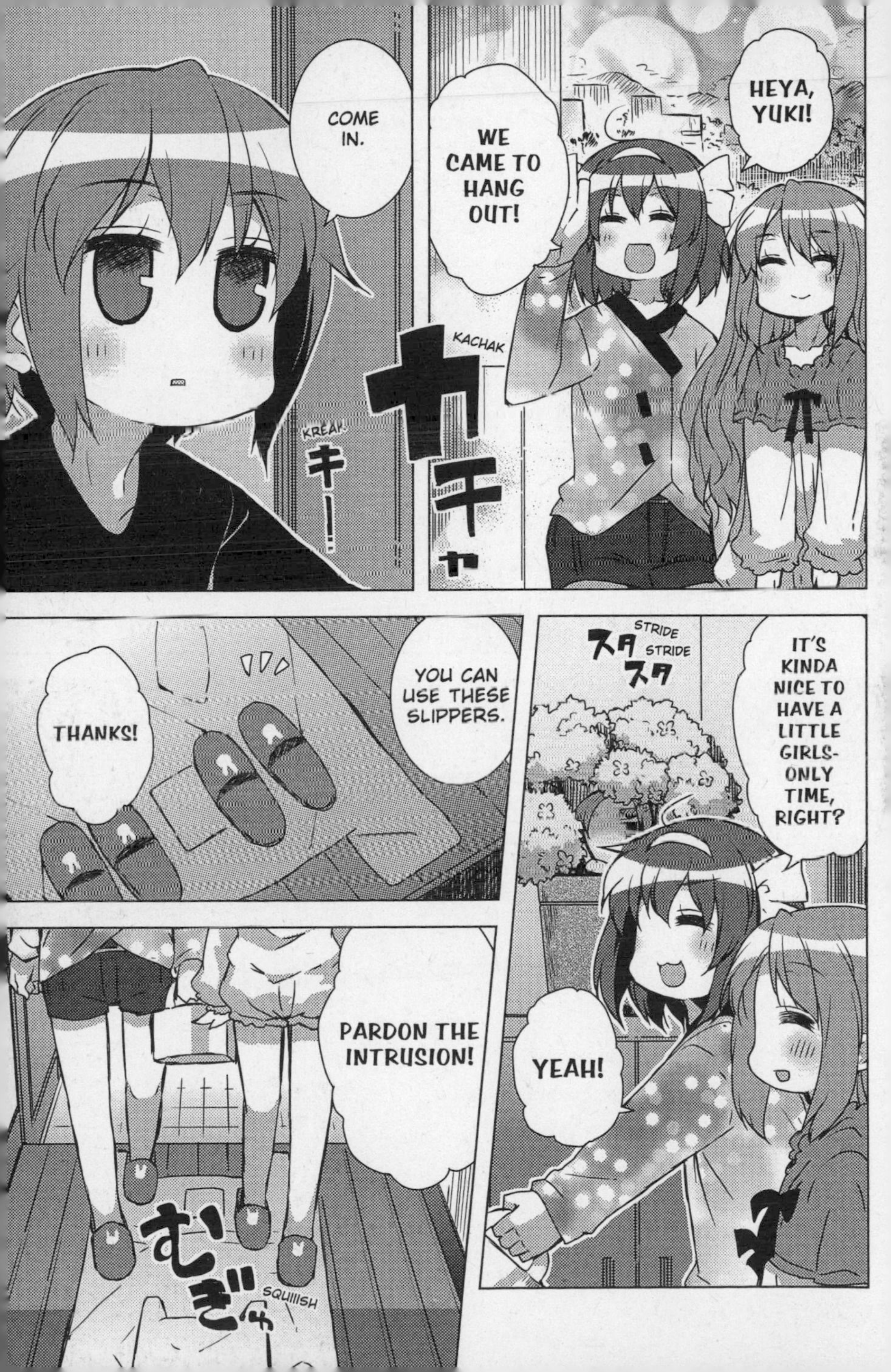
HEYA, YUKI!
WE CAME TO HANG OUT!
カチャ
KACHAK
COME IN.
キー!
KREAK
スタスタ
STRIDE STRIDE
IT'S KINDA NICE TO HAVE A LITTLE GIRLS-ONLY TIME, RIGHT?
YEAH!
YOU CAN USE THESE SLIPPERS.
THANKS!
PARDON THE INTRUSION!
むぎゅ
SQUIIISH

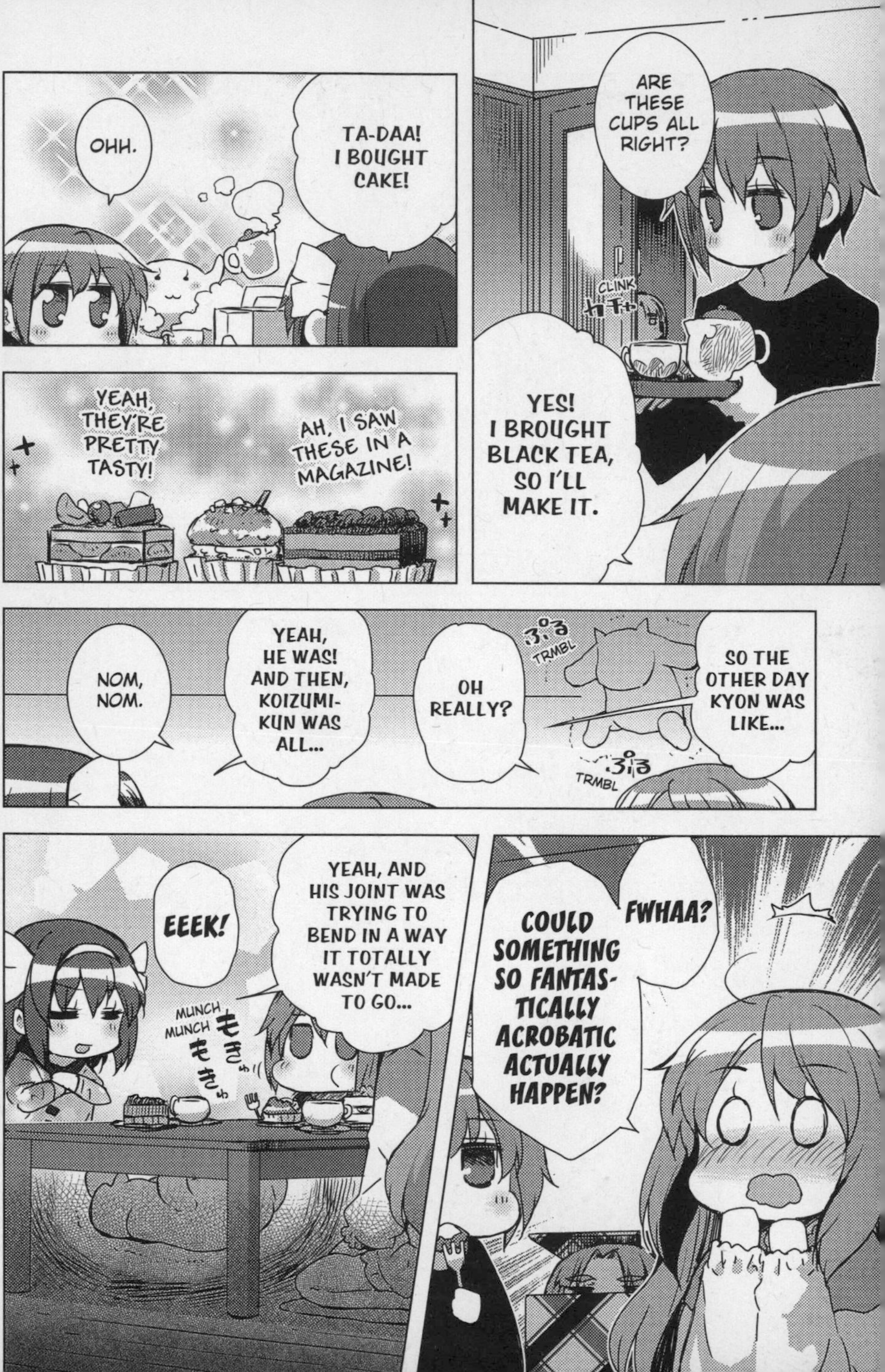
ARE THESE CUPS ALL RIGHT?
CLINK カチャ
YES! I BROUGHT BLACK TEA, SO I'LL MAKE IT.
TA-DAA! I BOUGHT CAKE!
OHH.
AH, I SAW THESE IN A MAGAZINE!
YEAH, THEY'RE PRETTY TASTY!
SO THE OTHER DAY KYON WAS LIKE...
ぷる TRMBL
ぷる TRMBL
OH REALLY?
YEAH, HE WAS! AND THEN, KOIZUMI-KUN WAS ALL...
NOM, NOM.
FWHAA?
COULD SOMETHING SO FANTASTICALLY ACROBATIC ACTUALLY HAPPEN?
YEAH, AND HIS JOINT WAS TRYING TO BEND IN A WAY IT TOTALLY WASN'T MADE TO GO...
EEEK!
MUNCH MUNCH もきゅもきゅ

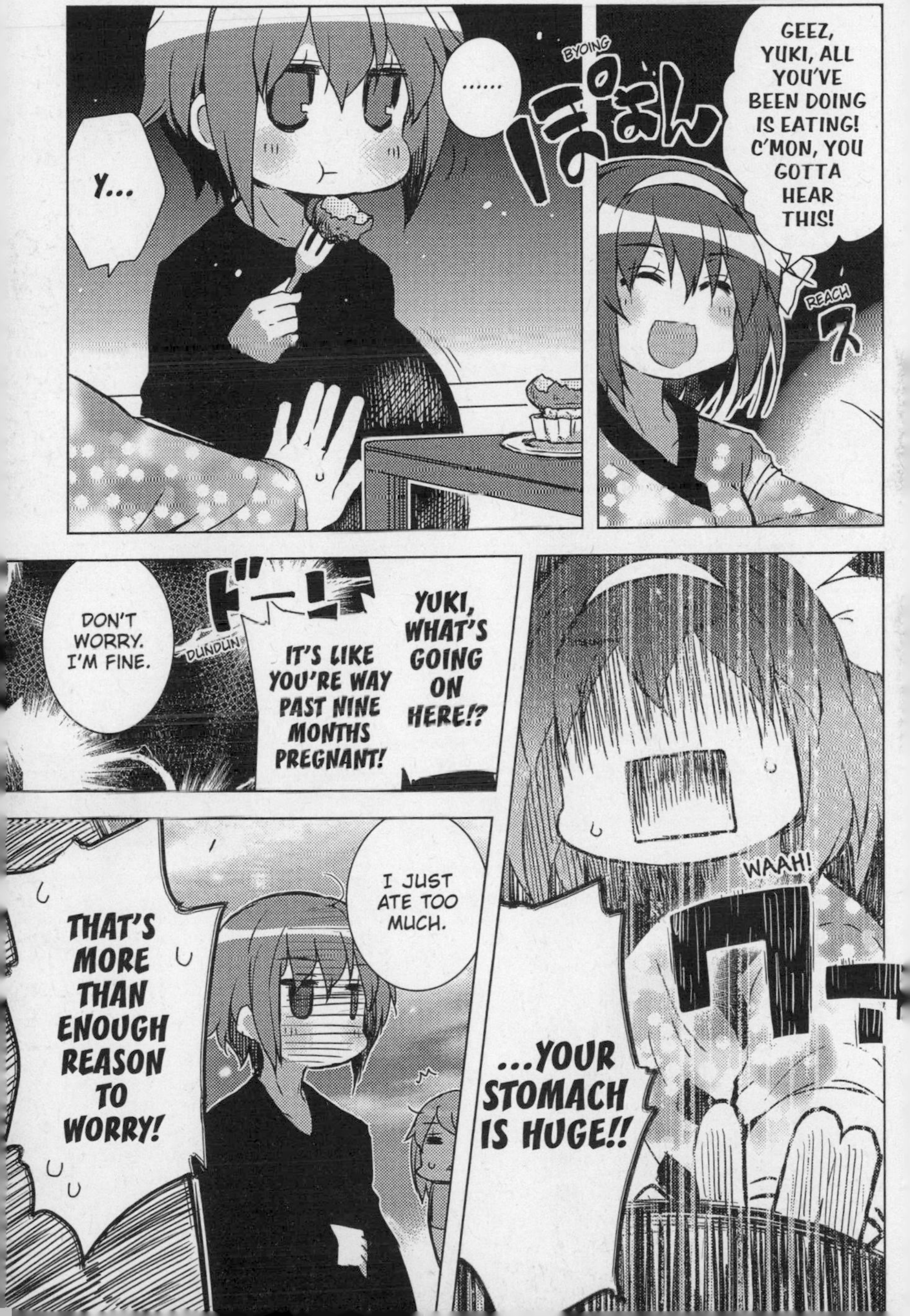
BYOING
GEEZ, YUKI, ALL YOU'VE BEEN DOING IS EATING! C'MON, YOU GOTTA HEAR THIS!
REACH
......
Y...
WAAH!
...YOUR STOMACH IS HUGE!!
YUKI, WHAT'S GOING ON HERE!?
IT'S LIKE YOU'RE WAY PAST NINE MONTHS PREGNANT!
DUNDUN
DON'T WORRY. I'M FINE.
I JUST ATE TOO MUCH.
THAT'S MORE THAN ENOUGH REASON TO WORRY!

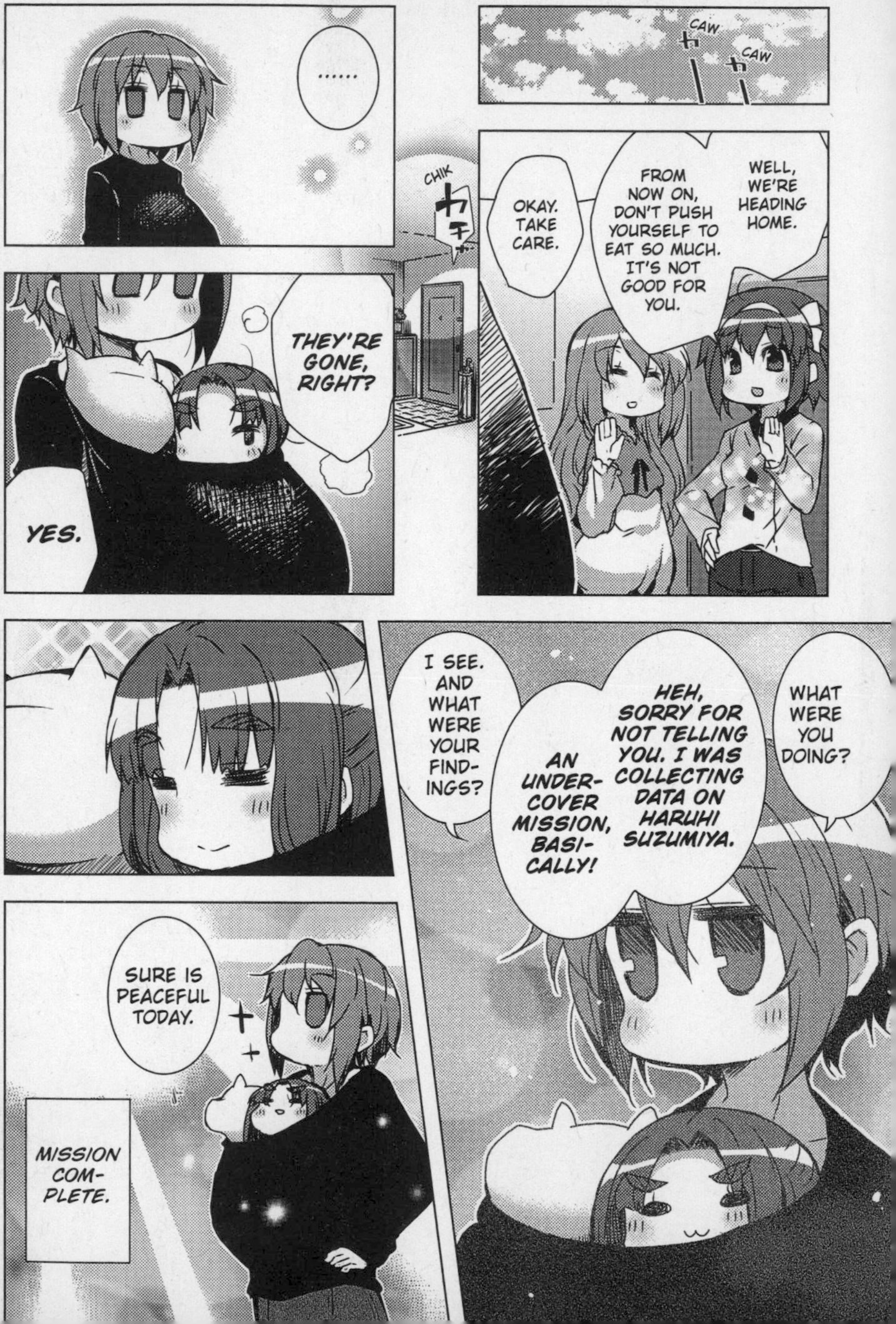
CAW
CAW
WELL, WE'RE HEADING HOME.
FROM NOW ON, DON'T PUSH YOURSELF TO EAT SO MUCH. IT'S NOT GOOD FOR YOU.
OKAY. TAKE CARE.
CHIK
......
THEY'RE GONE, RIGHT?
YES.
WHAT WERE YOU DOING?
HEH, SORRY FOR NOT TELLING YOU. I WAS COLLECTING DATA ON HARUHI SUZUMIYA.
AN UNDER-COVER MISSION, BASI-CALLY!
I SEE. AND WHAT WERE YOUR FIND-INGS?
SURE IS PEACEFUL TODAY.
MISSION COM-PLETE.

SPECIAL-ORDERED WITH A RIBBON

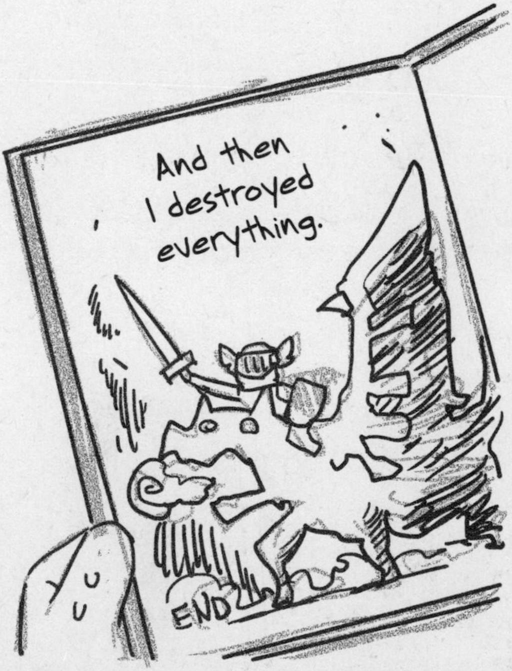
And then
I destroyed
everything.
END

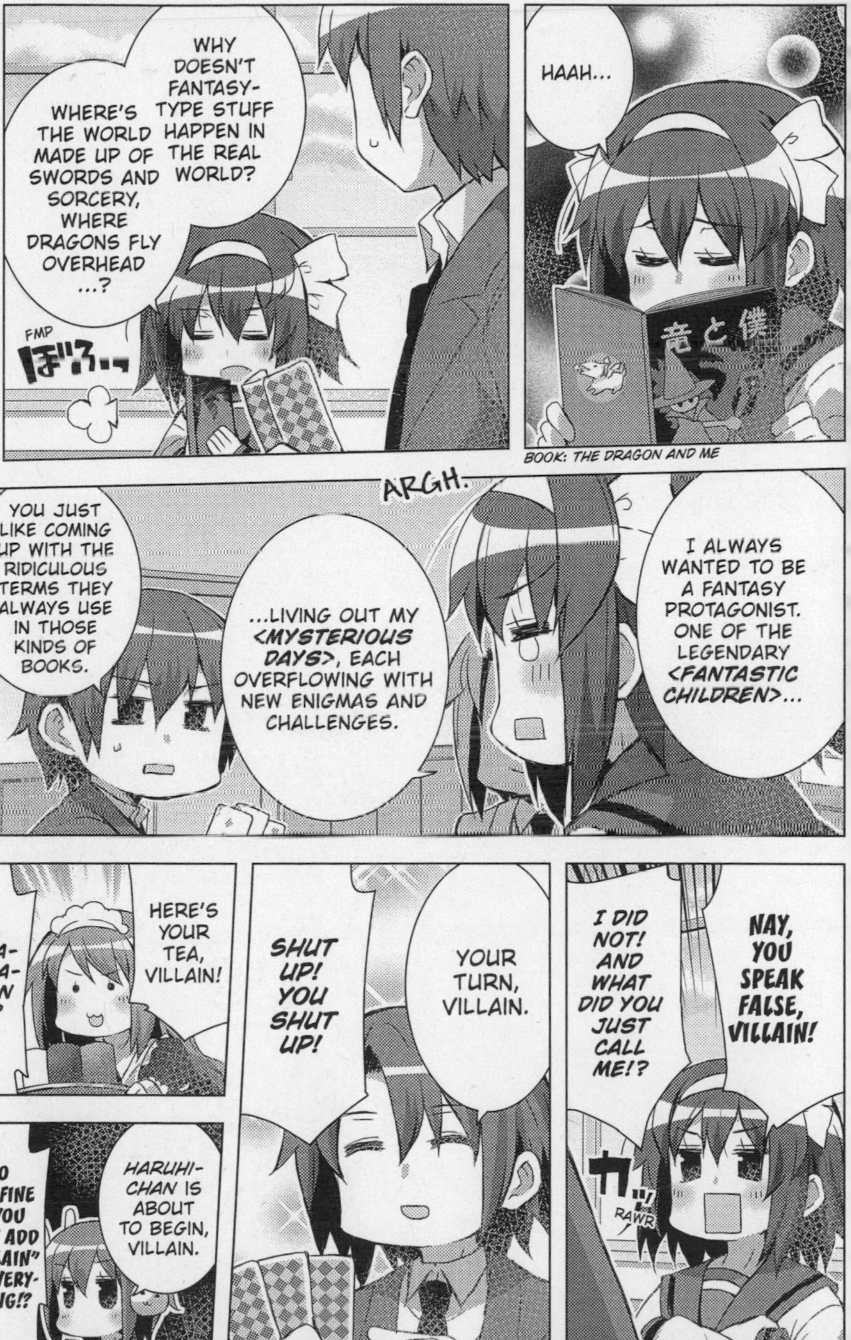

HAAH...
竜と僕
BOOK: THE DRAGON AND ME
WHY DOESN'T FANTASY-TYPE STUFF HAPPEN IN THE REAL WORLD?
WHERE'S THE WORLD MADE UP OF SWORDS AND SORCERY, WHERE DRAGONS FLY OVERHEAD ...?
FMP
ARGH.
I ALWAYS WANTED TO BE A FANTASY PROTAGONIST. ONE OF THE LEGENDARY <FANTASTIC CHILDREN>...
...LIVING OUT MY <MYSTERIOUS DAYS>, EACH OVERFLOWING WITH NEW ENIGMAS AND CHALLENGES.
YOU JUST LIKE COMING UP WITH THE RIDICULOUS TERMS THEY ALWAYS USE IN THOSE KINDS OF BOOKS.
NAY, YOU SPEAK FALSE, VILLAIN!
I DID NOT! AND WHAT DID YOU JUST CALL ME!?
RAWR
YOUR TURN, VILLAIN.
SHUT UP! YOU SHUT UP!
HERE'S YOUR TEA, VILLAIN!
ASA-HINA-SAN!?
HARUHI-CHAN IS ABOUT TO BEGIN, VILLAIN.
SO IT'S FINE IF YOU JUST ADD "VILLAIN" TO EVERY-THING!?

## A ROOM WITH DRAGONS FLYING OVERHEAD

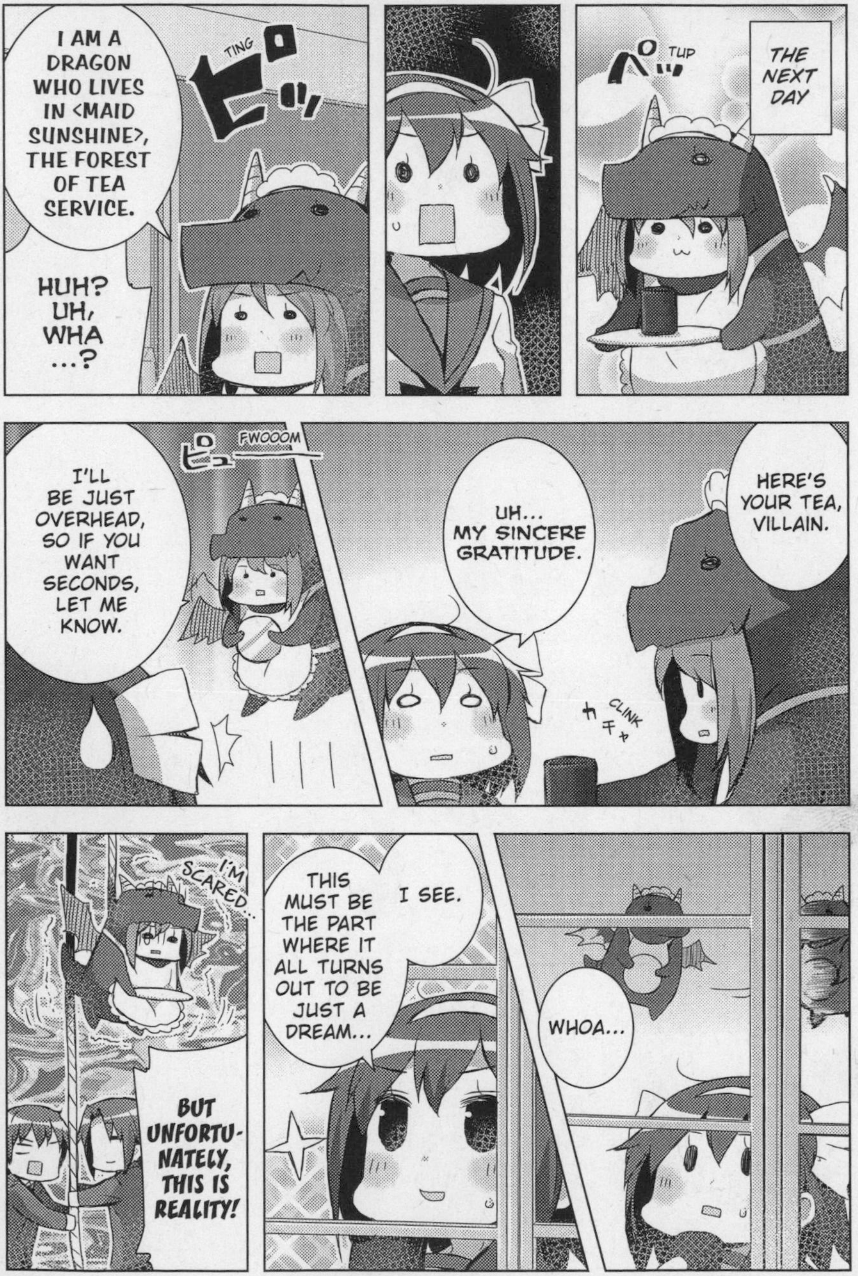
THE NEXT DAY
TUP
TING
I AM A DRAGON WHO LIVES IN <MAID SUNSHINE>, THE FOREST OF TEA SERVICE.
HUH? UH, WHA ...?
HERE'S YOUR TEA, VILLAIN.
CLINK
UH... MY SINCERE GRATITUDE.
FWOOOM
I'LL BE JUST OVERHEAD, SO IF YOU WANT SECONDS, LET ME KNOW.
WHOA...
I SEE.
THIS MUST BE THE PART WHERE IT ALL TURNS OUT TO BE JUST A DREAM...
I'M SCARED...
BUT UNFORTU-NATELY, THIS IS REALITY!

# A ROOM OF SWORDS AND SORCERY 1

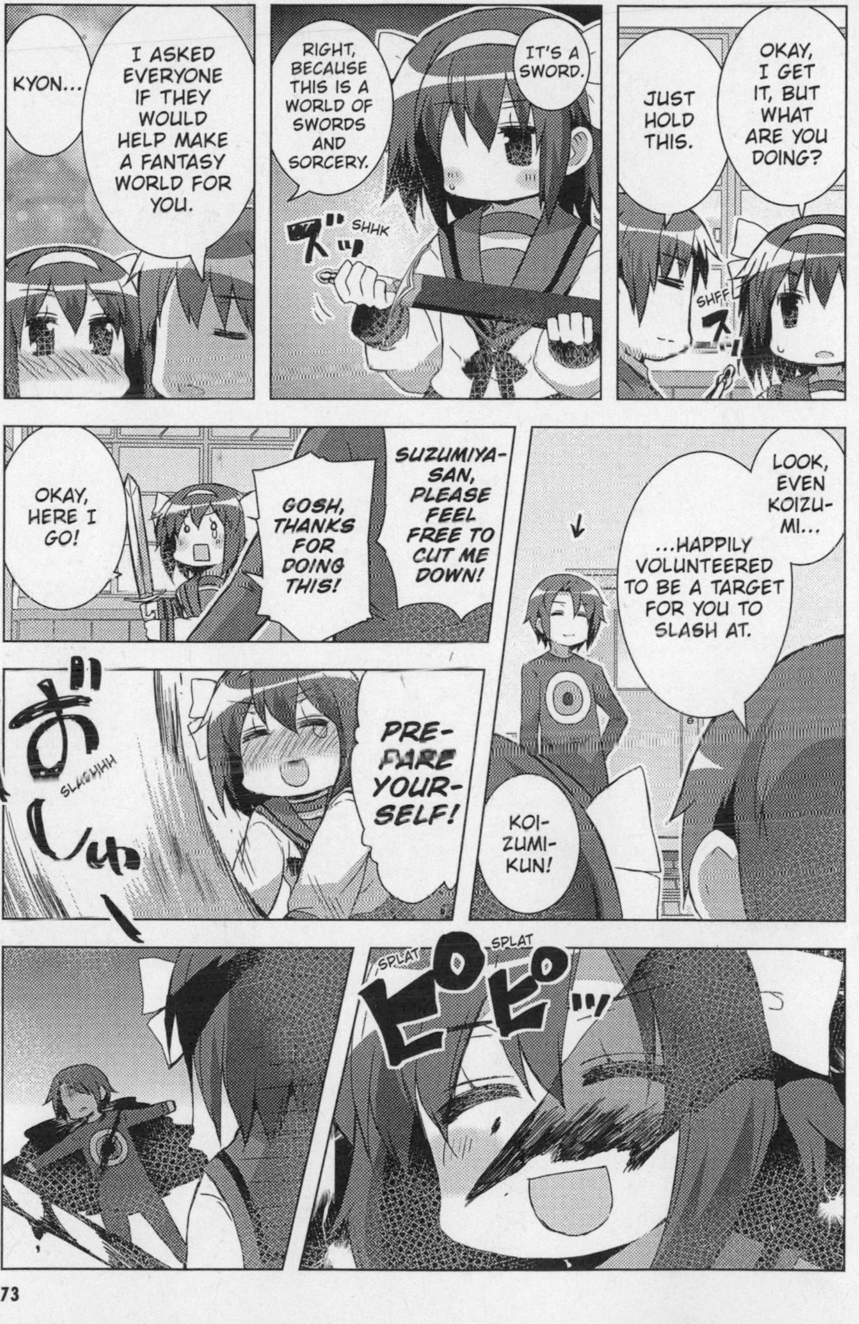
OKAY, I GET IT, BUT WHAT ARE YOU DOING?
JUST HOLD THIS.
SHFF
IT'S A SWORD.
RIGHT, BECAUSE THIS IS A WORLD OF SWORDS AND SORCERY.
SHHK
I ASKED EVERYONE IF THEY WOULD HELP MAKE A FANTASY WORLD FOR YOU.
KYON...
LOOK, EVEN KOIZUMI...
...HAPPILY VOLUNTEERED TO BE A TARGET FOR YOU TO SLASH AT.
KOI-ZUMI-KUN!
SUZUMIYA-SAN, PLEASE FEEL FREE TO CUT ME DOWN!
GOSH, THANKS FOR DOING THIS!
OKAY, HERE I GO!
PRE-PARE YOUR-SELF!
ばしゅ
SLASHHH
SPLAT
SPLAT

# A ROOM OF SWORDS AND SORCERY 2

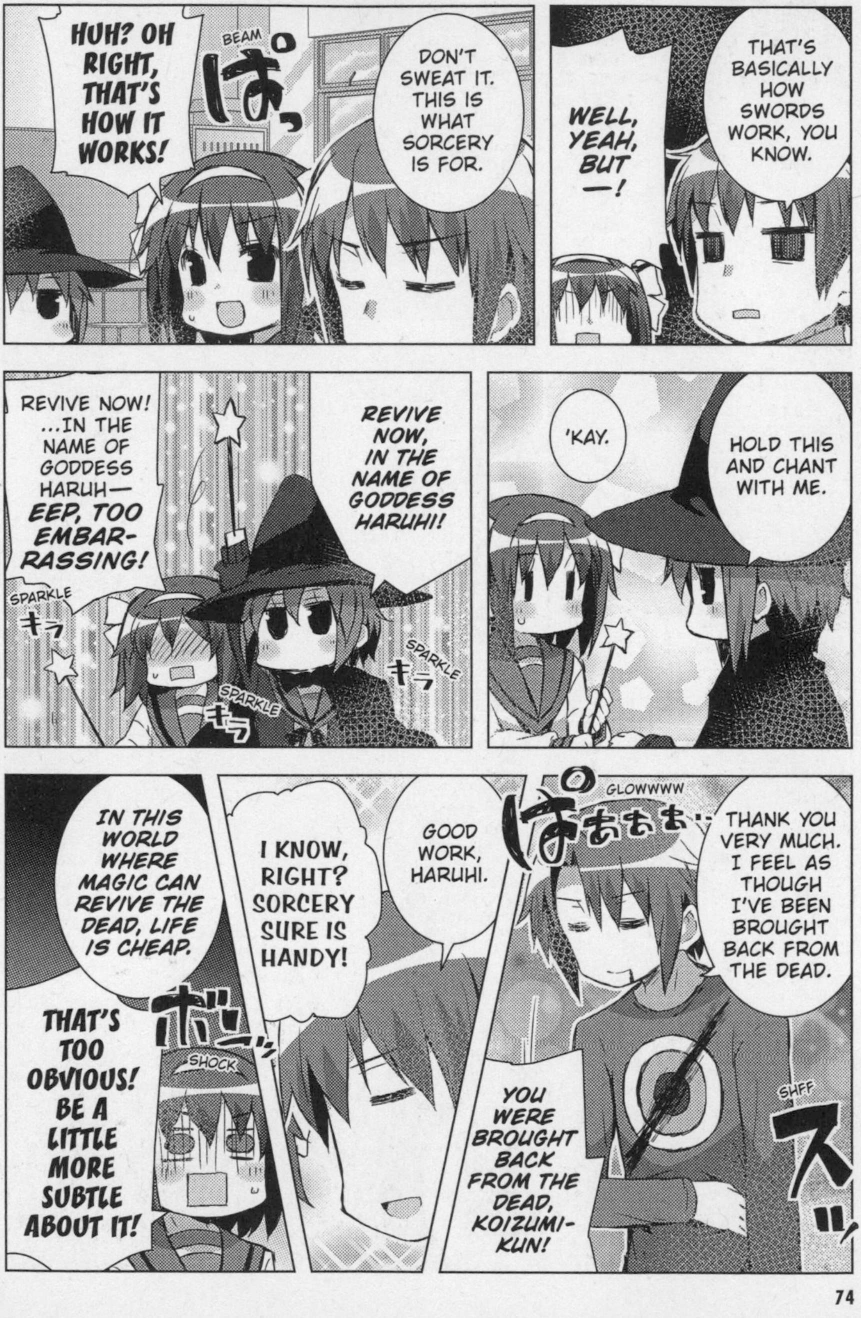

THAT'S BASICALLY HOW SWORDS WORK, YOU KNOW.
WELL, YEAH, BUT—!
DON'T SWEAT IT. THIS IS WHAT SORCERY IS FOR.
BEAM
ぱっ
HUH? OH RIGHT, THAT'S HOW IT WORKS!
HOLD THIS AND CHANT WITH ME.
'KAY.
REVIVE NOW, IN THE NAME OF GODDESS HARUHI!
REVIVE NOW! ...IN THE NAME OF GODDESS HARUH— EEP, TOO EMBARRASSING!
SPARKLE
キラ
SPARKLE
キラ
SPARKLE
キラ
GLOWWWW
ぱぁぁぁ…
THANK YOU VERY MUCH. I FEEL AS THOUGH I'VE BEEN BROUGHT BACK FROM THE DEAD.
GOOD WORK, HARUHI.
I KNOW, RIGHT? SORCERY SURE IS HANDY!
SHFF
ス"
YOU WERE BROUGHT BACK FROM THE DEAD, KOIZUMI-KUN!
IN THIS WORLD WHERE MAGIC CAN REVIVE THE DEAD, LIFE IS CHEAP.
SHOCK
THAT'S TOO OBVIOUS! BE A LITTLE MORE SUBTLE ABOUT IT!

# FANTASY WORLD

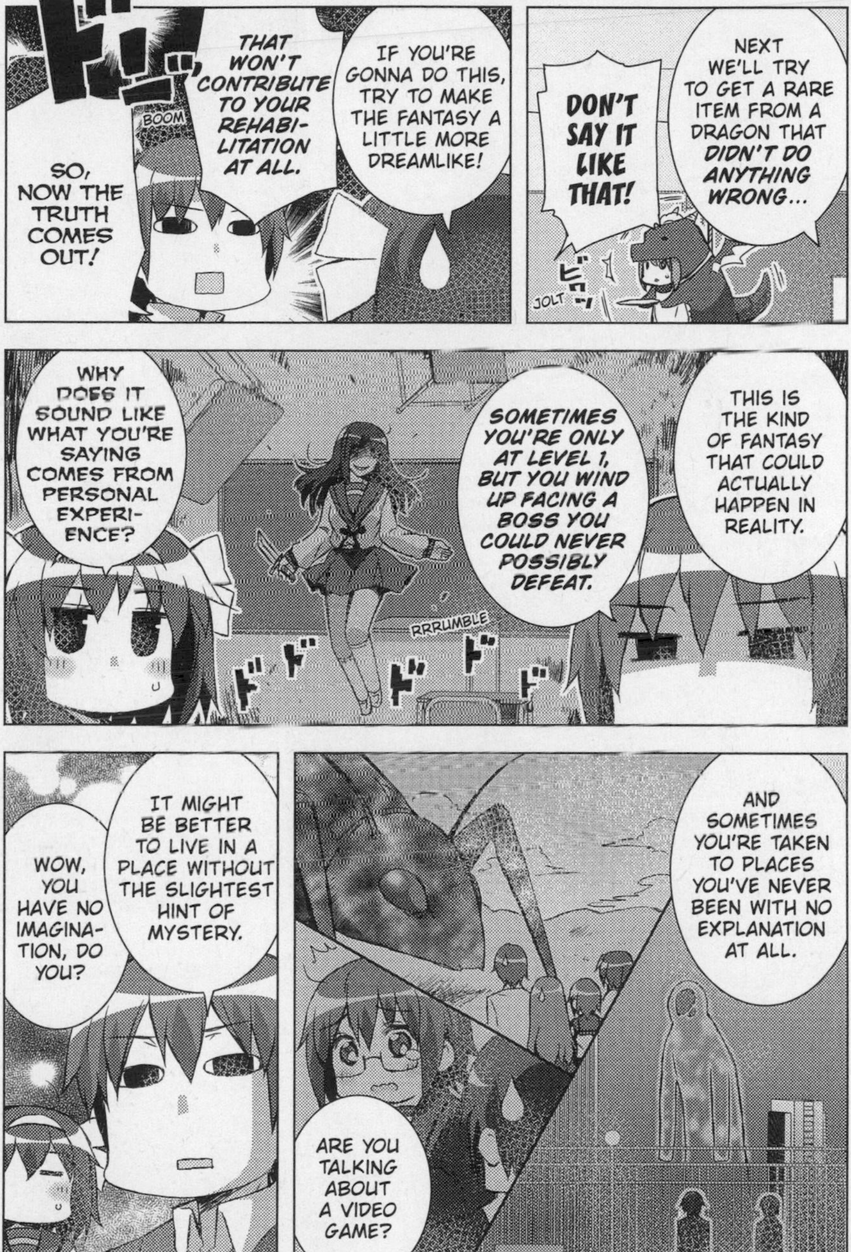
NEXT WE'LL TRY TO GET A RARE ITEM FROM A DRAGON THAT *DIDN'T DO ANYTHING WRONG*...
DON'T SAY IT LIKE THAT!
JOLT
IF YOU'RE GONNA DO THIS, TRY TO MAKE THE FANTASY A LITTLE MORE DREAMLIKE!
*THAT WON'T CONTRIBUTE TO YOUR REHABILITATION AT ALL.*
BOOM
SO, NOW THE TRUTH COMES OUT!
THIS IS THE KIND OF FANTASY THAT COULD ACTUALLY HAPPEN IN REALITY.
*SOMETIMES YOU'RE ONLY AT LEVEL 1, BUT YOU WIND UP FACING A BOSS YOU COULD NEVER POSSIBLY DEFEAT.*
RRRUMBLE
WHY DOES IT SOUND LIKE WHAT YOU'RE SAYING COMES FROM PERSONAL EXPERIENCE?
AND SOMETIMES YOU'RE TAKEN TO PLACES YOU'VE NEVER BEEN WITH NO EXPLANATION AT ALL.
ARE YOU TALKING ABOUT A VIDEO GAME?
IT MIGHT BE BETTER TO LIVE IN A PLACE WITHOUT THE SLIGHTEST HINT OF MYSTERY.
WOW, YOU HAVE NO IMAGINATION, DO YOU?

# DENIZENS OF FANTASY

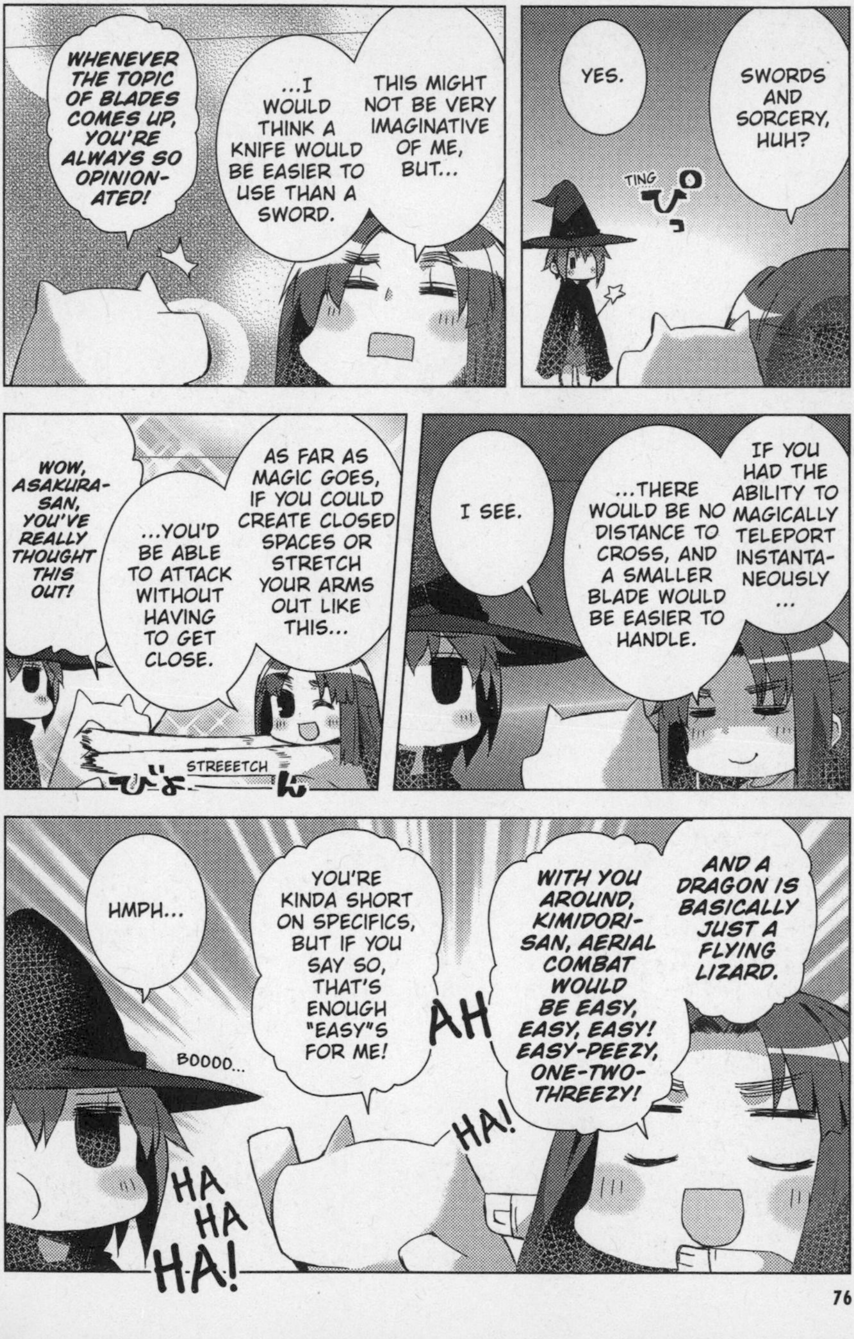

SWORDS AND SORCERY, HUH?
YES.
TING
THIS MIGHT NOT BE VERY IMAGINATIVE OF ME, BUT...
...I WOULD THINK A KNIFE WOULD BE EASIER TO USE THAN A SWORD.
WHENEVER THE TOPIC OF BLADES COMES UP, YOU'RE ALWAYS SO OPINION-ATED!
IF YOU HAD THE ABILITY TO MAGICALLY TELEPORT INSTANTA-NEOUSLY ...
...THERE WOULD BE NO DISTANCE TO CROSS, AND A SMALLER BLADE WOULD BE EASIER TO HANDLE.
I SEE.
AS FAR AS MAGIC GOES, IF YOU COULD CREATE CLOSED SPACES OR STRETCH YOUR ARMS OUT LIKE THIS...
...YOU'D BE ABLE TO ATTACK WITHOUT HAVING TO GET CLOSE.
WOW, ASAKURA-SAN, YOU'VE REALLY THOUGHT THIS OUT!
STREEETCH
AND A DRAGON IS BASICALLY JUST A FLYING LIZARD.
WITH YOU AROUND, KIMIDORI-SAN, AERIAL COMBAT WOULD BE EASY, EASY, EASY! EASY-PEEZY, ONE-TWO-THREEZY!
AH
HA!
YOU'RE KINDA SHORT ON SPECIFICS, BUT IF YOU SAY SO, THAT'S ENOUGH "EASY"S FOR ME!
HMPH...
BOOOO...
HA HA HA!

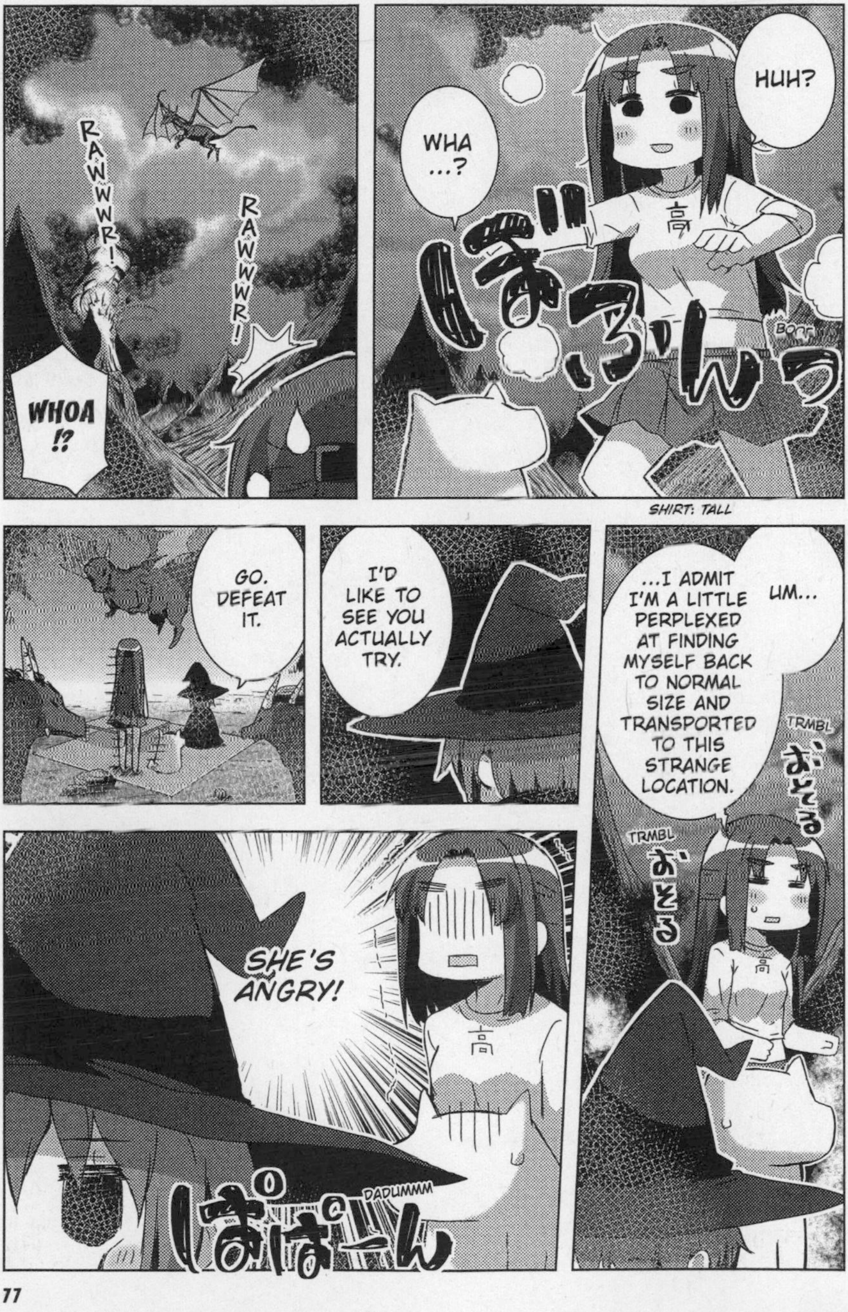
HUH?
WHA ...?
ぼふんっ
BOFF
SHIRT: TALL
RAWWWR!
RAWWWR!
WHOA !?
UM...
...I ADMIT I'M A LITTLE PERPLEXED AT FINDING MYSELF BACK TO NORMAL SIZE AND TRANSPORTED TO THIS STRANGE LOCATION.
TRMBL おそる
TRMBL おそる
I'D LIKE TO SEE YOU ACTUALLY TRY.
GO. DEFEAT IT.
SHE'S ANGRY!
DADUMMM
ぱぱーん

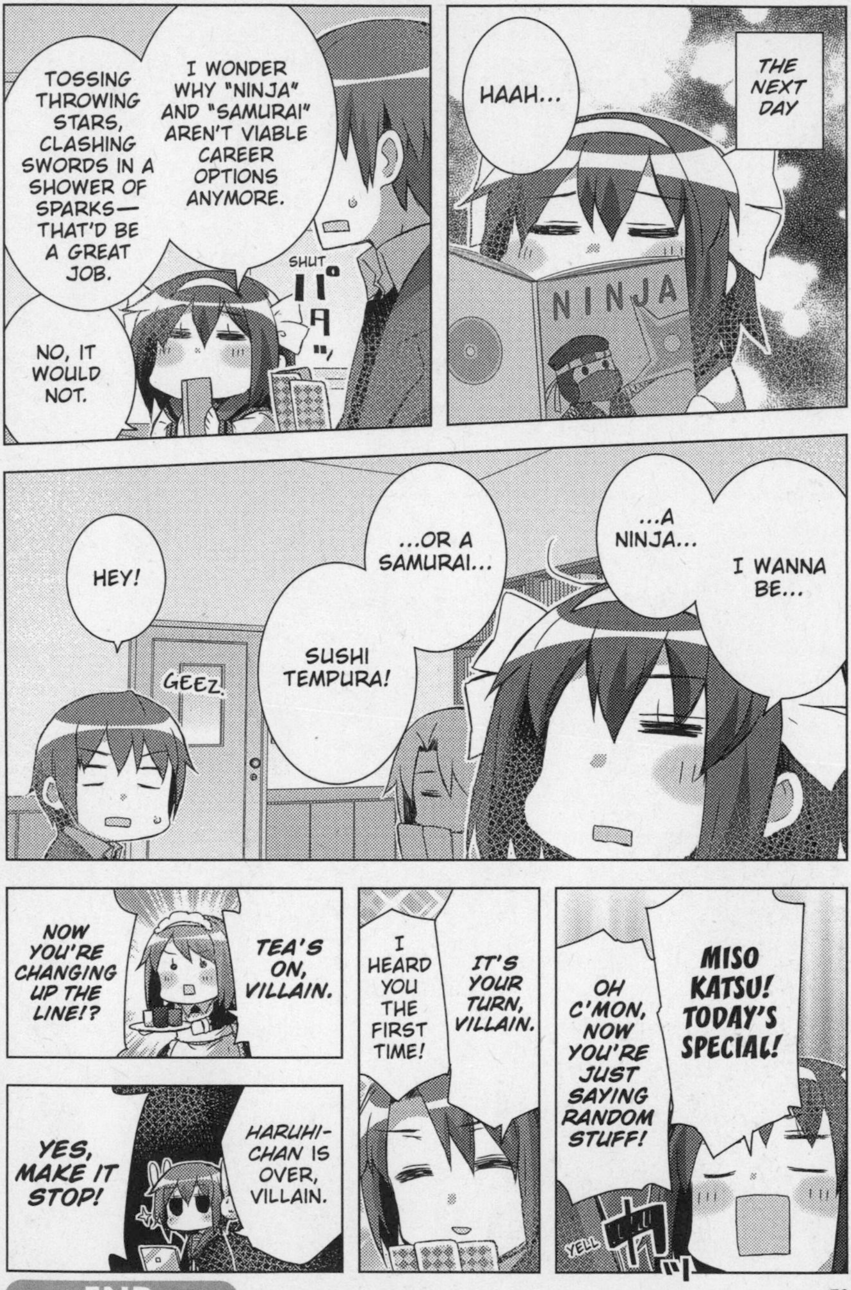
THE NEXT DAY
HAAH...
I WONDER WHY "NINJA" AND "SAMURAI" AREN'T VIABLE CAREER OPTIONS ANYMORE.
TOSSING THROWING STARS, CLASHING SWORDS IN A SHOWER OF SPARKS—THAT'D BE A GREAT JOB.
SHUT
NO, IT WOULD NOT.
I WANNA BE...
...A NINJA...
...OR A SAMURAI...
SUSHI TEMPURA!
HEY!
GEEZ.
MISO KATSU! TODAY'S SPECIAL!
OH C'MON, NOW YOU'RE JUST SAYING RANDOM STUFF!
YELL
IT'S YOUR TURN, VILLAIN.
I HEARD YOU THE FIRST TIME!
TEA'S ON, VILLAIN.
NOW YOU'RE CHANGING UP THE LINE!?
HARUHI-CHAN IS OVER, VILLAIN.
YES, MAKE IT STOP!

END

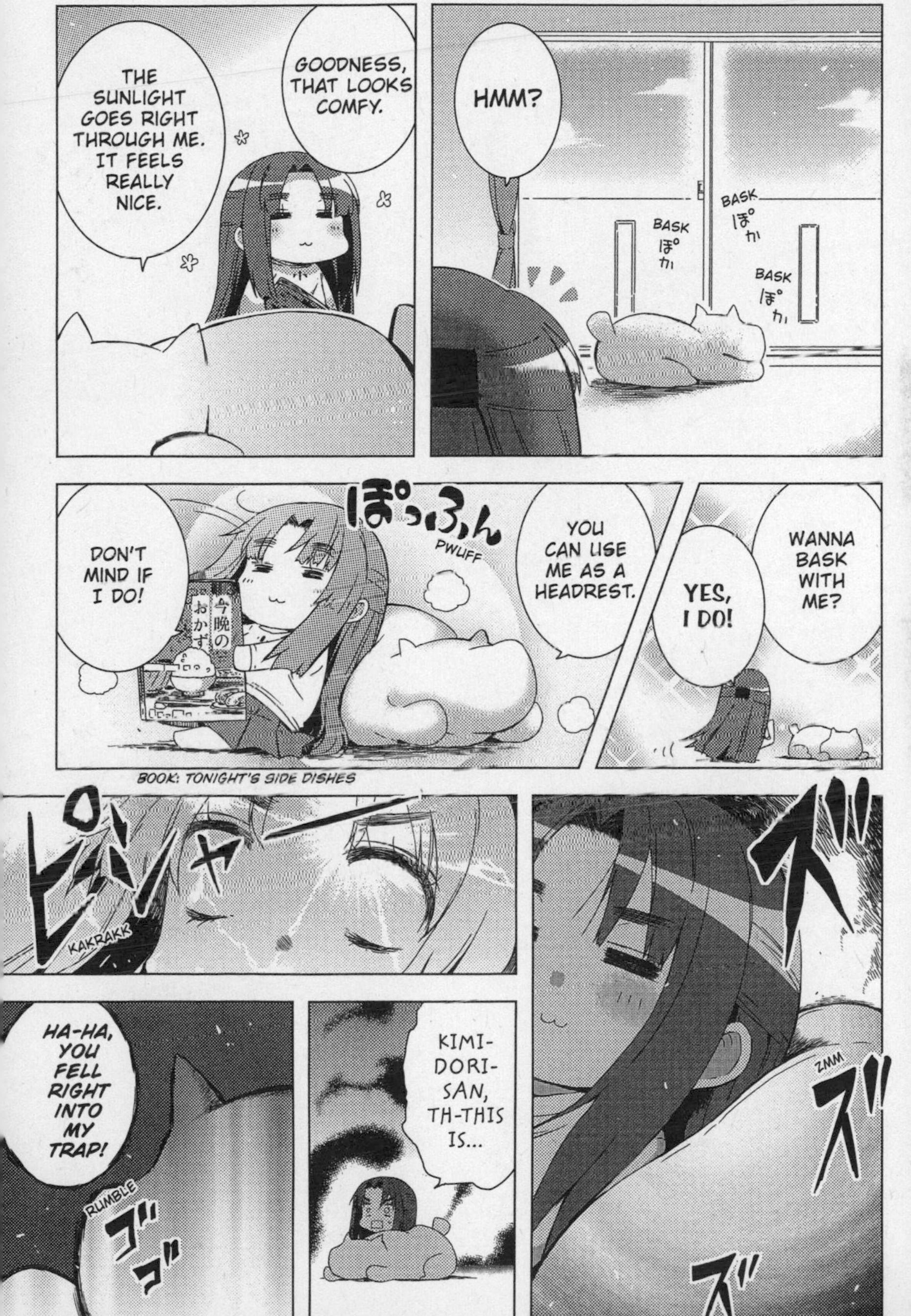
HMM?
BASK ぽか
BASK ぽか
BASK ぽか
GOODNESS, THAT LOOKS COMFY.
THE SUNLIGHT GOES RIGHT THROUGH ME. IT FEELS REALLY NICE.
WANNA BASK WITH ME?
YES, I DO!
YOU CAN USE ME AS A HEADREST.
ぽっふん
PWUFF
DON'T MIND IF I DO!
今晩のおかず
BOOK: TONIGHT'S SIDE DISHES
ズズズ
ZMM
ピシャ
KAKRAKK
KIMI-DORI-SAN, TH-THIS IS...
HA-HA, YOU FELL RIGHT INTO MY TRAP!
RUMBLE
ゴゴ

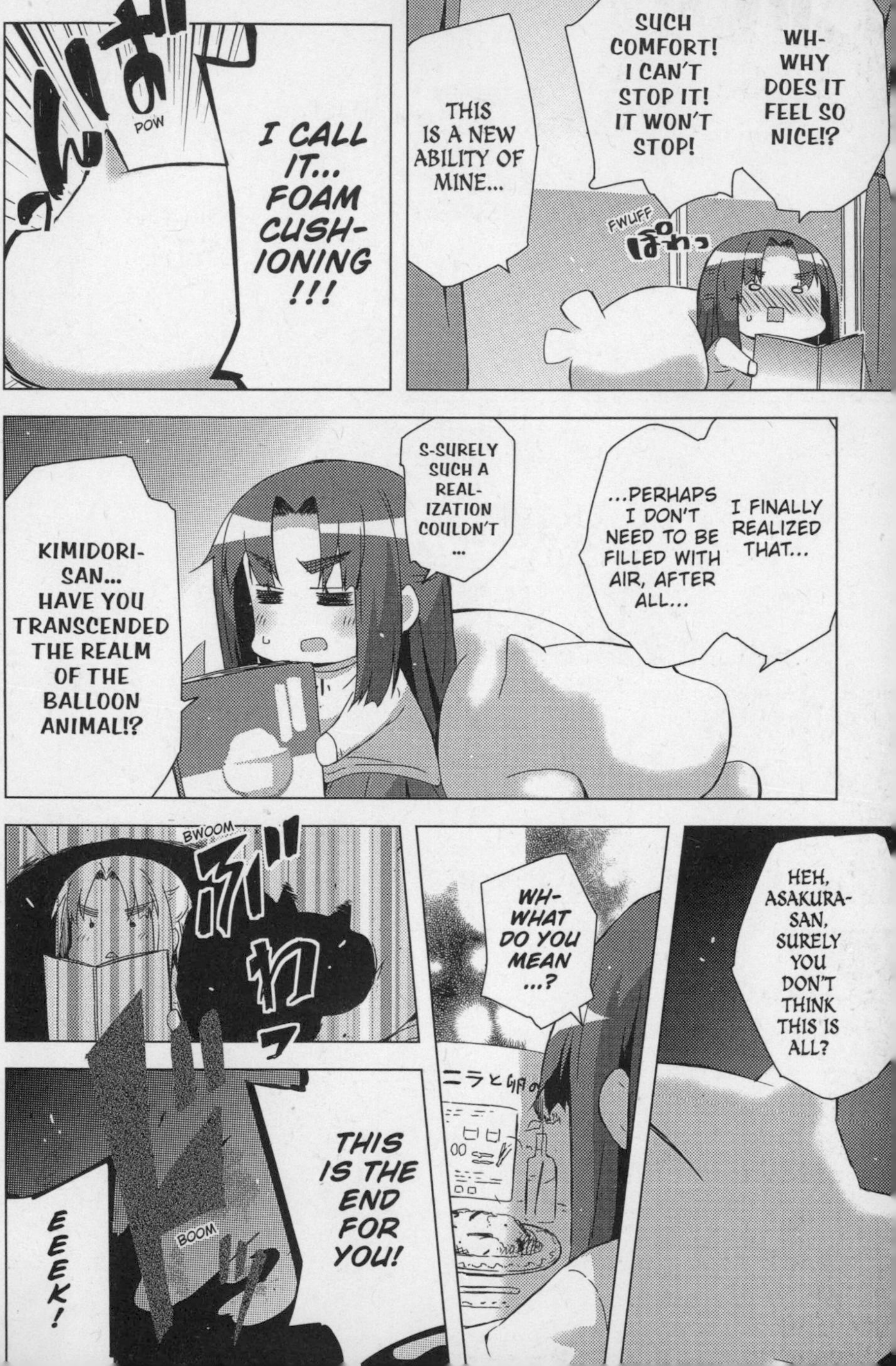
WH-WHY DOES IT FEEL SO NICE!?
SUCH COMFORT! I CAN'T STOP IT! IT WON'T STOP!
THIS IS A NEW ABILITY OF MINE...
FWUFF
ぽわっ
I CALL IT... FOAM CUSHIONING!!!
POW
I FINALLY REALIZED THAT...
...PERHAPS I DON'T NEED TO BE FILLED WITH AIR, AFTER ALL...
S-SURELY SUCH A REAL-IZATION COULDN'T ...
KIMIDORI-SAN... HAVE YOU TRANSCENDED THE REALM OF THE BALLOON ANIMAL!?
HEH, ASAKURA-SAN, SURELY YOU DON'T THINK THIS IS ALL?
WH-WHAT DO YOU MEAN ...?
BWOOM
ぶわっ
THIS IS THE END FOR YOU!
BOOM
EEEEK!

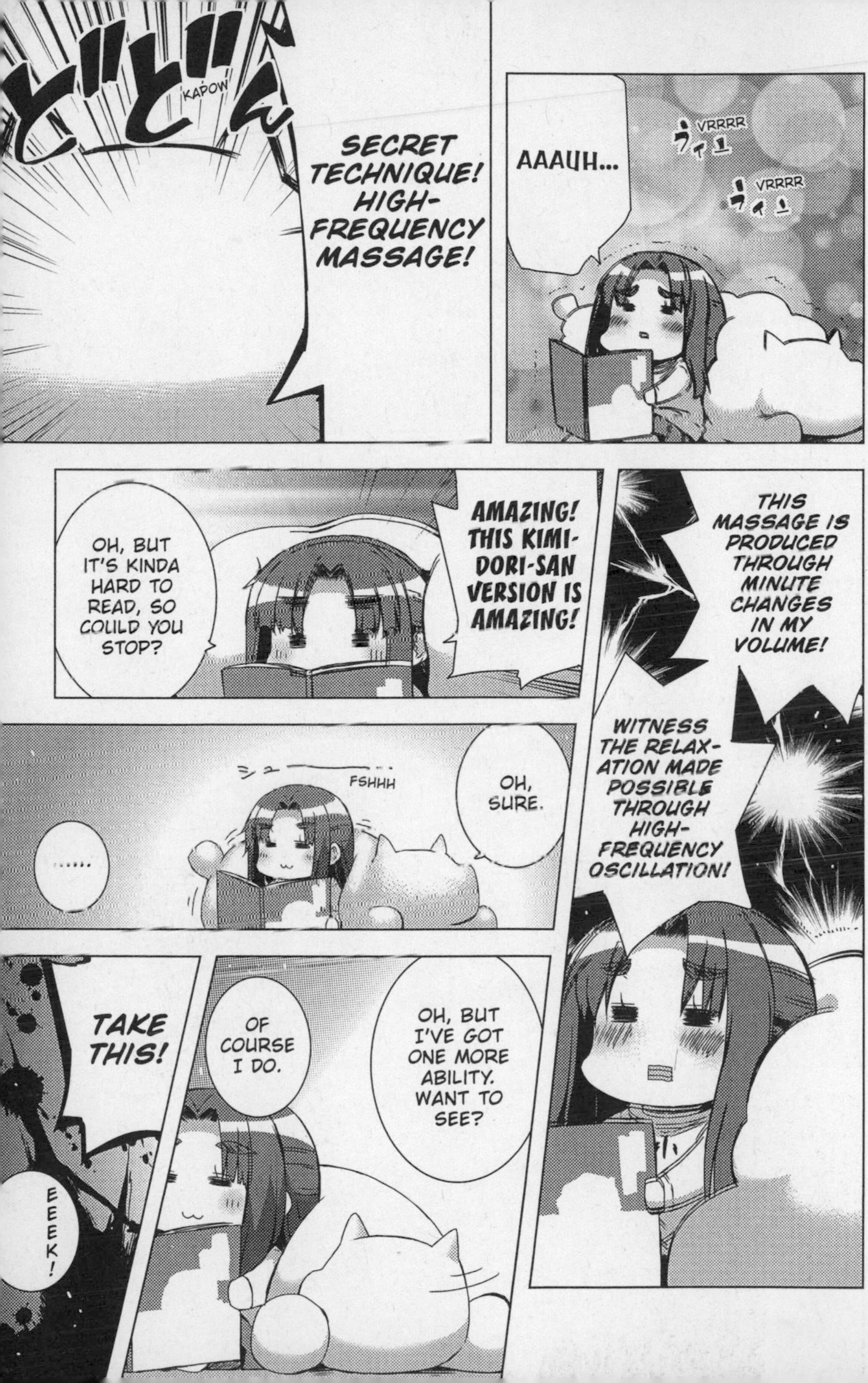
VRRRR
VRRRR
AAAUH...
KAPOW
SECRET TECHNIQUE! HIGH-FREQUENCY MASSAGE!
THIS MASSAGE IS PRODUCED THROUGH MINUTE CHANGES IN MY VOLUME!
WITNESS THE RELAXATION MADE POSSIBLE THROUGH HIGH-FREQUENCY OSCILLATION!
AMAZING! THIS KIMIDORI-SAN VERSION IS AMAZING!
OH, BUT IT'S KINDA HARD TO READ, SO COULD YOU STOP?
OH, SURE.
FSHHH
......
OH, BUT I'VE GOT ONE MORE ABILITY. WANT TO SEE?
OF COURSE I DO.
TAKE THIS!
EEEEK!

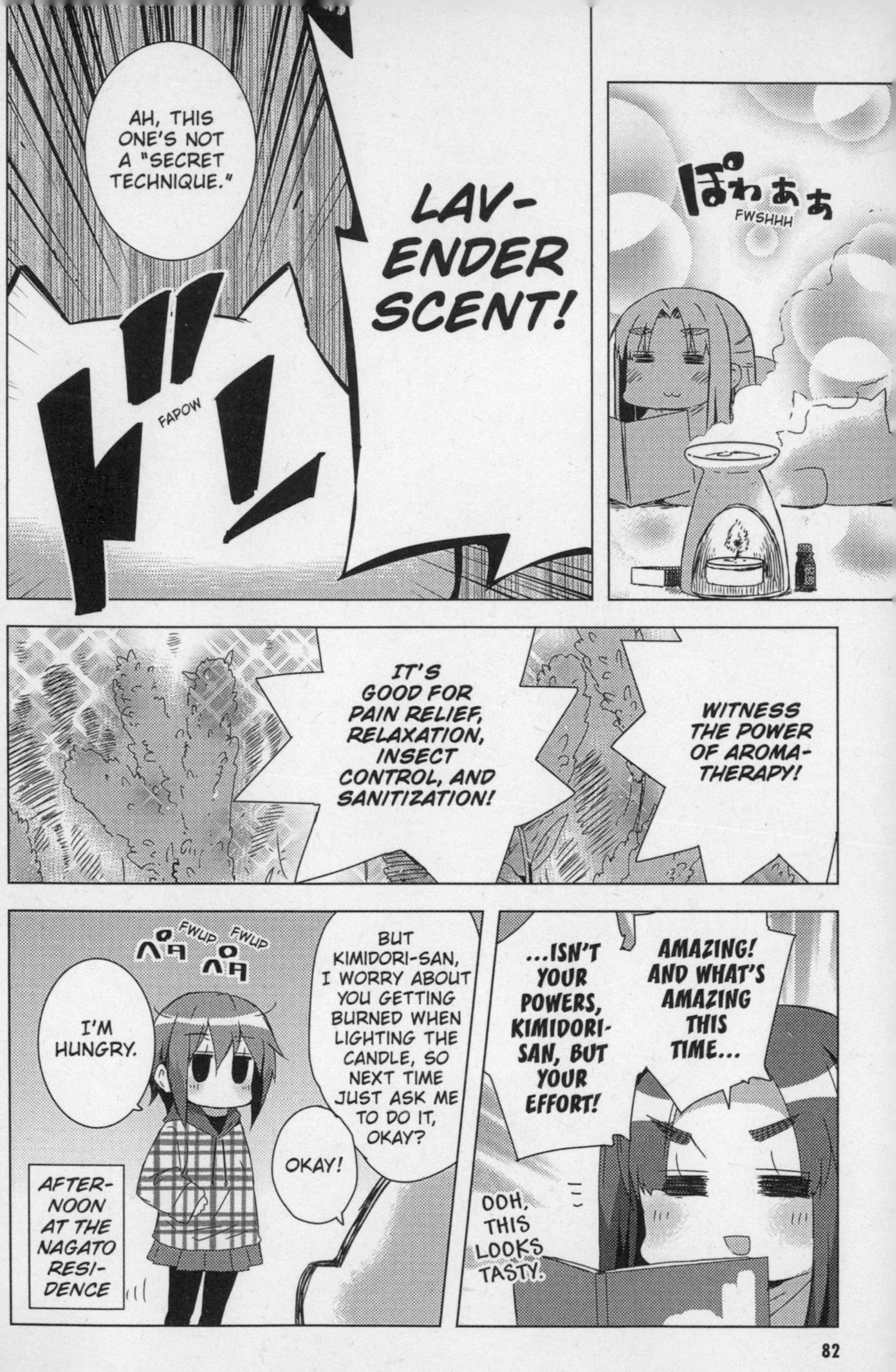

ぽわぁぁ
FWSHHH
AH, THIS ONE'S NOT A "SECRET TECHNIQUE."
LAV-ENDER SCENT!
ドン
FAPOW
WITNESS THE POWER OF AROMA-THERAPY!
IT'S GOOD FOR PAIN RELIEF, RELAXATION, INSECT CONTROL, AND SANITIZATION!
AMAZING! AND WHAT'S AMAZING THIS TIME...
...ISN'T YOUR POWERS, KIMIDORI-SAN, BUT YOUR EFFORT!
OOH, THIS LOOKS TASTY.
BUT KIMIDORI-SAN, I WORRY ABOUT YOU GETTING BURNED WHEN LIGHTING THE CANDLE, SO NEXT TIME JUST ASK ME TO DO IT, OKAY?
OKAY!
ぺタ ぺタ
FWUP FWUP
I'M HUNGRY.
AFTER-NOON AT THE NAGATO RESI-DENCE

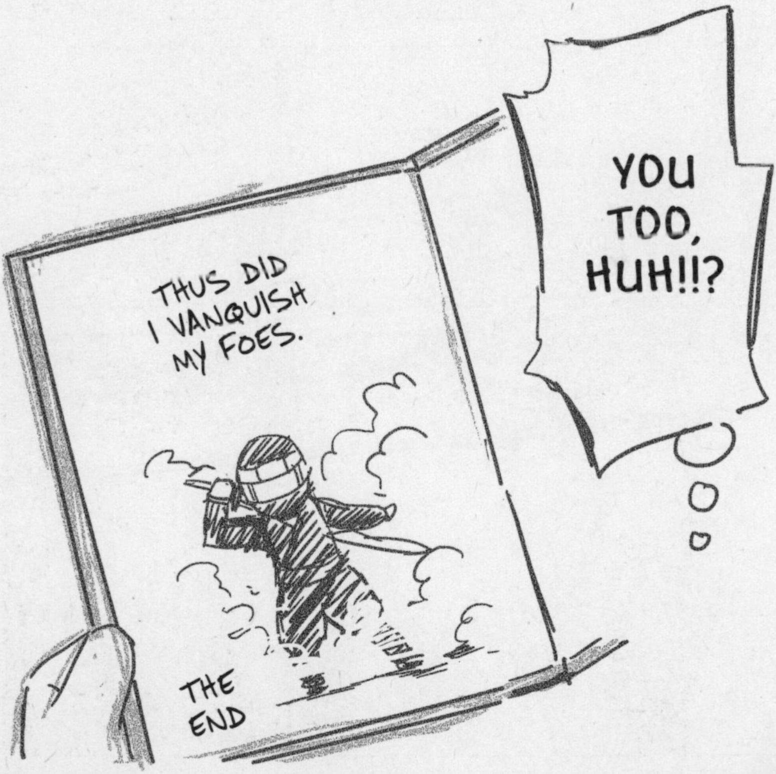
YOU TOO, HUH!!?
THUS DID I VANQUISH MY FOES.
THE END

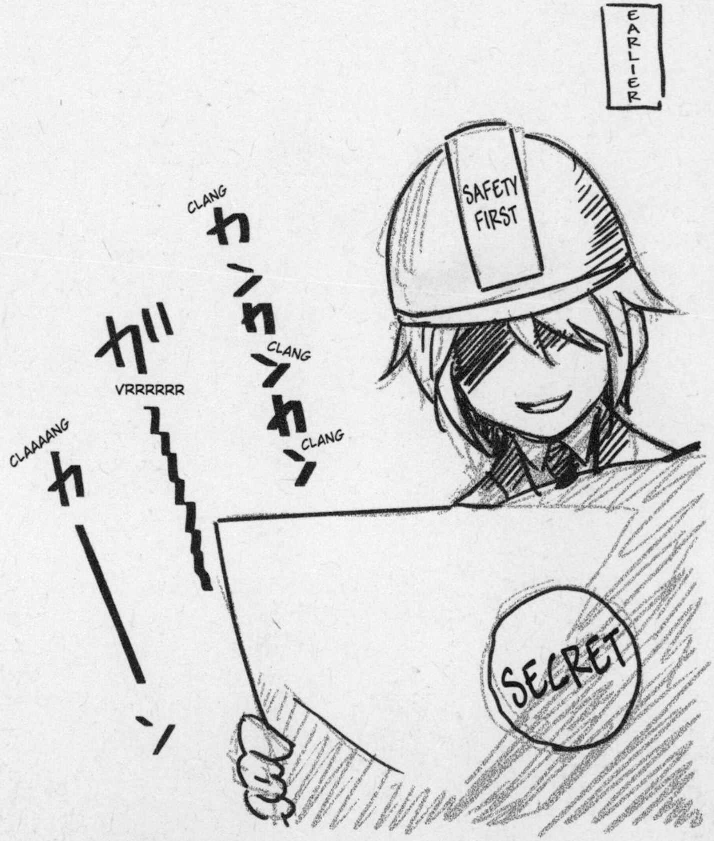
EARLIER
SAFETY FIRST
CLANG
カンカンカン
CLANG
CLANG
VRRRRRR
ガ〜
CLAAAANG
カーン
SECRET

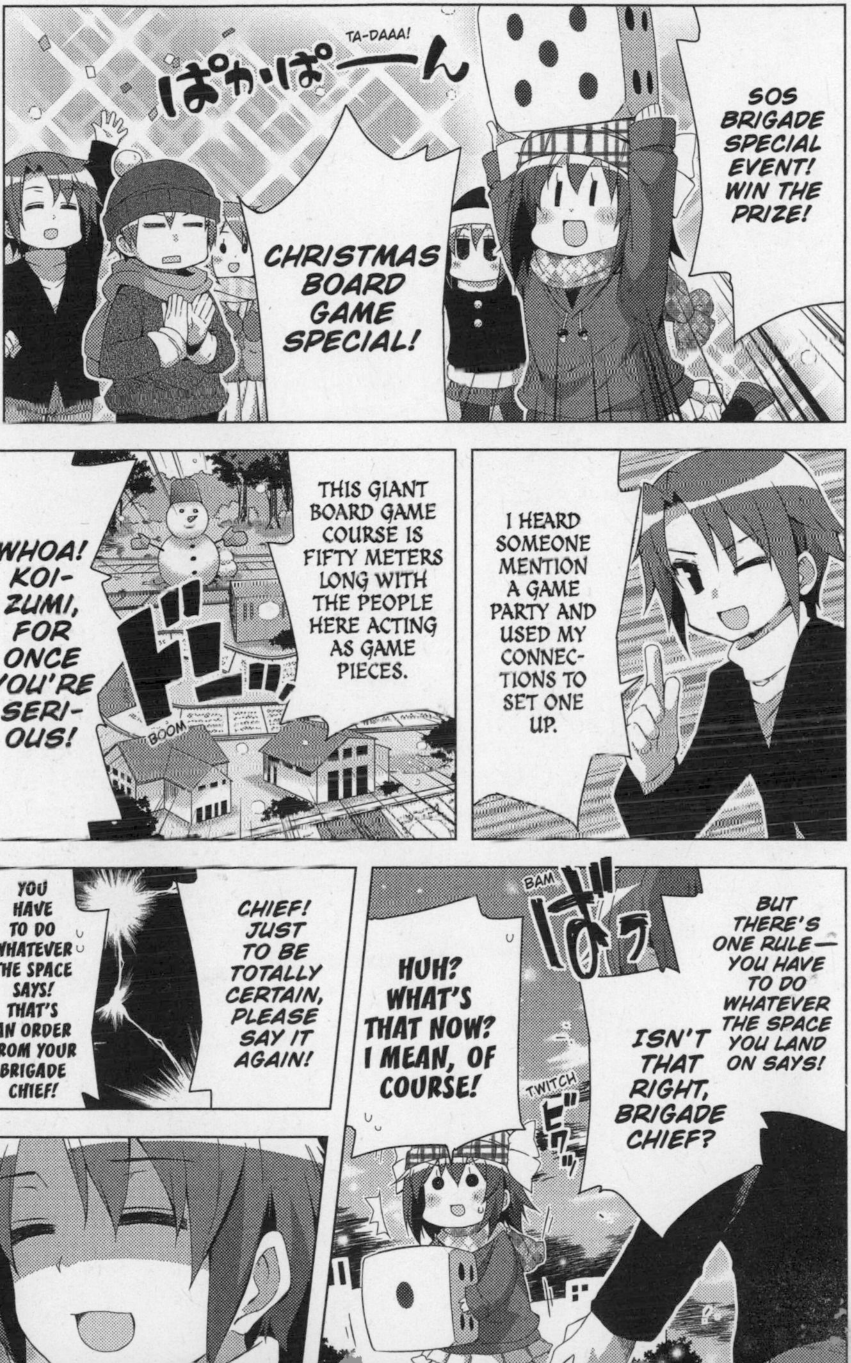
SOS BRIGADE SPECIAL EVENT! WIN THE PRIZE!
TA-DAAA!
CHRISTMAS BOARD GAME SPECIAL!
I HEARD SOMEONE MENTION A GAME PARTY AND USED MY CONNEC-TIONS TO SET ONE UP.
THIS GIANT BOARD GAME COURSE IS FIFTY METERS LONG WITH THE PEOPLE HERE ACTING AS GAME PIECES.
WHOA! KOI-ZUMI, FOR ONCE YOU'RE SERI-OUS!
BOOM
BAM
BUT THERE'S ONE RULE— YOU HAVE TO DO WHATEVER THE SPACE YOU LAND ON SAYS!
ISN'T THAT RIGHT, BRIGADE CHIEF?
TWITCH
HUH? WHAT'S THAT NOW? I MEAN, OF COURSE!
CHIEF! JUST TO BE TOTALLY CERTAIN, PLEASE SAY IT AGAIN!
YOU HAVE TO DO WHATEVER THE SPACE SAYS! THAT'S AN ORDER FROM YOUR BRIGADE CHIEF!

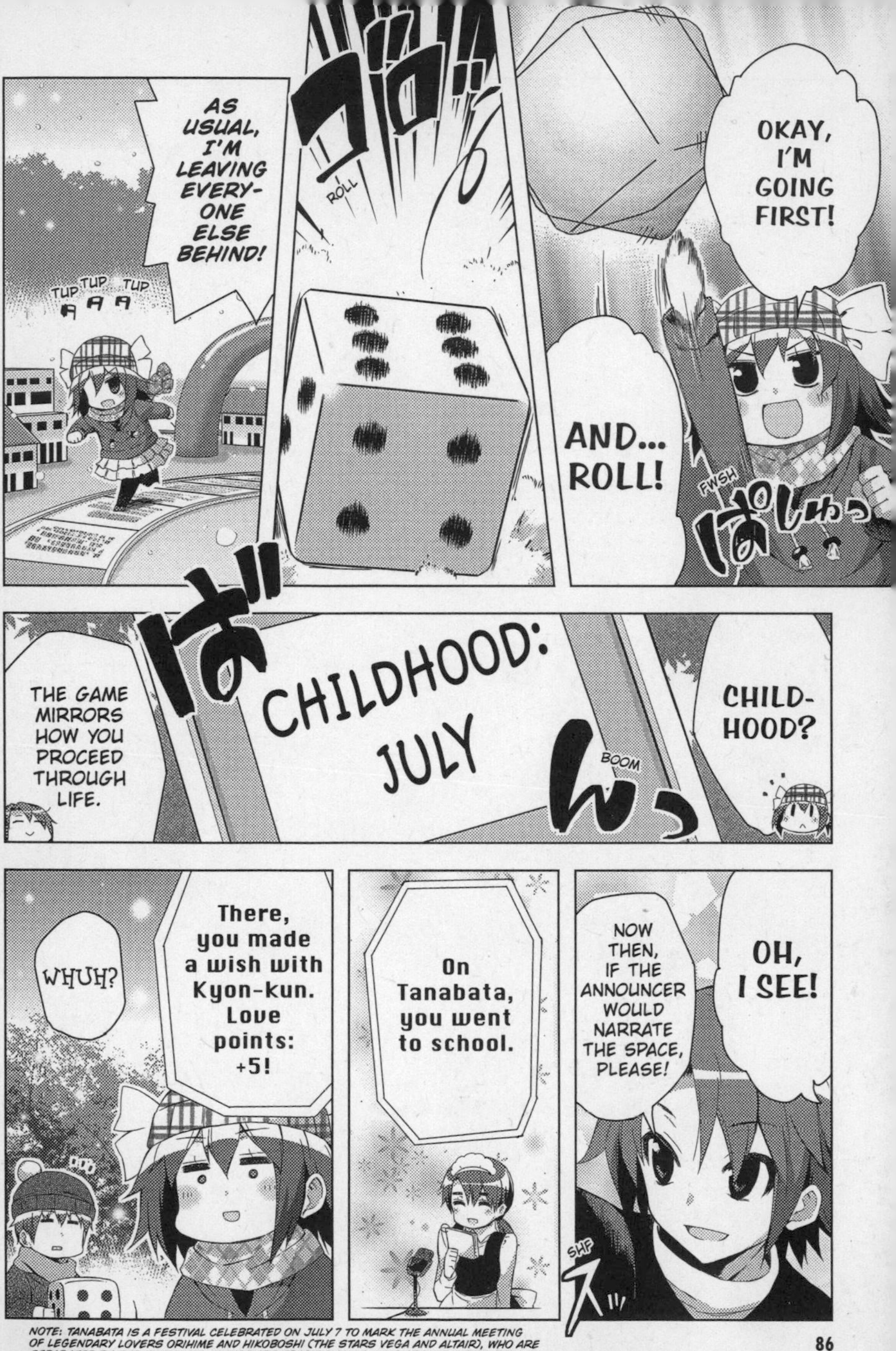
OKAY, I'M GOING FIRST!
AND... ROLL!
FWSH
ROLL
AS USUAL, I'M LEAVING EVERY-ONE ELSE BEHIND!
TUP TUP TUP
CHILD-HOOD?
BOOM
CHILDHOOD: JULY
THE GAME MIRRORS HOW YOU PROCEED THROUGH LIFE.
OH, I SEE!
NOW THEN, IF THE ANNOUNCER WOULD NARRATE THE SPACE, PLEASE!
SHP
On Tanabata, you went to school.
There, you made a wish with Kyon-kun. Love points: +5!
WHUH?

*NOTE: TANABATA IS A FESTIVAL CELEBRATED ON JULY 7 TO MARK THE ANNUAL MEETING OF LEGENDARY LOVERS ORIHIME AND HIKOBOSHI (THE STARS VEGA AND ALTAIR), WHO ARE SEPARATED BY THE MILKY WAY. WISHES ARE TRADITIONALLY HUNG FROM BAMBOO STALKS, AND FESTIVALS ARE HELD IN MANY AREAS.*

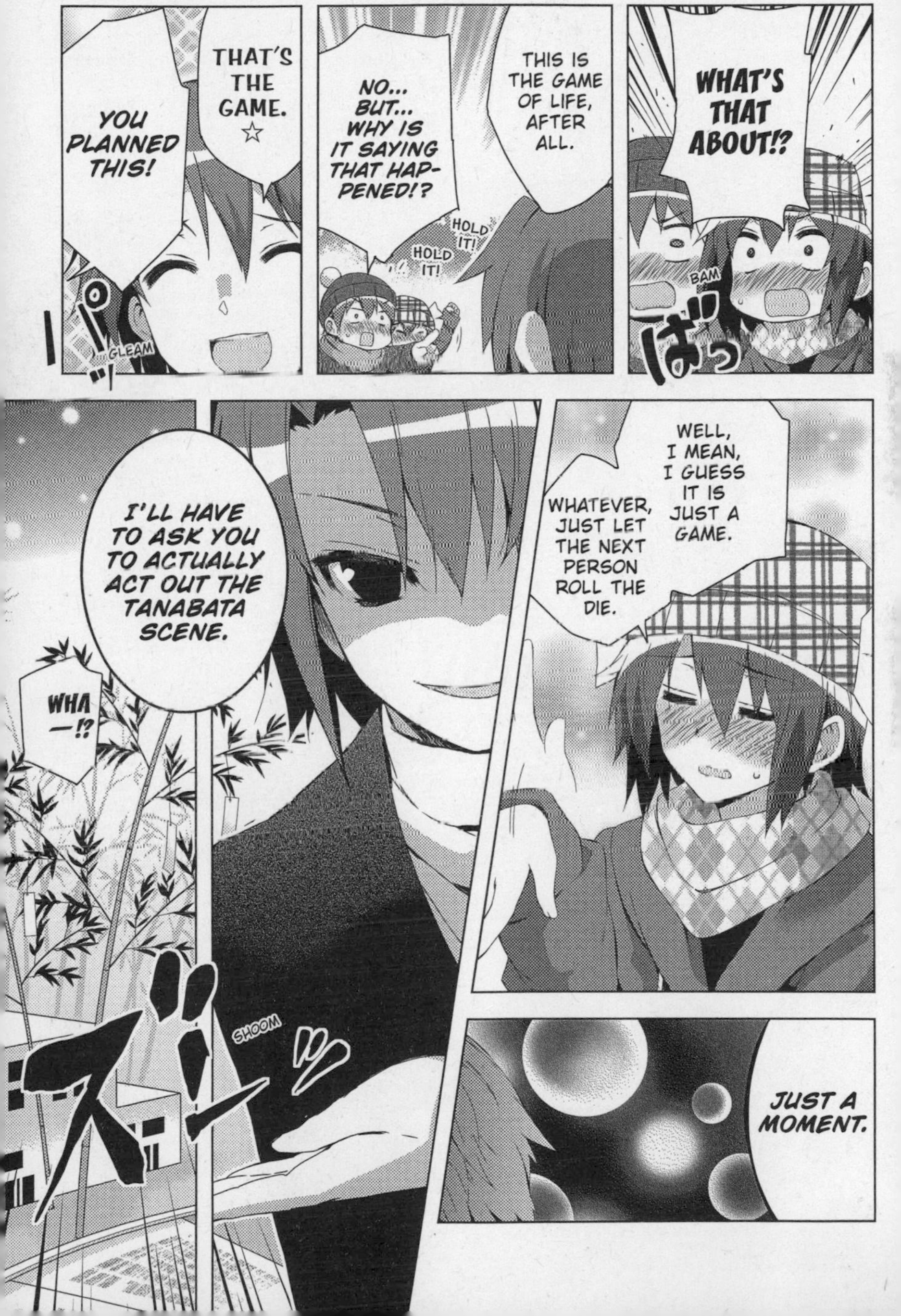
WHAT'S THAT ABOUT!?
BAM
ばっ
THIS IS THE GAME OF LIFE, AFTER ALL.
NO... BUT... WHY IS IT SAYING THAT HAPPENED!?
HOLD IT!
HOLD IT!
THAT'S THE GAME. ☆
YOU PLANNED THIS!
GLEAM
WELL, I MEAN, I GUESS IT IS JUST A GAME.
WHATEVER, JUST LET THE NEXT PERSON ROLL THE DIE.
JUST A MOMENT.
I'LL HAVE TO ASK YOU TO ACTUALLY ACT OUT THE TANABATA SCENE.
WHA—!?
SHOOM

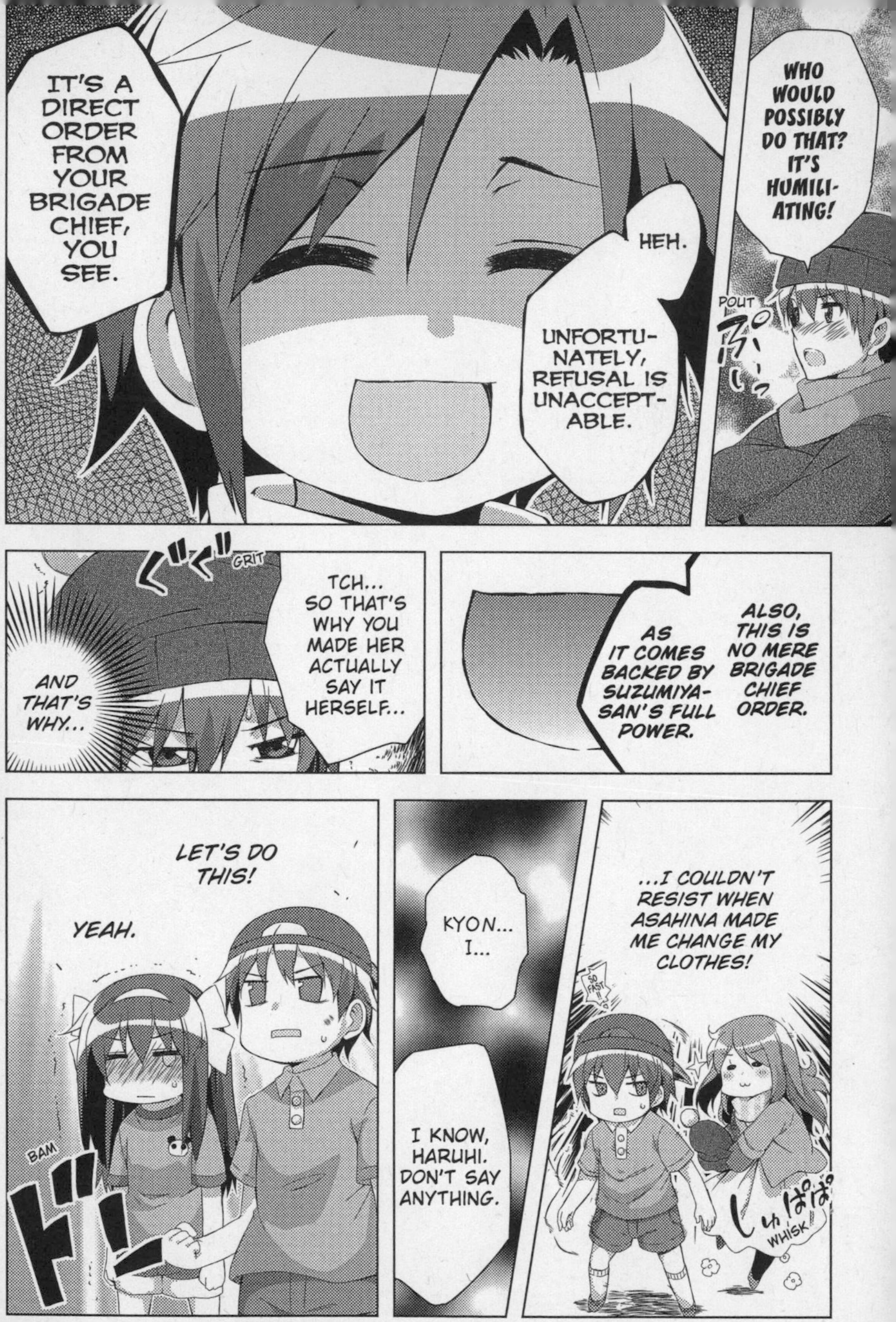
WHO WOULD POSSIBLY DO THAT? IT'S HUMILI-ATING!
POUT
HEH.
UNFORTU-NATELY, REFUSAL IS UNACCEPT-ABLE.
IT'S A DIRECT ORDER FROM YOUR BRIGADE CHIEF, YOU SEE.
ALSO, THIS IS NO MERE BRIGADE CHIEF ORDER.
AS IT COMES BACKED BY SUZUMIYA-SAN'S FULL POWER.
GRIT
TCH... SO THAT'S WHY YOU MADE HER ACTUALLY SAY IT HERSELF...
AND THAT'S WHY...
...I COULDN'T RESIST WHEN ASAHINA MADE ME CHANGE MY CLOTHES!
SO FAST!!
WHISK
KYON... I...
I KNOW, HARUHI. DON'T SAY ANYTHING.
LET'S DO THIS!
YEAH.
BAM

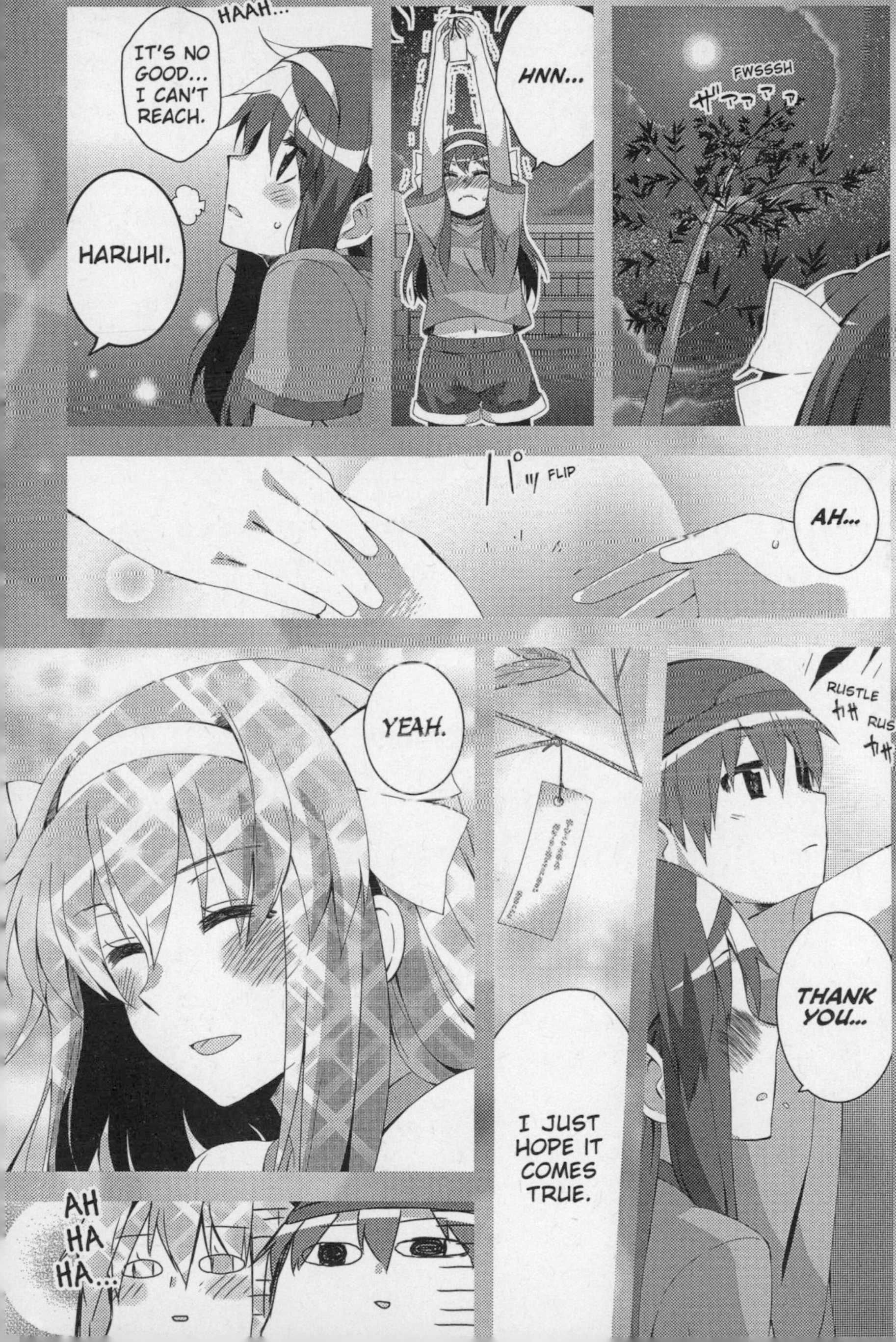
FWSSSH
HNN...
HAAH...
IT'S NO GOOD... I CAN'T REACH.
HARUHI.
AH...
FLIP
RUSTLE
RUSTLE
THANK YOU...
I JUST HOPE IT COMES TRUE.
YEAH.
AH HA HA...

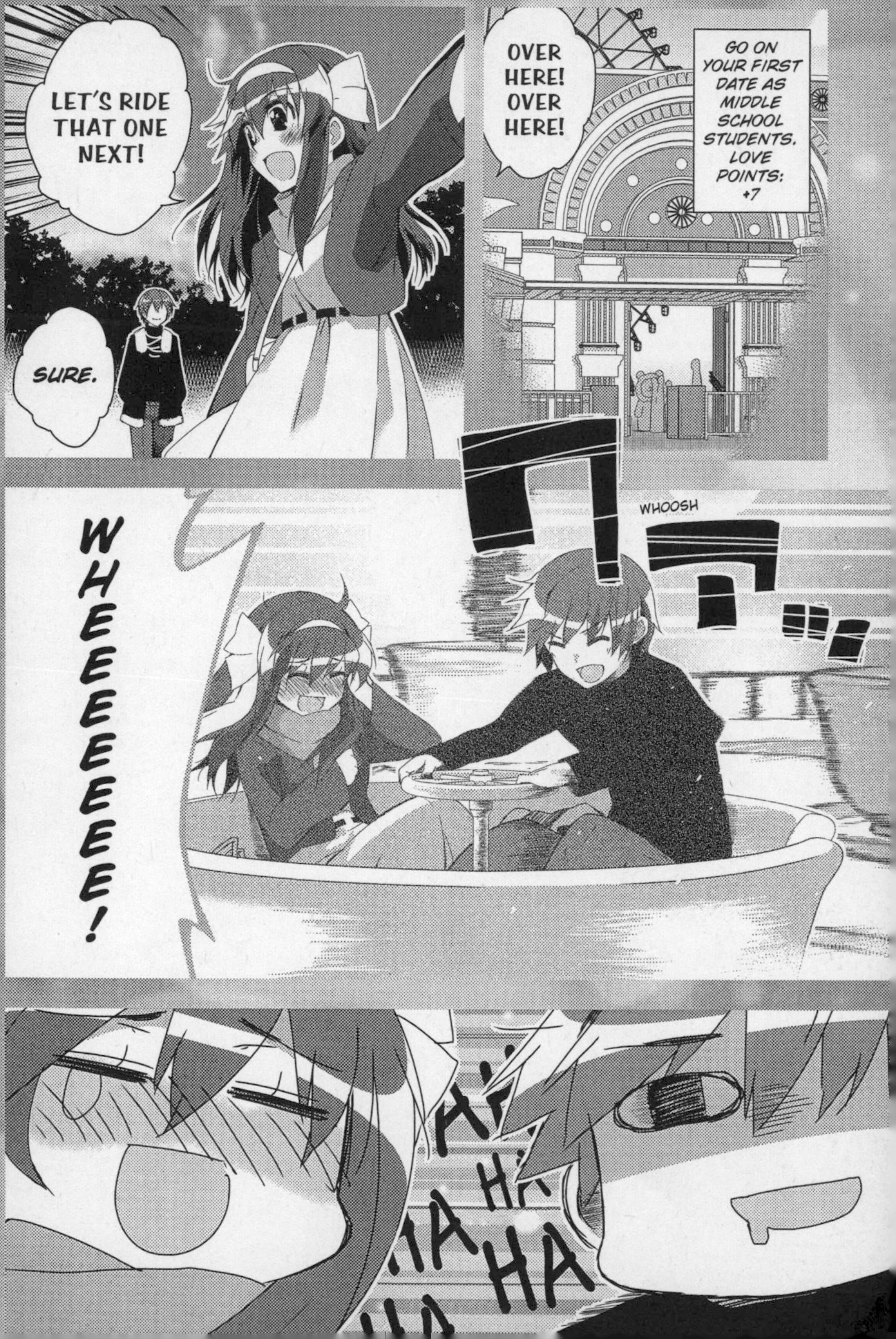
GO ON YOUR FIRST DATE AS MIDDLE SCHOOL STUDENTS. LOVE POINTS: +7
OVER HERE! OVER HERE!
LET'S RIDE THAT ONE NEXT!
SURE.
WHOOSH
WHEEEEEEEEE!
HA HA HA HA

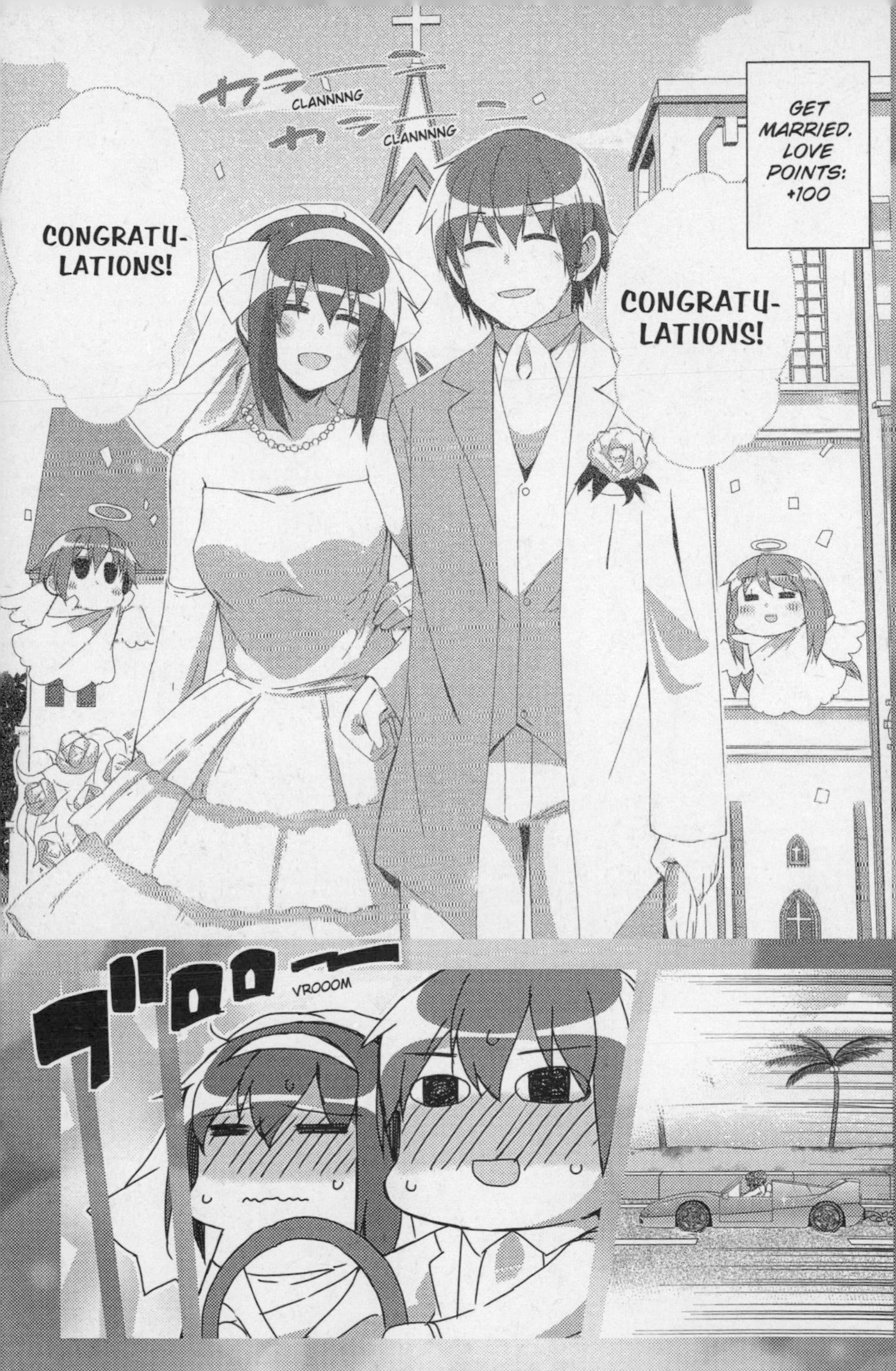
GET MARRIED. LOVE POINTS: +100
CLANNNNG
CLANNNNG
CONGRATU-LATIONS!
CONGRATU-LATIONS!
VROOM

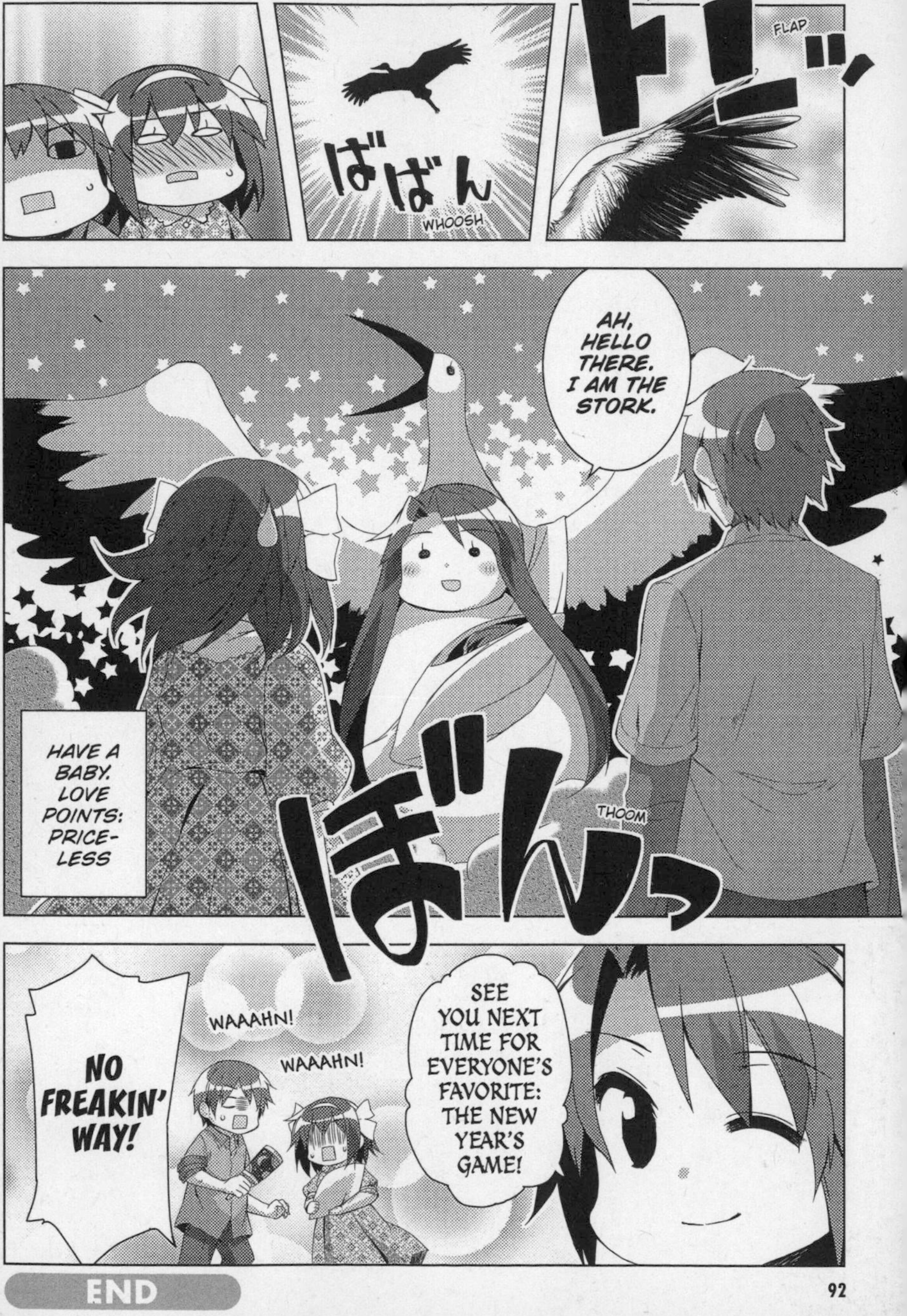
FLAP
ばばん
WHOOSH
AH, HELLO THERE. I AM THE STORK.
ぼんっ
THOOM
HAVE A BABY. LOVE POINTS: PRICE-LESS
SEE YOU NEXT TIME FOR EVERYONE'S FAVORITE: THE NEW YEAR'S GAME!
WAAAHN!
WAAAHN!
NO FREAKIN' WAY!

END

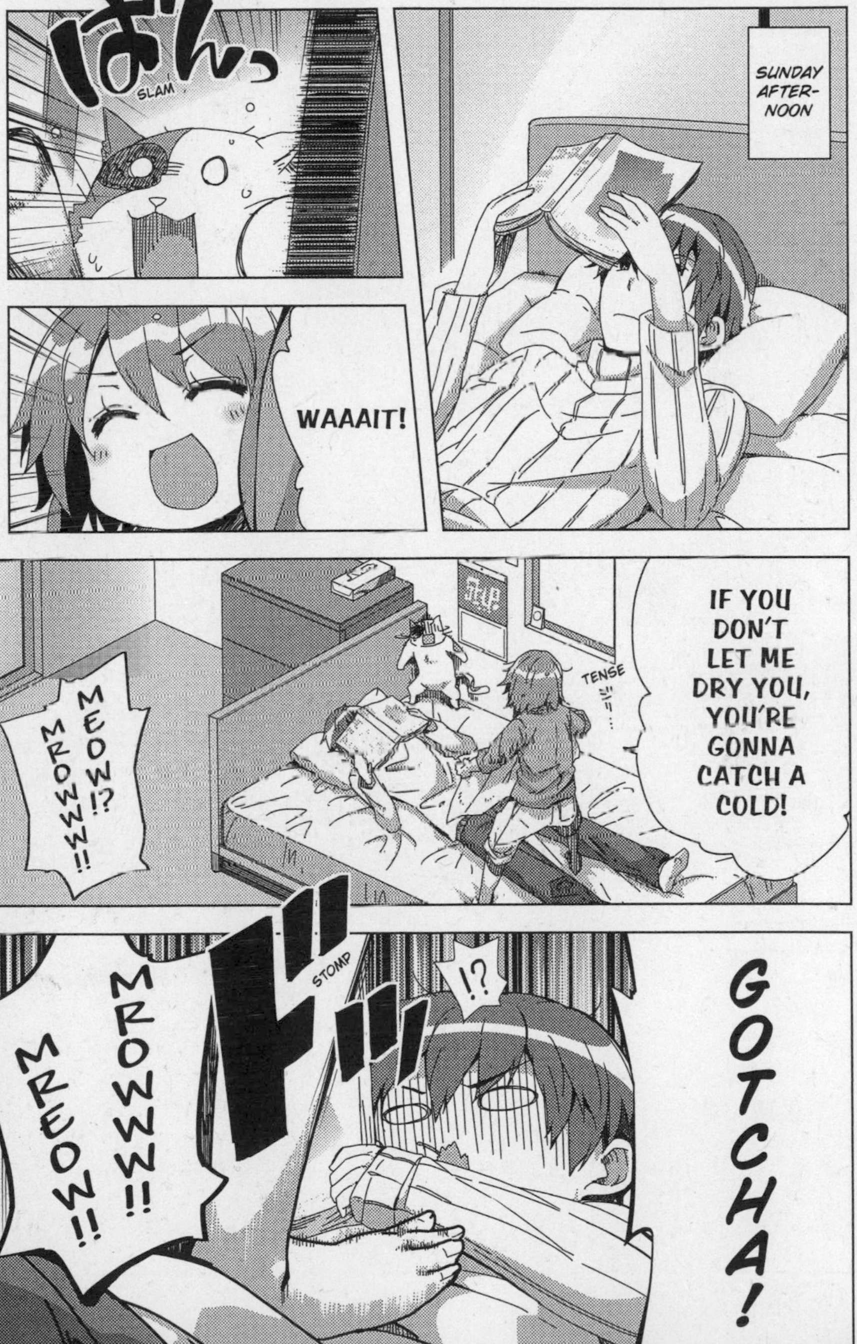
SUNDAY AFTER-NOON
ばんっ
SLAM
WAAAIT!
IF YOU DON'T LET ME DRY YOU, YOU'RE GONNA CATCH A COLD!
TENSE
MEOW!? MROWWW!!
GOTCHA!
!?
STOMP
MROWWW!! MREOW!!

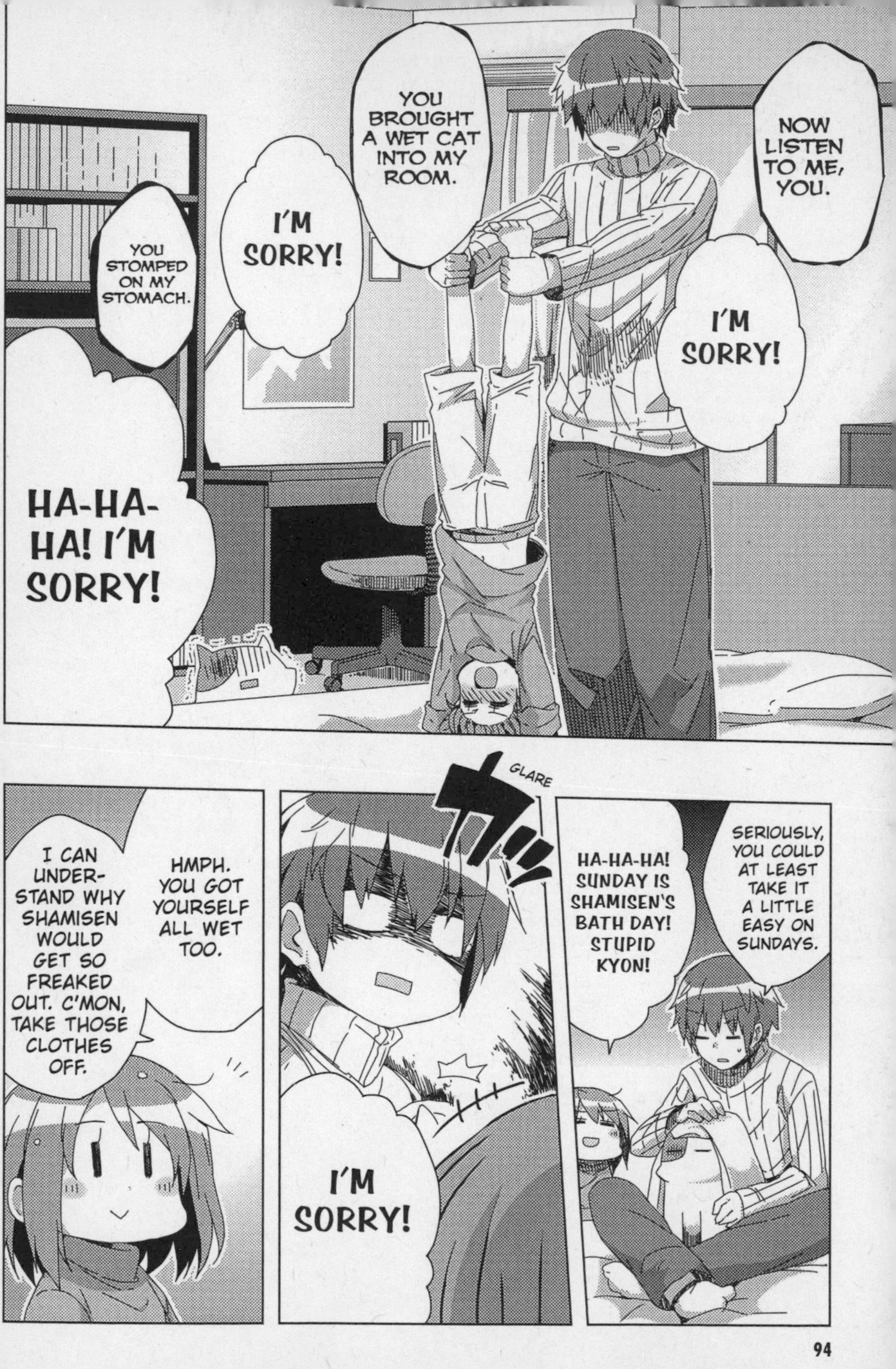
NOW LISTEN TO ME, YOU.
I'M SORRY!
YOU BROUGHT A WET CAT INTO MY ROOM.
I'M SORRY!
YOU STOMPED ON MY STOMACH.
HA-HA-HA! I'M SORRY!
SERIOUSLY, YOU COULD AT LEAST TAKE IT A LITTLE EASY ON SUNDAYS.
HA-HA-HA! SUNDAY IS SHAMISEN'S BATH DAY! STUPID KYON!
GLARE
I'M SORRY!
HMPH. YOU GOT YOURSELF ALL WET TOO.
I CAN UNDER-STAND WHY SHAMISEN WOULD GET SO FREAKED OUT. C'MON, TAKE THOSE CLOTHES OFF.

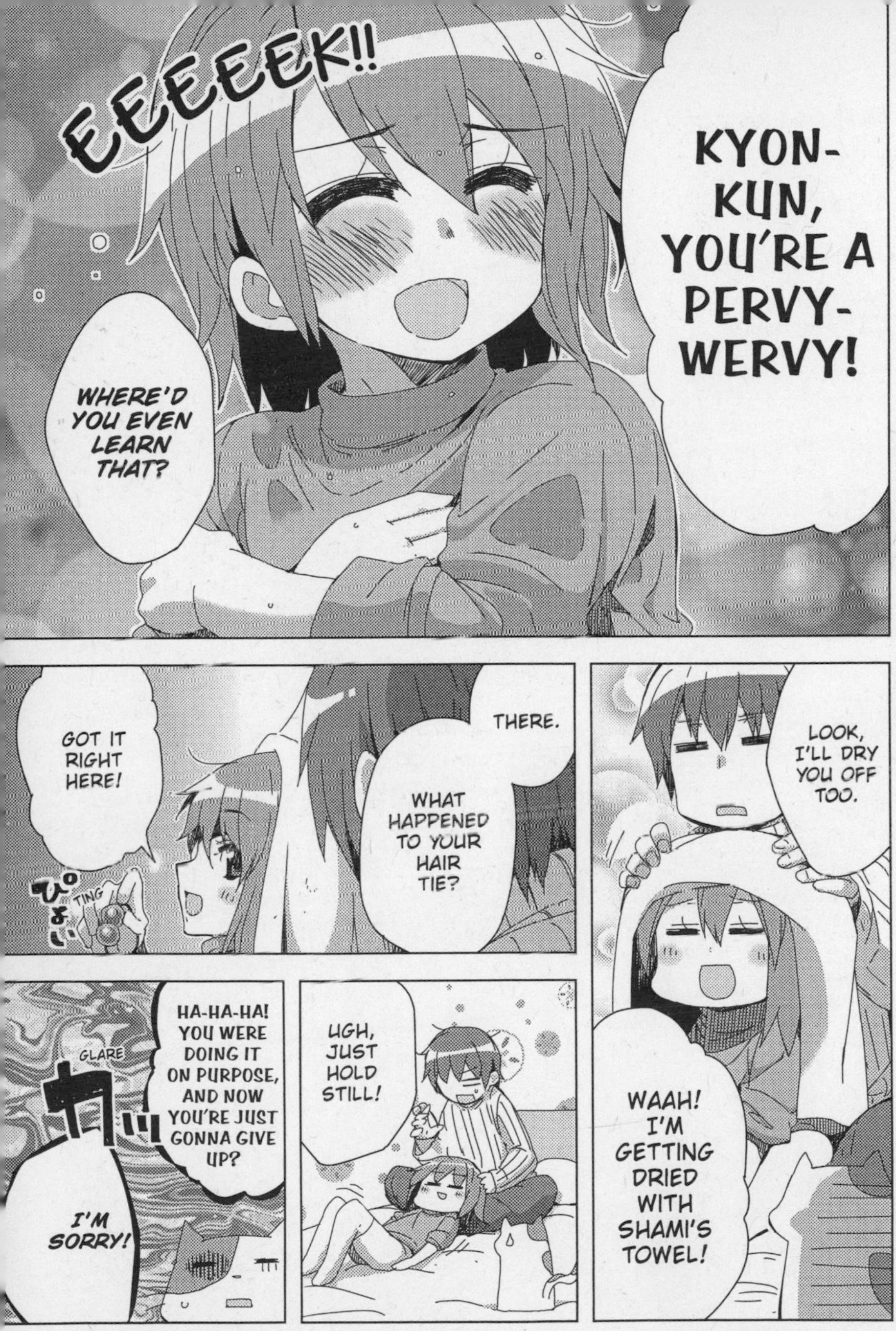
KYON-KUN, YOU'RE A PERVY-WERVY!
EEEEEEK!!
WHERE'D YOU EVEN LEARN THAT?
LOOK, I'LL DRY YOU OFF TOO.
WAAH! I'M GETTING DRIED WITH SHAMI'S TOWEL!
THERE.
WHAT HAPPENED TO YOUR HAIR TIE?
GOT IT RIGHT HERE!
TING
UGH, JUST HOLD STILL!
HA-HA-HA! YOU WERE DOING IT ON PURPOSE, AND NOW YOU'RE JUST GONNA GIVE UP?
GLARE
I'M SORRY!

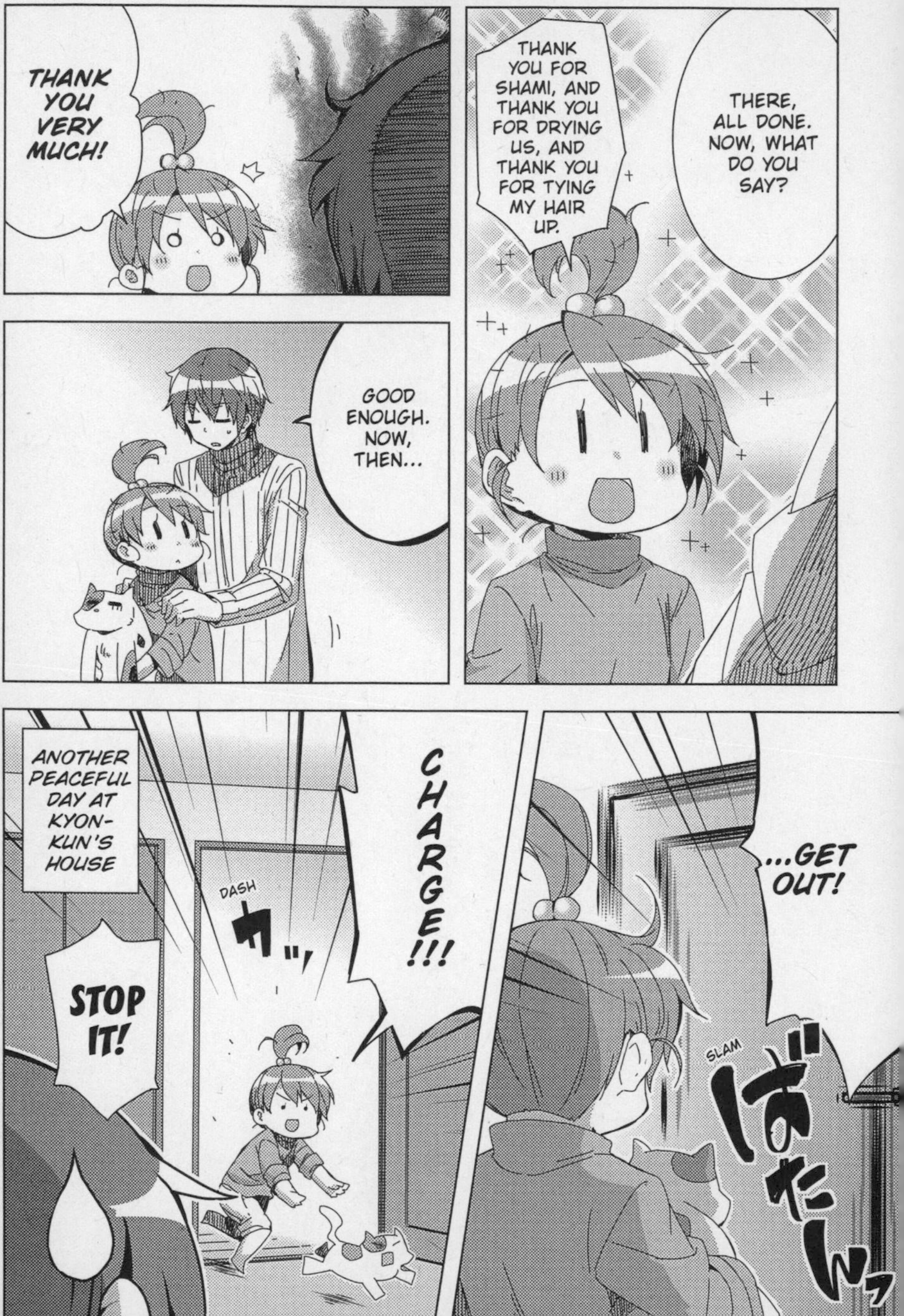
THERE, ALL DONE. NOW, WHAT DO YOU SAY?
THANK YOU FOR SHAMI, AND THANK YOU FOR DRYING US, AND THANK YOU FOR TYING MY HAIR UP.
THANK YOU VERY MUCH!
GOOD ENOUGH. NOW, THEN...
...GET OUT!
SLAM
ばたんっ
CHARGE!!!
ANOTHER PEACEFUL DAY AT KYON-KUN'S HOUSE
DASH
STOP IT!

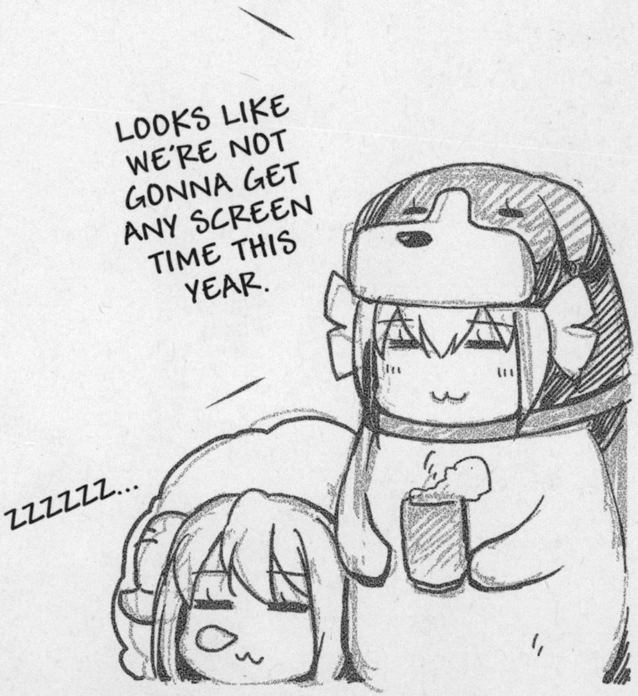
LOOKS LIKE WE'RE NOT GONNA GET ANY SCREEN TIME THIS YEAR.
ZZZZZZ...

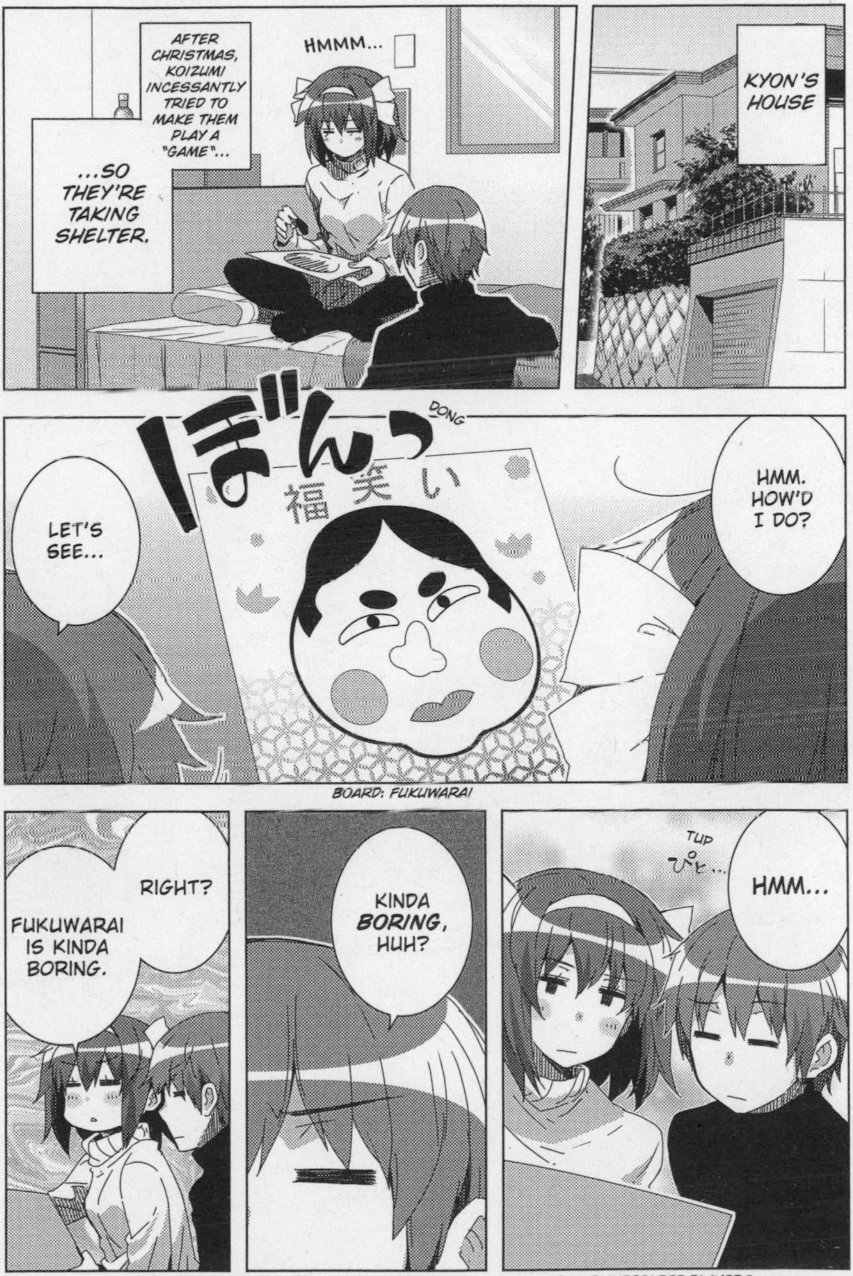
KYON'S HOUSE
HMMM...
AFTER CHRISTMAS, KOIZUMI INCESSANTLY TRIED TO MAKE THEM PLAY A "GAME"...
...SO THEY'RE TAKING SHELTER.
HMM. HOW'D I DO?
ぼんっ
DONG
福笑い
LET'S SEE...
BOARD: FUKUWARAI
HMM...
ぴと...
TUP
KINDA BORING, HUH?
RIGHT?
FUKUWARAI IS KINDA BORING.

NOTE: SIMILAR TO PIN THE TAIL ON THE DONKEY, IN FUKUWARAI, BLINDFOLDED PLAYERS ATTEMPT TO PLACE FACIAL FEATURES ON A BLANK FACE WITH HUMOROUS RESULTS.

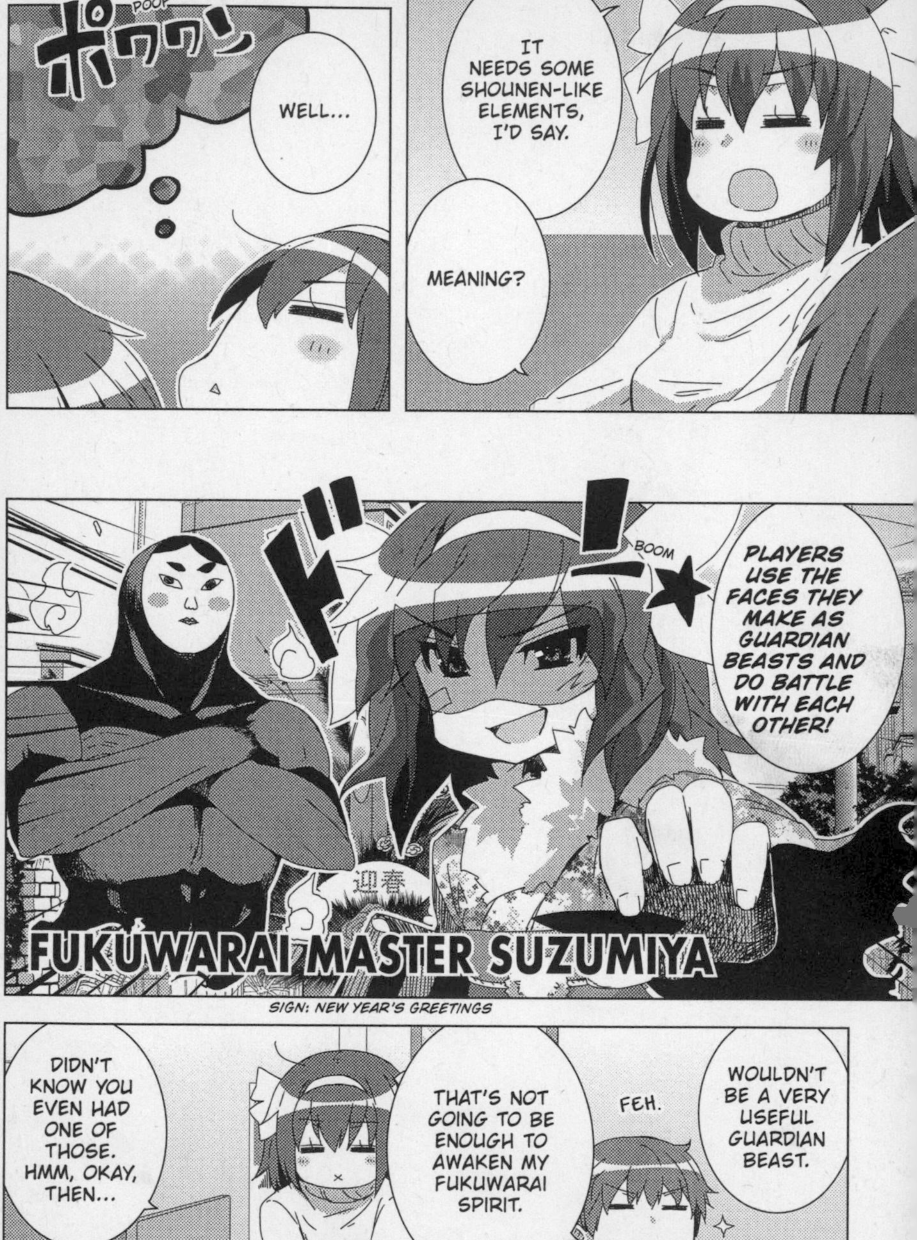
IT NEEDS SOME SHOUNEN-LIKE ELEMENTS, I'D SAY.
MEANING?
POOF
ポワワン
WELL...
ド
BOOM
PLAYERS USE THE FACES THEY MAKE AS GUARDIAN BEASTS AND DO BATTLE WITH EACH OTHER!
迎春
FUKUWARAI MASTER SUZUMIYA
SIGN: NEW YEAR'S GREETINGS
WOULDN'T BE A VERY USEFUL GUARDIAN BEAST.
FEH.
THAT'S NOT GOING TO BE ENOUGH TO AWAKEN MY FUKUWARAI SPIRIT.
DIDN'T KNOW YOU EVEN HAD ONE OF THOSE. HMM, OKAY, THEN...

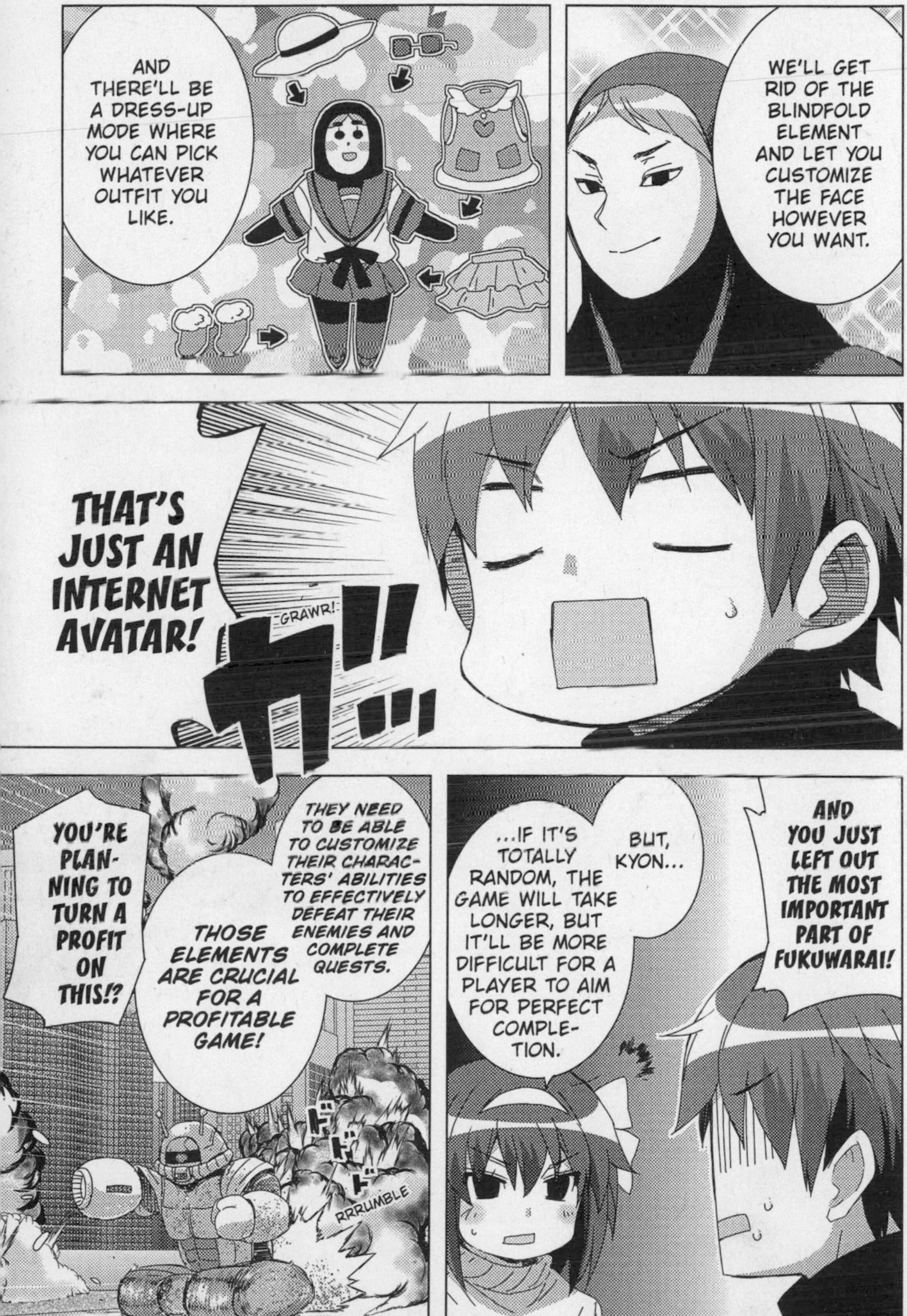
WE'LL GET RID OF THE BLINDFOLD ELEMENT AND LET YOU CUSTOMIZE THE FACE HOWEVER YOU WANT.
AND THERE'LL BE A DRESS-UP MODE WHERE YOU CAN PICK WHATEVER OUTFIT YOU LIKE.
THAT'S JUST AN INTERNET AVATAR!
GRAWR!
AND YOU JUST LEFT OUT THE MOST IMPORTANT PART OF FUKUWARAI!
BUT, KYON...
...IF IT'S TOTALLY RANDOM, THE GAME WILL TAKE LONGER, BUT IT'LL BE MORE DIFFICULT FOR A PLAYER TO AIM FOR PERFECT COMPLE-TION.
THEY NEED TO BE ABLE TO CUSTOMIZE THEIR CHARAC-TERS' ABILITIES TO EFFECTIVELY DEFEAT THEIR ENEMIES AND COMPLETE QUESTS.
THOSE ELEMENTS ARE CRUCIAL FOR A PROFITABLE GAME!
YOU'RE PLAN-NING TO TURN A PROFIT ON THIS!?
RRRUMBLE

# MEANWHILE, KOIZUMI...

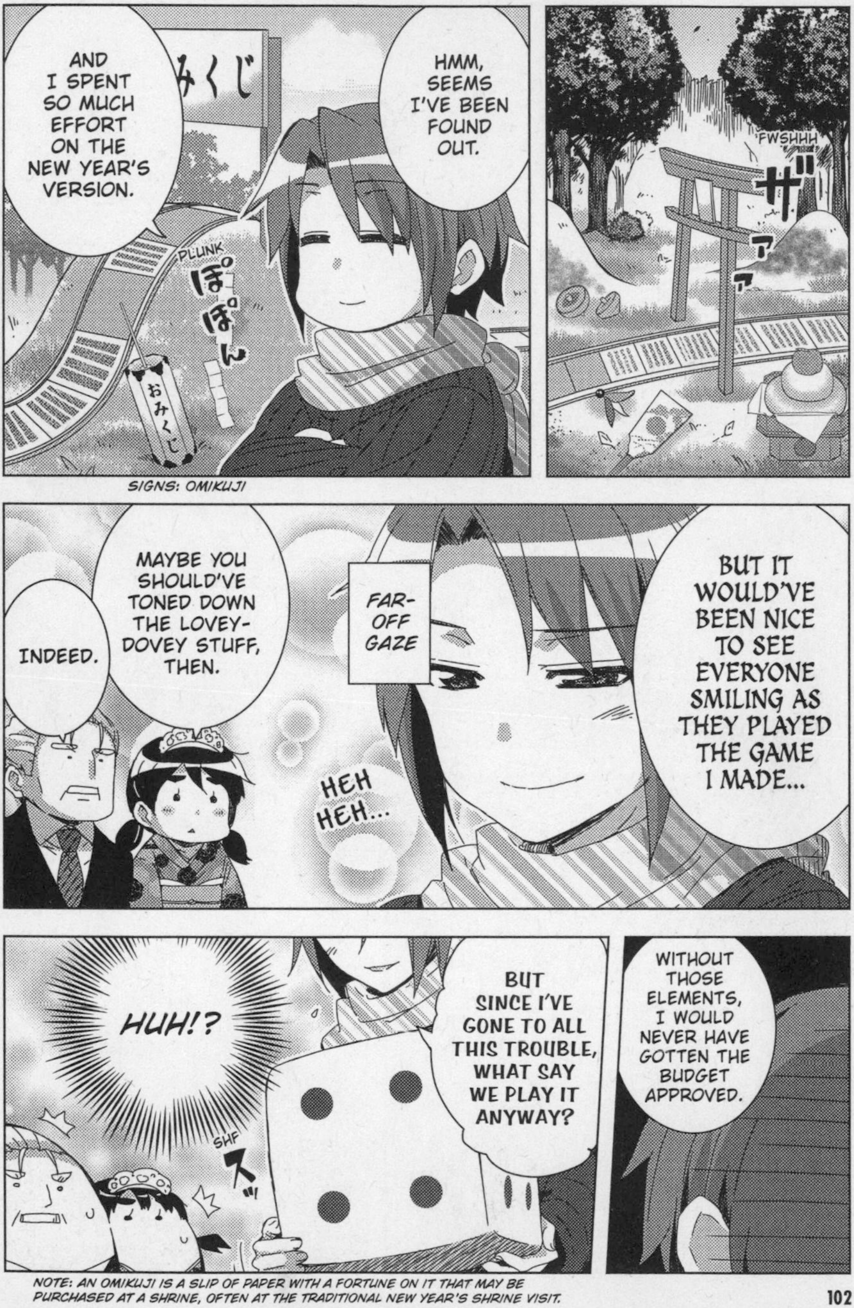
FWSHHH
ザアァ
HMM, SEEMS I'VE BEEN FOUND OUT.
AND I SPENT SO MUCH EFFORT ON THE NEW YEAR'S VERSION.
みくじ
PLUNK
ぽぽん
おみくじ
SIGNS: OMIKUJI
BUT IT WOULD'VE BEEN NICE TO SEE EVERYONE SMILING AS THEY PLAYED THE GAME I MADE...
FAR-OFF GAZE
HEH HEH...
MAYBE YOU SHOULD'VE TONED DOWN THE LOVEY-DOVEY STUFF, THEN.
INDEED.
WITHOUT THOSE ELEMENTS, I WOULD NEVER HAVE GOTTEN THE BUDGET APPROVED.
BUT SINCE I'VE GONE TO ALL THIS TROUBLE, WHAT SAY WE PLAY IT ANYWAY?
HUH!?
SHF
スッ

*NOTE: AN OMIKUJI IS A SLIP OF PAPER WITH A FORTUNE ON IT THAT MAY BE PURCHASED AT A SHRINE, OFTEN AT THE TRADITIONAL NEW YEAR'S SHRINE VISIT.*

# MEANWHILE, ASAHINA...

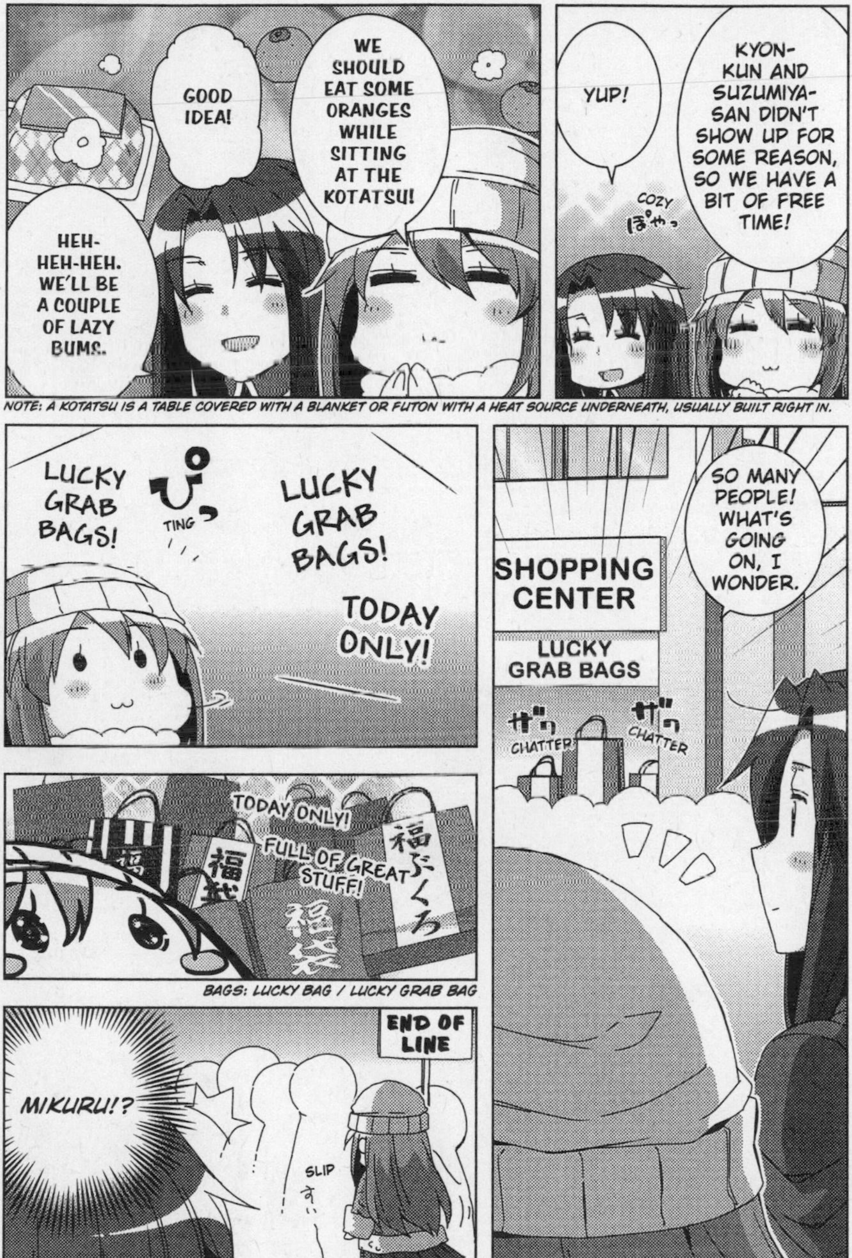
KYON-KUN AND SUZUMIYA-SAN DIDN'T SHOW UP FOR SOME REASON, SO WE HAVE A BIT OF FREE TIME!
YUP!
COZY
ぽやっ
WE SHOULD EAT SOME ORANGES WHILE SITTING AT THE KOTATSU!
GOOD IDEA!
HEH-HEH-HEH. WE'LL BE A COUPLE OF LAZY BUMS.
SO MANY PEOPLE! WHAT'S GOING ON, I WONDER.
SHOPPING CENTER
LUCKY GRAB BAGS
ザワ
CHATTER
ザワ
CHATTER
LUCKY GRAB BAGS!
LUCKY GRAB BAGS!
ぴっ
TING
TODAY ONLY!
TODAY ONLY!
FULL OF GREAT STUFF!
福ぶくろ
福袋
END OF LINE
MIKURU!?
SLIP
すい

NOTE: A KOTATSU IS A TABLE COVERED WITH A BLANKET OR FUTON WITH A HEAT SOURCE UNDERNEATH, USUALLY BUILT RIGHT IN.

BAGS: LUCKY BAG / LUCKY GRAB BAG

## MEANWHILE, AT THE NAGATO RESIDENCE...

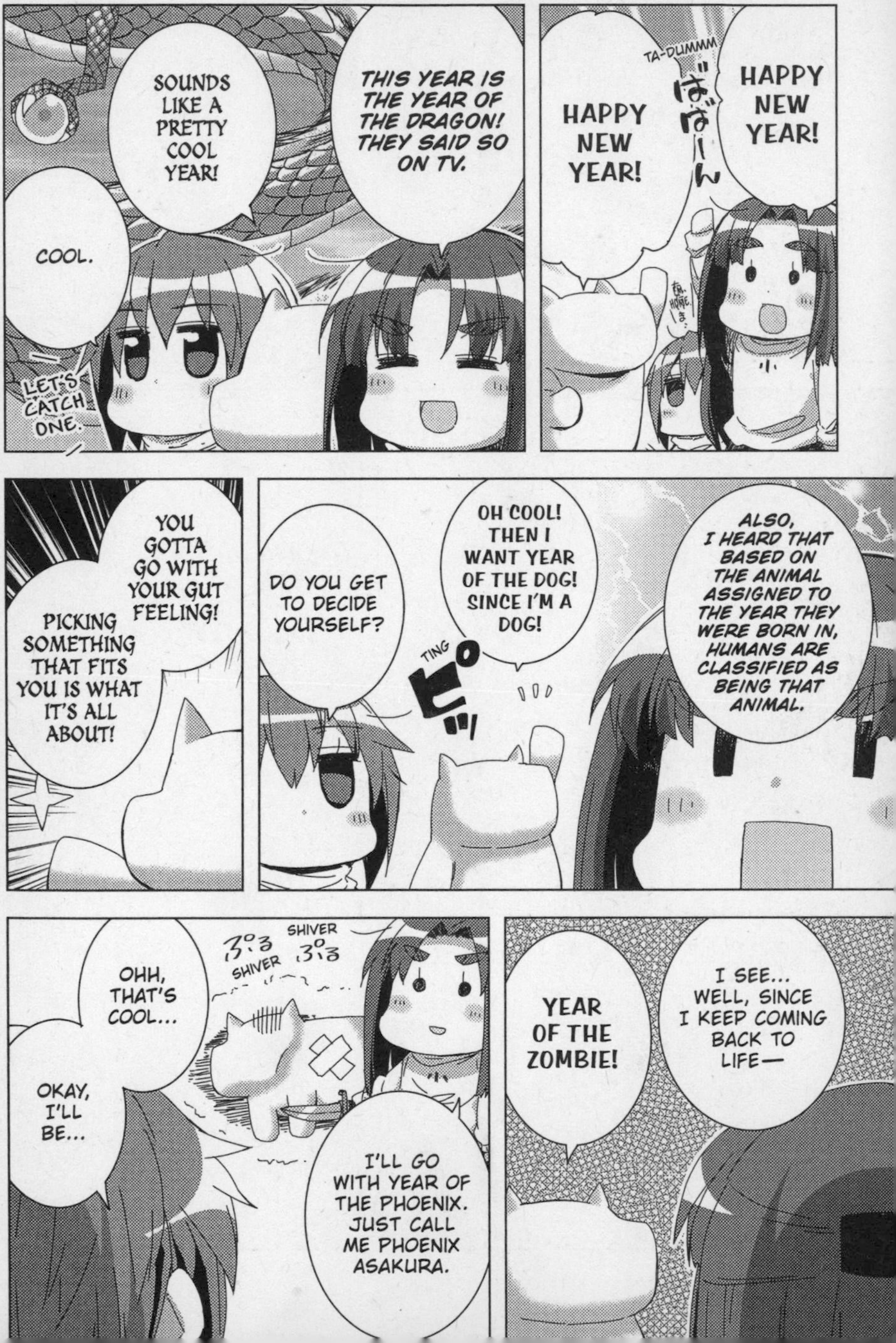
HAPPY NEW YEAR!
TA-DUMMM
ばばーん
HAPPY NEW YEAR!
THIS YEAR IS THE YEAR OF THE DRAGON! THEY SAID SO ON TV.
SOUNDS LIKE A PRETTY COOL YEAR!
COOL.
LET'S CATCH ONE.
ALSO, I HEARD THAT BASED ON THE ANIMAL ASSIGNED TO THE YEAR THEY WERE BORN IN, HUMANS ARE CLASSIFIED AS BEING THAT ANIMAL.
OH COOL! THEN I WANT YEAR OF THE DOG! SINCE I'M A DOG!
TING
ピッ
DO YOU GET TO DECIDE YOURSELF?
YOU GOTTA GO WITH YOUR GUT FEELING!
PICKING SOMETHING THAT FITS YOU IS WHAT IT'S ALL ABOUT!
I SEE... WELL, SINCE I KEEP COMING BACK TO LIFE—
YEAR OF THE ZOMBIE!
SHIVER
ぷる
SHIVER
ぷる
OHH, THAT'S COOL...
I'LL GO WITH YEAR OF THE PHOENIX. JUST CALL ME PHOENIX ASAKURA.
OKAY, I'LL BE...

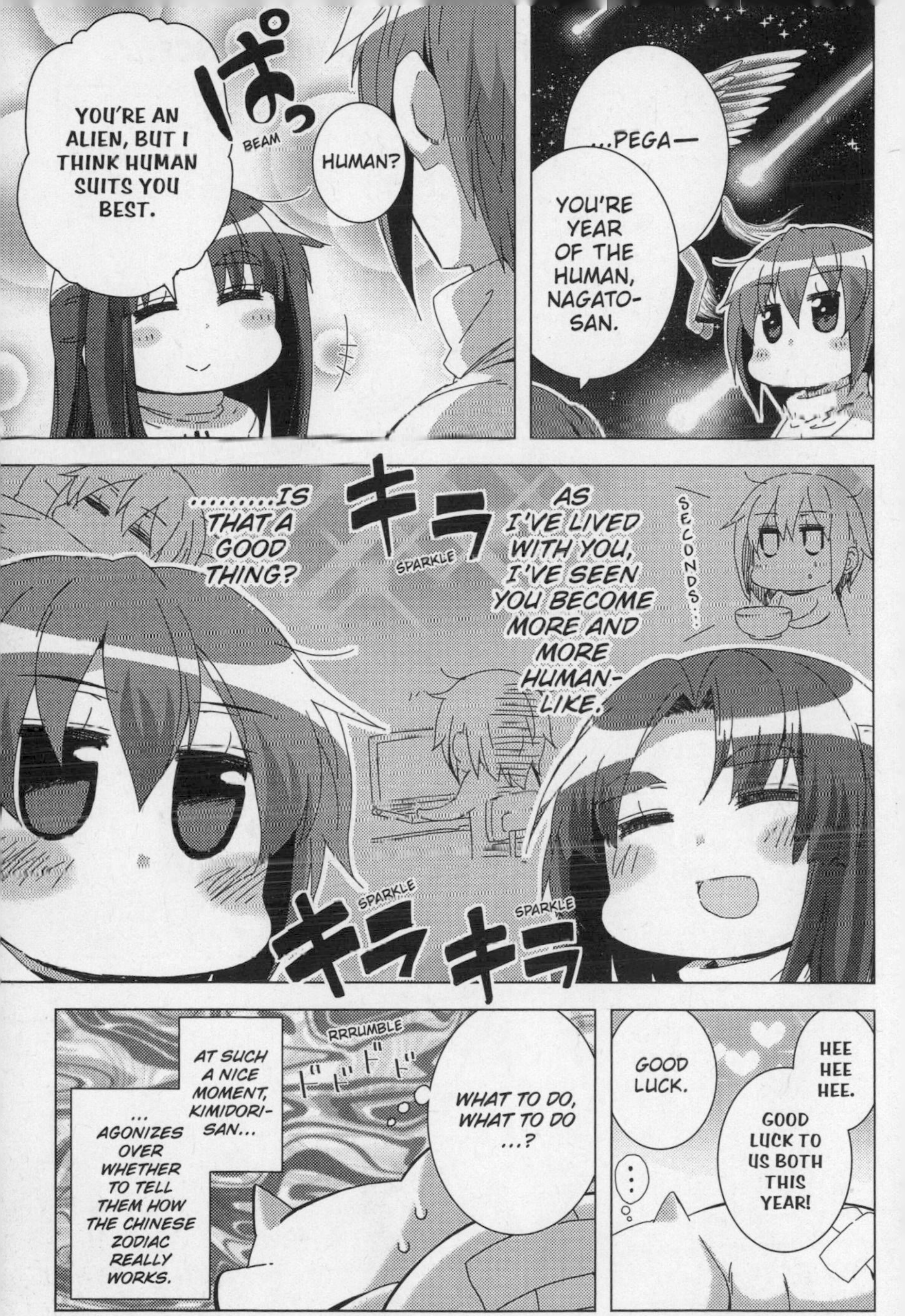
...PEGA—
YOU'RE YEAR OF THE HUMAN, NAGATO-SAN.
HUMAN?
ぱっ
BEAM
YOU'RE AN ALIEN, BUT I THINK HUMAN SUITS YOU BEST.
SECONDS...
AS I'VE LIVED WITH YOU, I'VE SEEN YOU BECOME MORE AND MORE HUMAN-LIKE.
キラ
SPARKLE
..........IS THAT A GOOD THING?
キラ
SPARKLE
キラ
SPARKLE
HEE HEE HEE.
GOOD LUCK TO US BOTH THIS YEAR!
GOOD LUCK.
...
WHAT TO DO, WHAT TO DO ...?
ドドド
RRRUMBLE
AT SUCH A NICE MOMENT, KIMIDORI-SAN...
... AGONIZES OVER WHETHER TO TELL THEM HOW THE CHINESE ZODIAC REALLY WORKS.

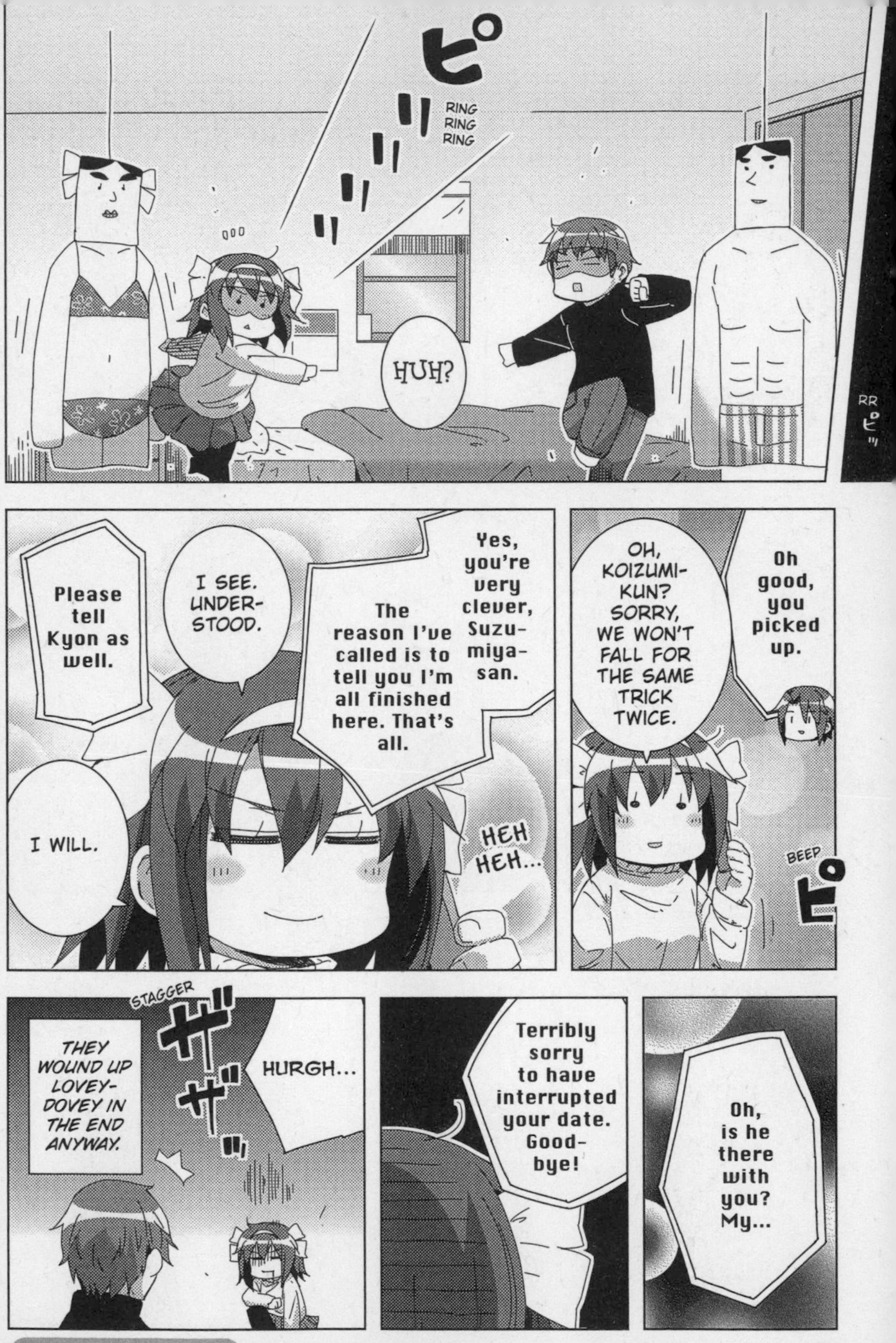
ピ
RING RING RING
HUH?
RR ピッ
Oh good, you picked up.
OH, KOIZUMI-KUN? SORRY, WE WON'T FALL FOR THE SAME TRICK TWICE.
BEEP ピ
Yes, you're very clever, Suzumiya-san.
The reason I've called is to tell you I'm all finished here. That's all.
I SEE. UNDERSTOOD.
Please tell Kyon as well.
HEH HEH...
I WILL.
Oh, is he there with you? My...
Terribly sorry to have interrupted your date. Good-bye!
HURGH...
STAGGER ザザッ
THEY WOUND UP LOVEY-DOVEY IN THE END ANYWAY.

END

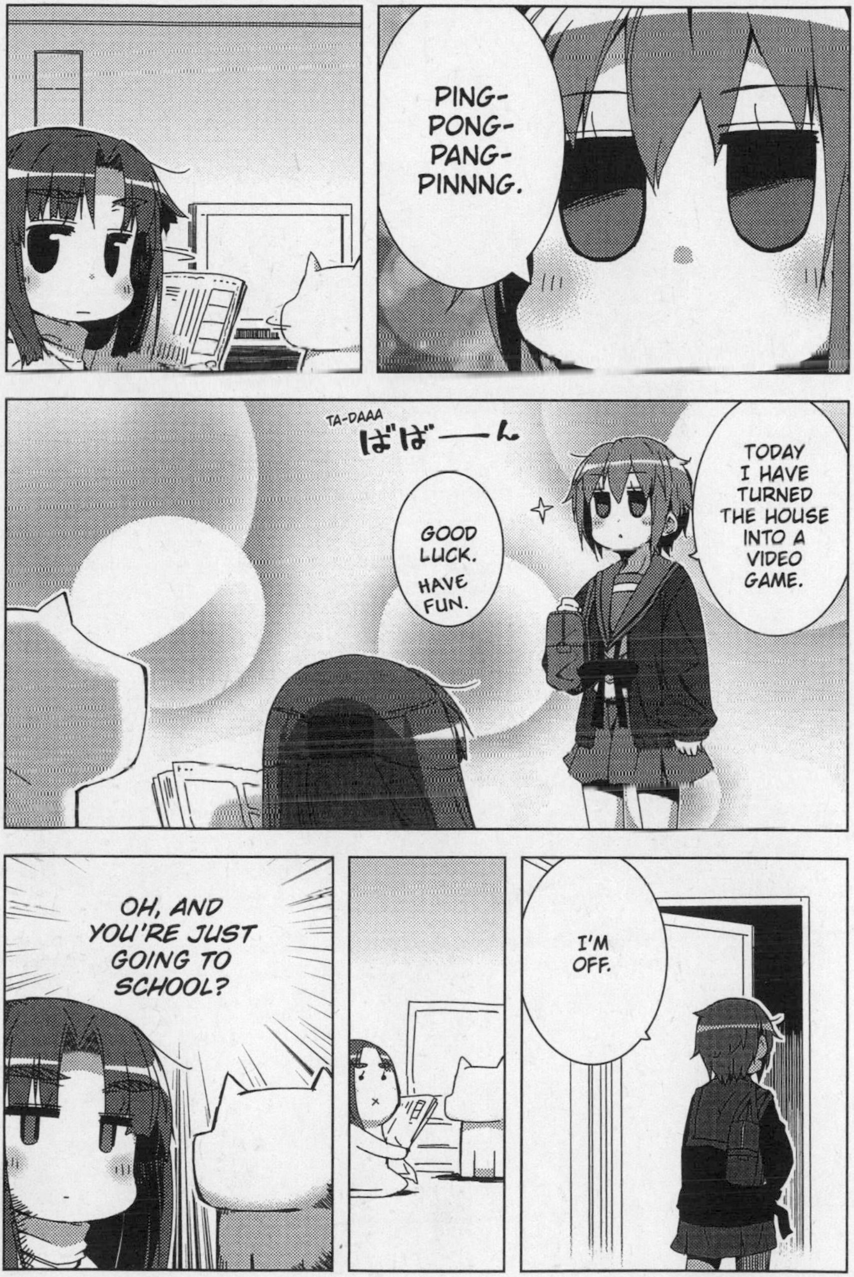
PING-PONG-PANG-PINNNG.
TODAY I HAVE TURNED THE HOUSE INTO A VIDEO GAME.
TA-DAAA
ばばーん
GOOD LUCK. HAVE FUN.
I'M OFF.
OH, AND YOU'RE JUST GOING TO SCHOOL?

## MIDDAY

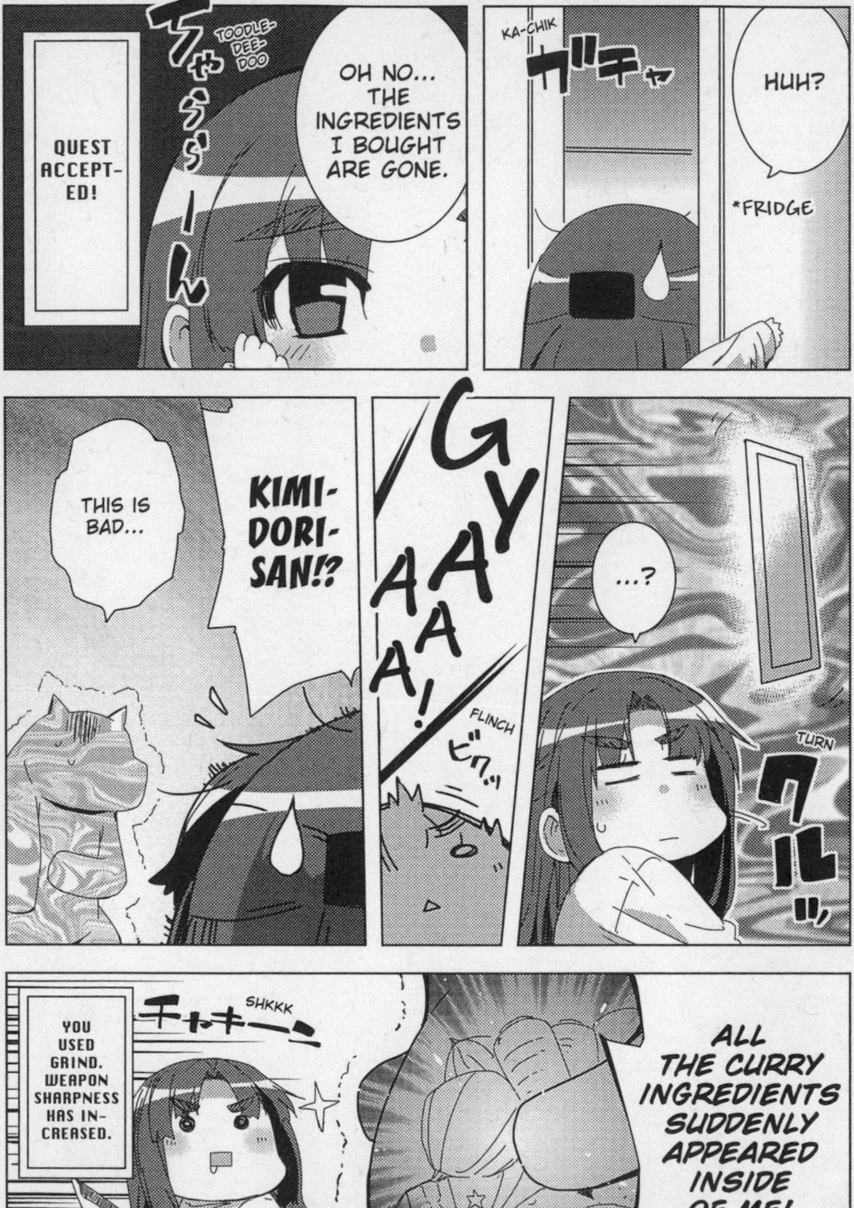
HUH?
KA-CHIK
*FRIDGE
OH NO... THE INGREDIENTS I BOUGHT ARE GONE.
TOODLE-DEE-DOO
QUEST ACCEPTED!
...?
TURN
GYAAAAA!
FLINCH
KIMI-DORI-SAN!?
THIS IS BAD...
ALL THE CURRY INGREDIENTS SUDDENLY APPEARED INSIDE OF ME!
SHKKK
YOU USED GRIND. WEAPON SHARPNESS HAS INCREASED.

## EVENING

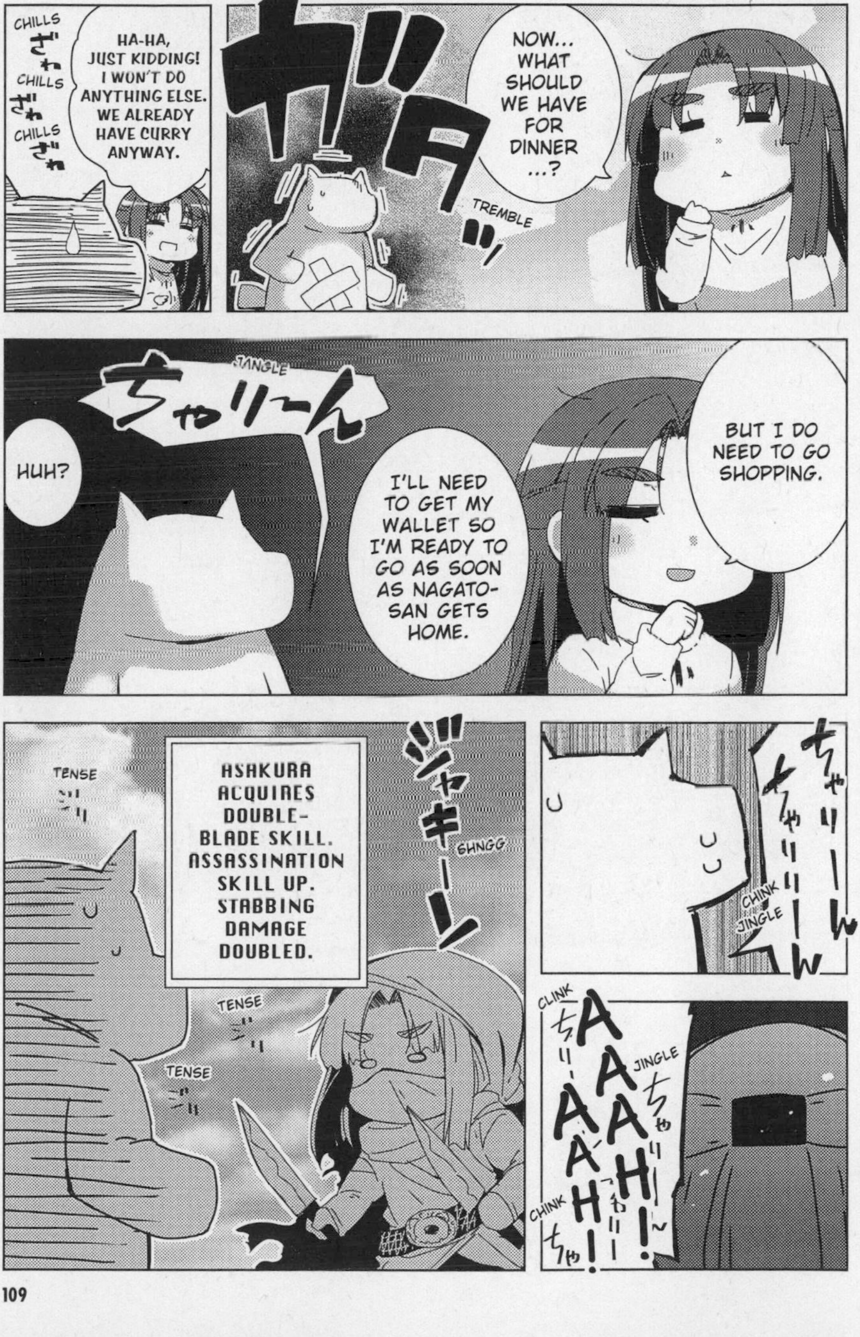

NOW... WHAT SHOULD WE HAVE FOR DINNER ...?
ガタ
TREMBLE
HA-HA, JUST KIDDING! I WON'T DO ANYTHING ELSE. WE ALREADY HAVE CURRY ANYWAY.
CHILLS ざわ CHILLS ざわ CHILLS ざわ
BUT I DO NEED TO GO SHOPPING.
I'LL NEED TO GET MY WALLET SO I'M READY TO GO AS SOON AS NAGATO-SAN GETS HOME.
JANGLE
ちゃりーん
HUH?
ちゃりーん ちゃりりーん
CHINK JINGLE
AAAAH!
CLINK
JINGLE
CHINK
ASAKURA ACQUIRES DOUBLE-BLADE SKILL. ASSASSINATION SKILL UP. STABBING DAMAGE DOUBLED.
ジャキーン
SHNGG
TENSE
TENSE
TENSE

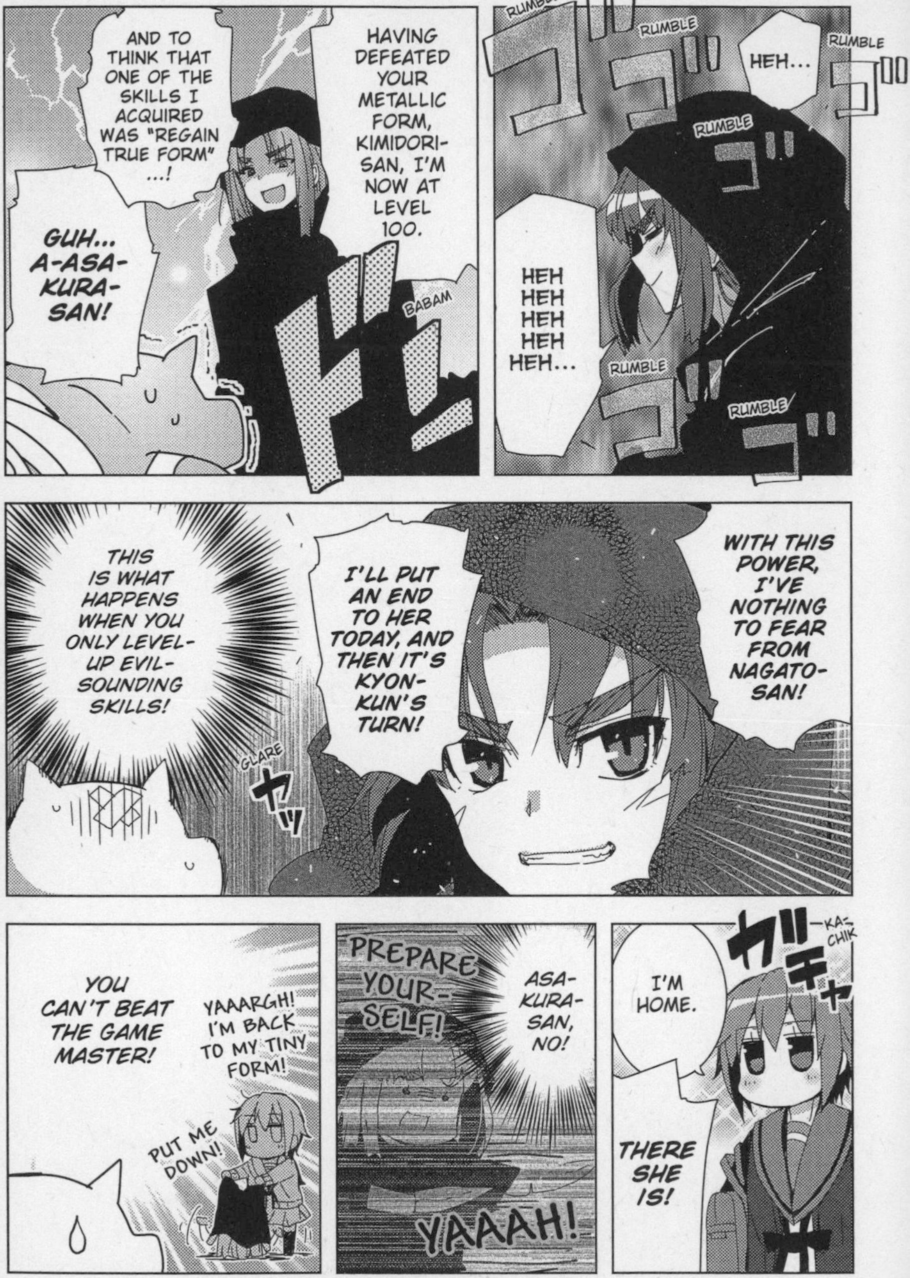
RUMBLE
RUMBLE
RUMBLE
HEH...
RUMBLE
HEH HEH HEH HEH HEH...
RUMBLE
RUMBLE
HAVING DEFEATED YOUR METALLIC FORM, KIMIDORI-SAN, I'M NOW AT LEVEL 100.
AND TO THINK THAT ONE OF THE SKILLS I ACQUIRED WAS "REGAIN TRUE FORM"...!
BABAM
GUH... A-ASA-KURA-SAN!
WITH THIS POWER, I'VE NOTHING TO FEAR FROM NAGATO-SAN!
I'LL PUT AN END TO HER TODAY, AND THEN IT'S KYON-KUN'S TURN!
THIS IS WHAT HAPPENS WHEN YOU ONLY LEVEL-UP EVIL-SOUNDING SKILLS!
GLARE
KA-CHIK
I'M HOME.
THERE SHE IS!
ASA-KURA-SAN, NO!
PREPARE YOUR-SELF!
YAAAH!
YOU CAN'T BEAT THE GAME MASTER!
YAAARGH! I'M BACK TO MY TINY FORM!
PUT ME DOWN!

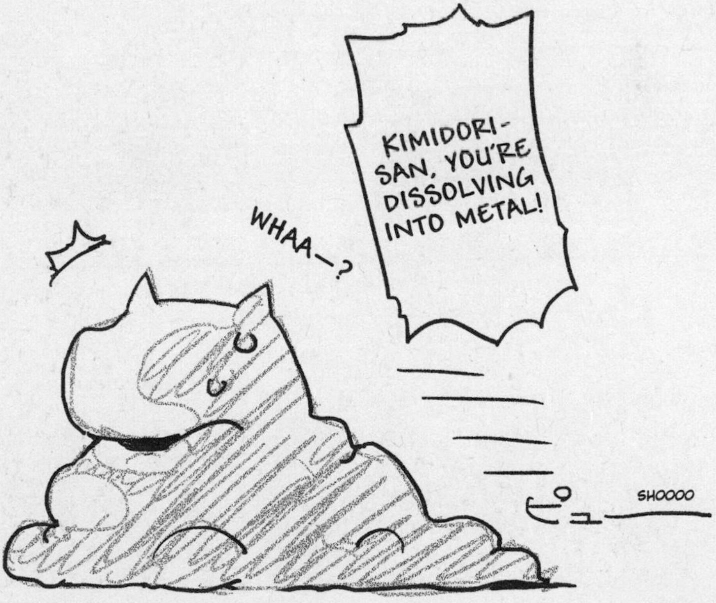
KIMIDORI-SAN, YOU'RE DISSOLVING INTO METAL!
WHAA—?
ピュー
SHOOOO

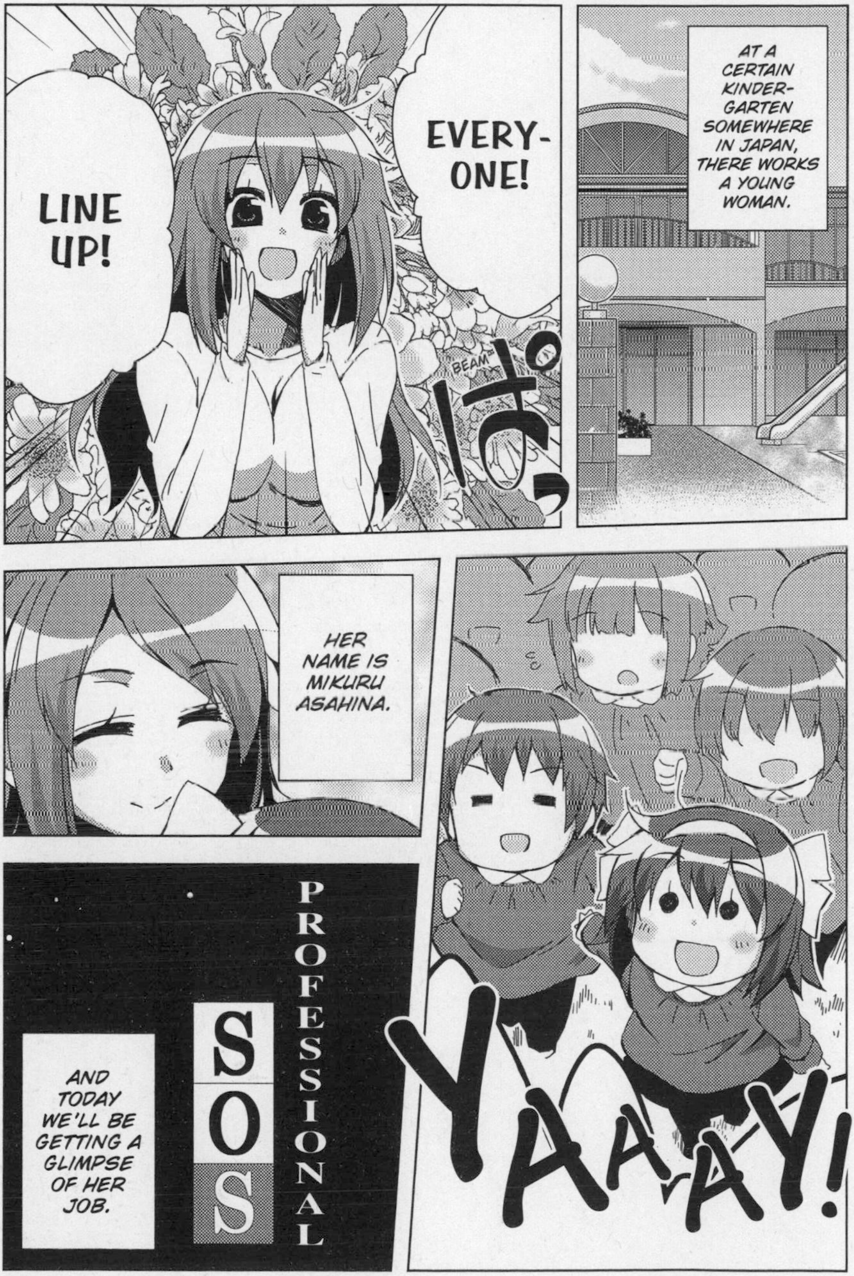
AT A CERTAIN KINDER-GARTEN SOMEWHERE IN JAPAN, THERE WORKS A YOUNG WOMAN.
EVERY-ONE!
LINE UP!
BEAM
YAAAY!
HER NAME IS MIKURU ASAHINA.
PROFESSIONAL SOS
AND TODAY WE'LL BE GETTING A GLIMPSE OF HER JOB.

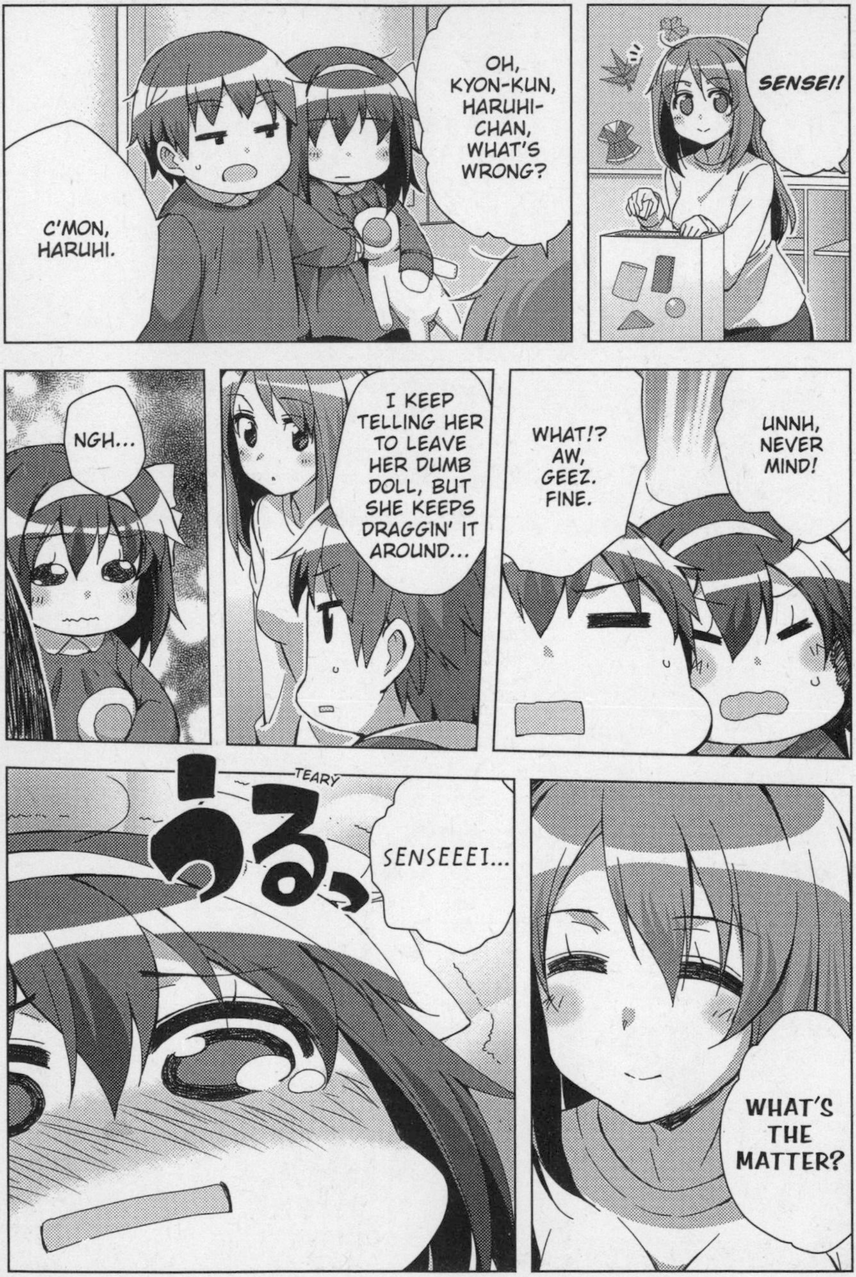
SENSEI!
OH, KYON-KUN, HARUHI-CHAN, WHAT'S WRONG?
C'MON, HARUHI.
UNNH, NEVER MIND!
WHAT!? AW, GEEZ. FINE.
I KEEP TELLING HER TO LEAVE HER DUMB DOLL, BUT SHE KEEPS DRAGGIN' IT AROUND...
NGH...
WHAT'S THE MATTER?
SENSEEEI...
うるっ
TEARY

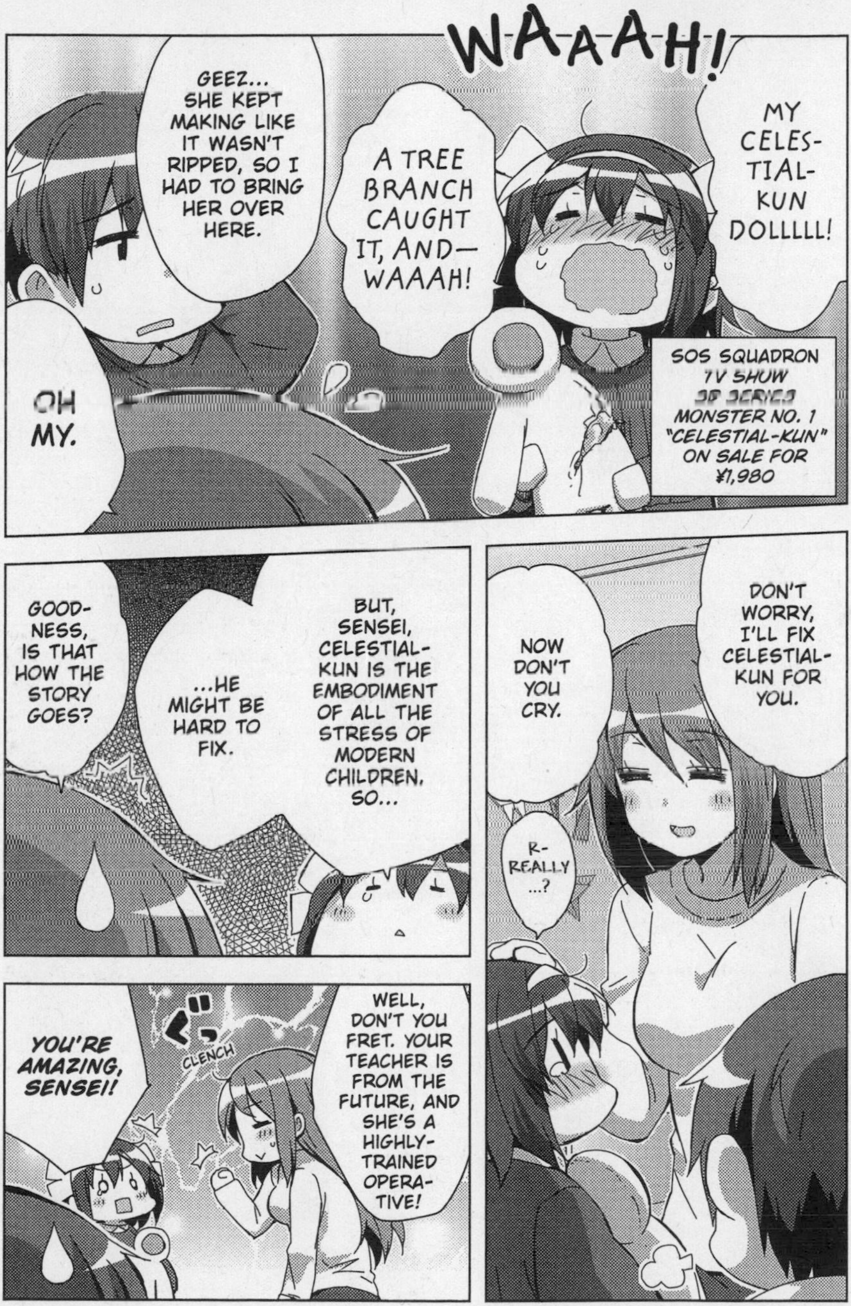
MY CELES-TIAL-KUN DOLLLLL!
WAAAH!
SOS SQUADRON TV SHOW 3D SERIES MONSTER NO. 1 "CELESTIAL-KUN" ON SALE FOR ¥1,980
A TREE BRANCH CAUGHT IT, AND—WAAAH!
GEEZ... SHE KEPT MAKING LIKE IT WASN'T RIPPED, SO I HAD TO BRING HER OVER HERE.
OH MY.
DON'T WORRY, I'LL FIX CELESTIAL-KUN FOR YOU.
NOW DON'T YOU CRY.
R-REALLY ...?
BUT, SENSEI, CELESTIAL-KUN IS THE EMBODIMENT OF ALL THE STRESS OF MODERN CHILDREN, SO...
...HE MIGHT BE HARD TO FIX.
GOOD-NESS, IS THAT HOW THE STORY GOES?
WELL, DON'T YOU FRET. YOUR TEACHER IS FROM THE FUTURE, AND SHE'S A HIGHLY-TRAINED OPERA-TIVE!
CLENCH
YOU'RE AMAZING, SENSEI!

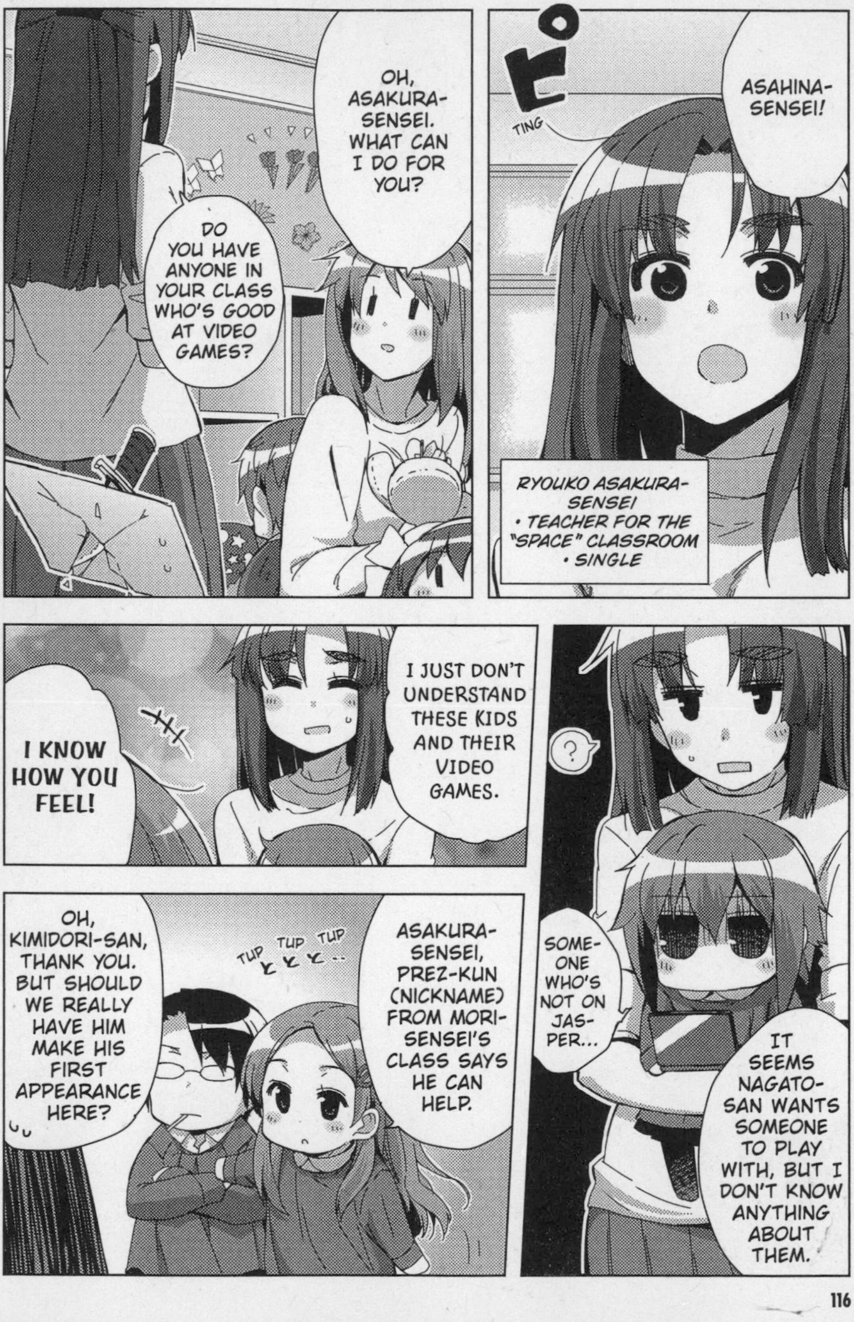

ASAHINA-SENSEI!
TING
RYOUKO ASAKURA-SENSEI • TEACHER FOR THE "SPACE" CLASSROOM • SINGLE
OH, ASAKURA-SENSEI. WHAT CAN I DO FOR YOU?
DO YOU HAVE ANYONE IN YOUR CLASS WHO'S GOOD AT VIDEO GAMES?
?
I JUST DON'T UNDERSTAND THESE KIDS AND THEIR VIDEO GAMES.
I KNOW HOW YOU FEEL!
SOME-ONE WHO'S NOT ON JAS-PER...
IT SEEMS NAGATO-SAN WANTS SOMEONE TO PLAY WITH, BUT I DON'T KNOW ANYTHING ABOUT THEM.
ASAKURA-SENSEI, PREZ-KUN (NICKNAME) FROM MORI-SENSEI'S CLASS SAYS HE CAN HELP.
TUP TUP TUP
OH, KIMIDORI-SAN, THANK YOU. BUT SHOULD WE REALLY HAVE HIM MAKE HIS FIRST APPEARANCE HERE?

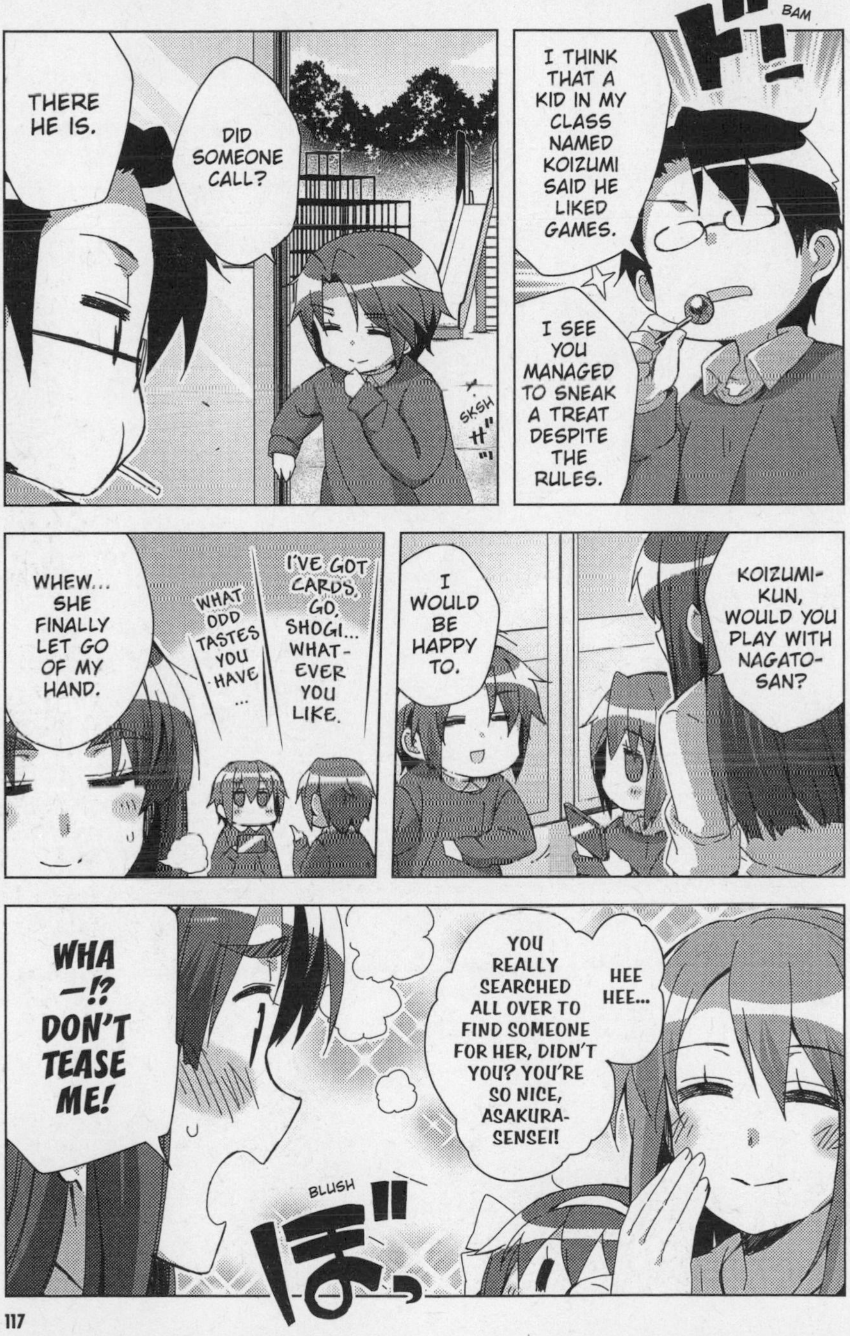
BAM
I THINK THAT A KID IN MY CLASS NAMED KOIZUMI SAID HE LIKED GAMES.
I SEE YOU MANAGED TO SNEAK A TREAT DESPITE THE RULES.
THERE HE IS.
DID SOMEONE CALL?
SKSH
KOIZUMI-KUN, WOULD YOU PLAY WITH NAGATO-SAN?
I WOULD BE HAPPY TO.
I'VE GOT CARDS, GO, SHOGI... WHATEVER YOU LIKE.
WHAT ODD TASTES YOU HAVE ...
WHEW... SHE FINALLY LET GO OF MY HAND.
HEE HEE...
YOU REALLY SEARCHED ALL OVER TO FIND SOMEONE FOR HER, DIDN'T YOU? YOU'RE SO NICE, ASAKURA-SENSEI!
BLUSH
WHA—!? DON'T TEASE ME!

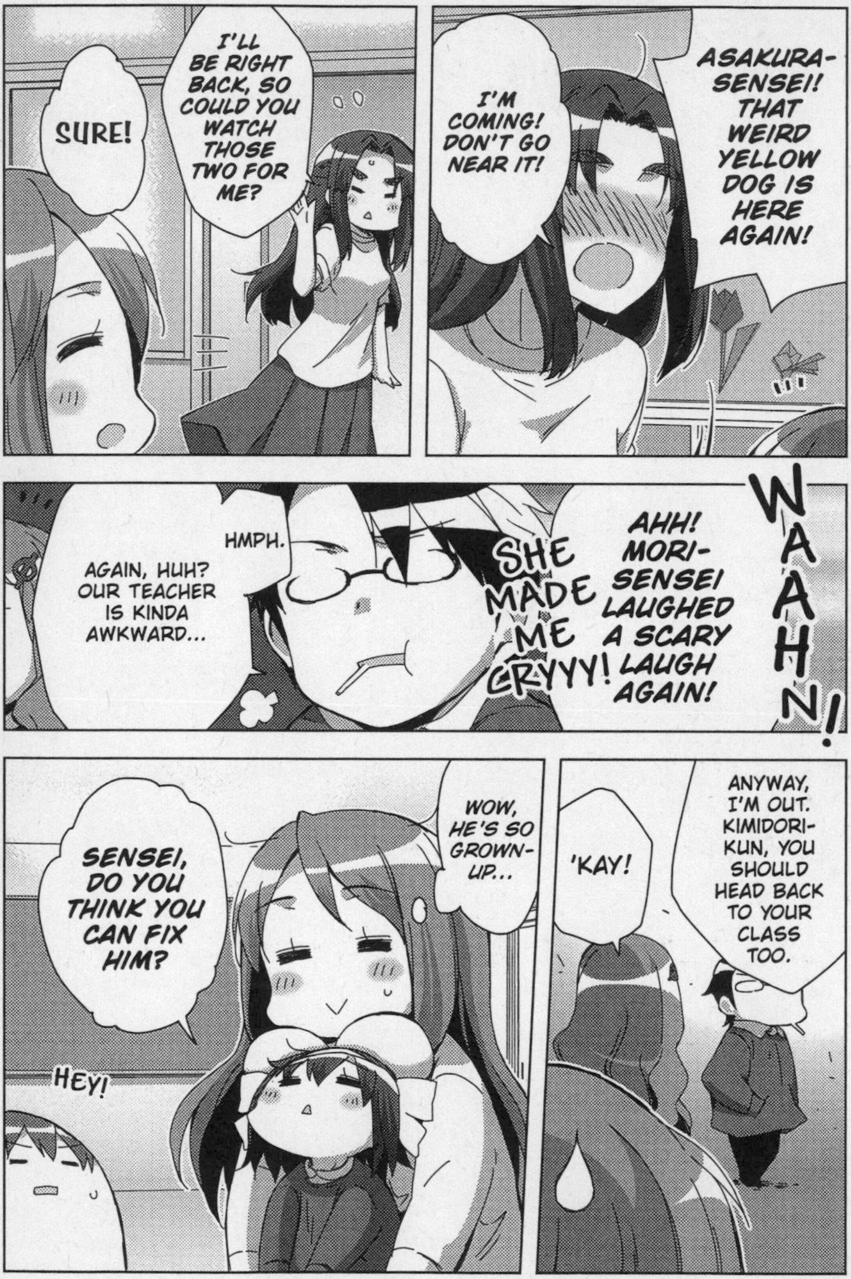
ASAKURA-SENSEI! THAT WEIRD YELLOW DOG IS HERE AGAIN!
I'M COMING! DON'T GO NEAR IT!
I'LL BE RIGHT BACK, SO COULD YOU WATCH THOSE TWO FOR ME?
SURE!
WAAHN!
AHH! MORI-SENSEI LAUGHED A SCARY LAUGH AGAIN!
SHE MADE ME CRYYY!
HMPH.
AGAIN, HUH? OUR TEACHER IS KINDA AWKWARD...
ANYWAY, I'M OUT. KIMIDORI-KUN, YOU SHOULD HEAD BACK TO YOUR CLASS TOO.
'KAY!
WOW, HE'S SO GROWN-UP...
SENSEI, DO YOU THINK YOU CAN FIX HIM?
HEY!

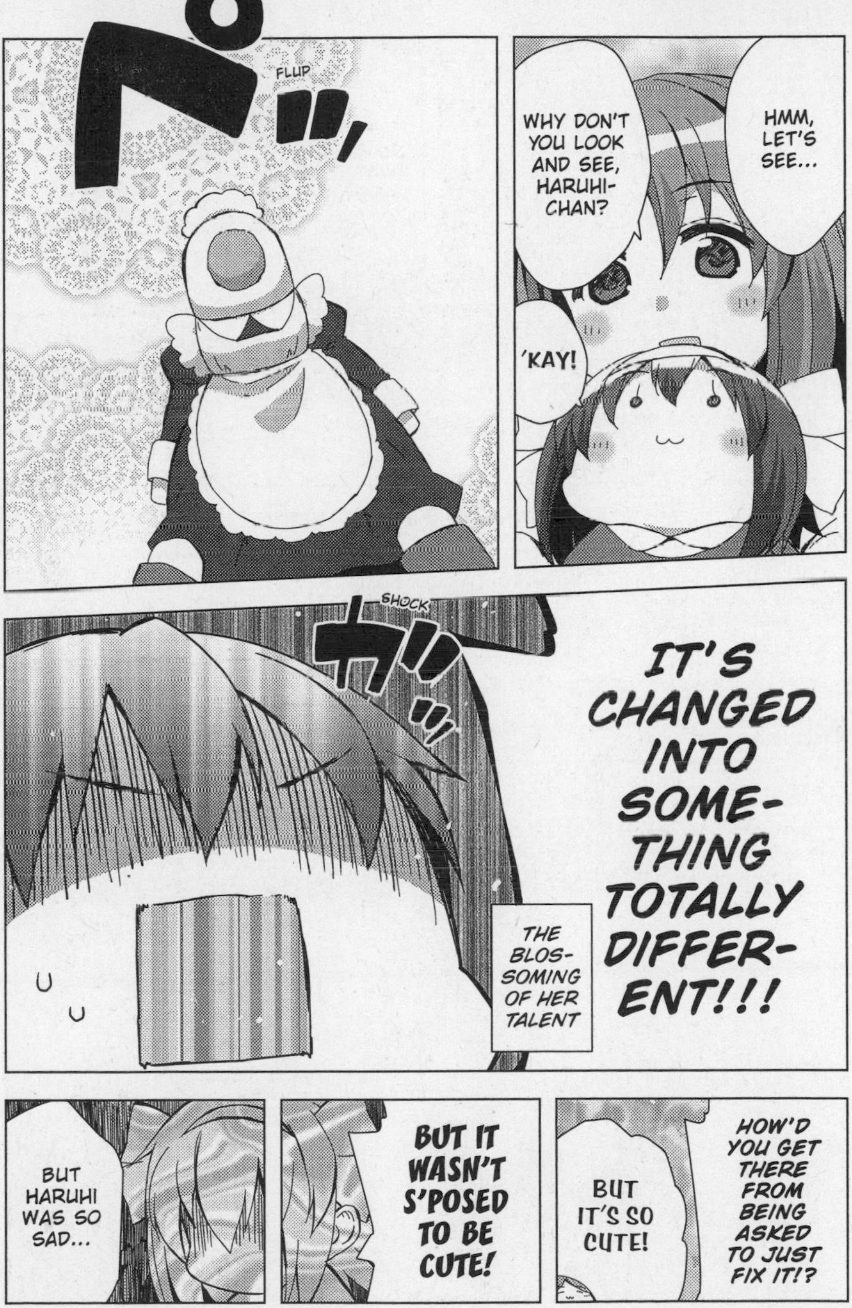
HMM, LET'S SEE...
WHY DON'T YOU LOOK AND SEE, HARUHI-CHAN?
'KAY!
FLUP
SHOCK
IT'S CHANGED INTO SOME-THING TOTALLY DIFFER-ENT!!!
THE BLOS-SOMING OF HER TALENT
HOW'D YOU GET THERE FROM BEING ASKED TO JUST FIX IT!?
BUT IT'S SO CUTE!
BUT IT WASN'T S'POSED TO BE CUTE!
BUT HARUHI WAS SO SAD...

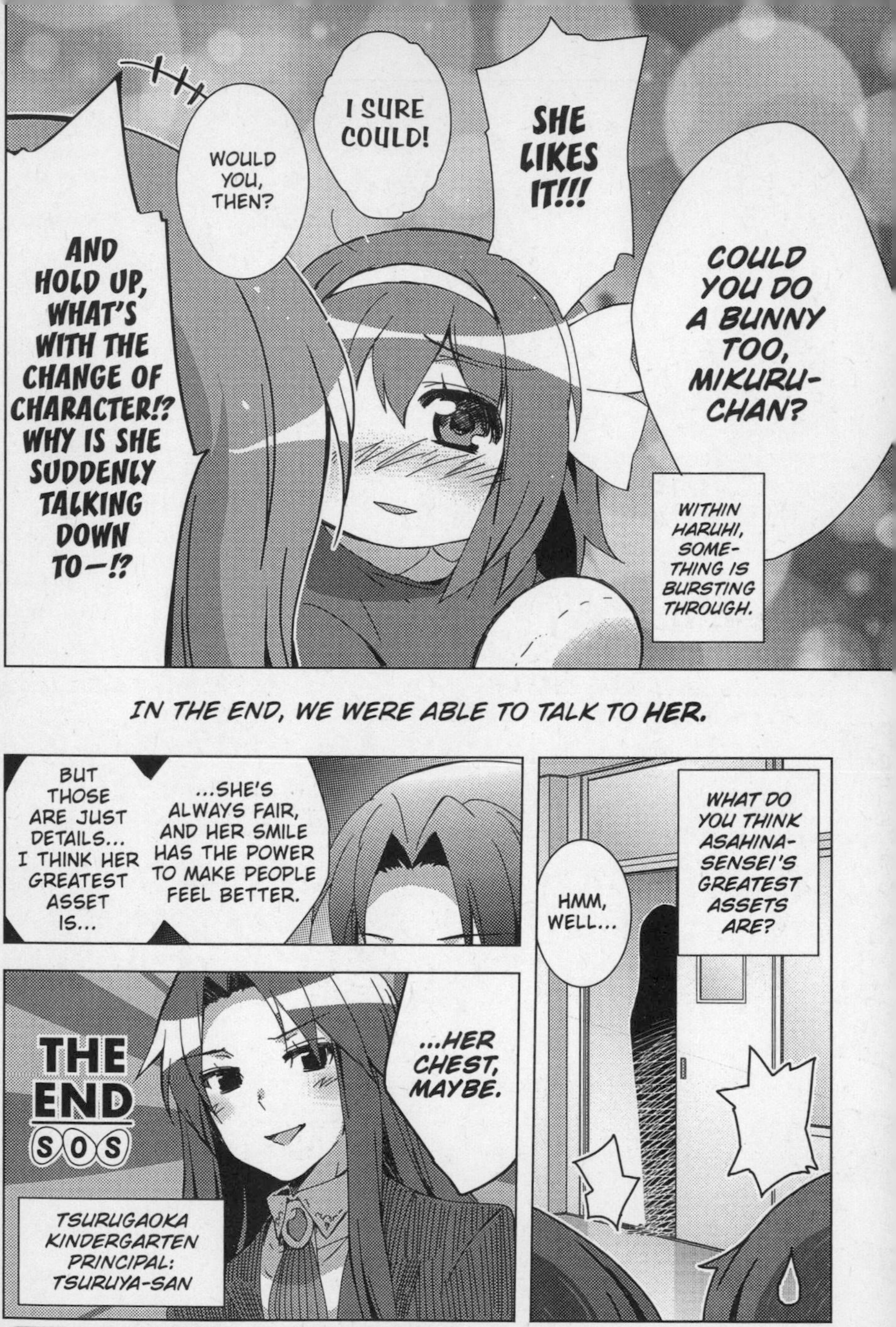
COULD YOU DO A BUNNY TOO, MIKURU-CHAN?
I SURE COULD!
SHE LIKES IT!!!
WOULD YOU, THEN?
AND HOLD UP, WHAT'S WITH THE CHANGE OF CHARACTER!? WHY IS SHE SUDDENLY TALKING DOWN TO—!?
WITHIN HARUHI, SOMETHING IS BURSTING THROUGH.
IN THE END, WE WERE ABLE TO TALK TO HER.
WHAT DO YOU THINK ASAHINA-SENSEI'S GREATEST ASSETS ARE?
HMM, WELL...
...SHE'S ALWAYS FAIR, AND HER SMILE HAS THE POWER TO MAKE PEOPLE FEEL BETTER.
BUT THOSE ARE JUST DETAILS... I THINK HER GREATEST ASSET IS...
...HER CHEST, MAYBE.
THE END
SOS
TSURUGAOKA KINDERGARTEN PRINCIPAL: TSURUYA-SAN

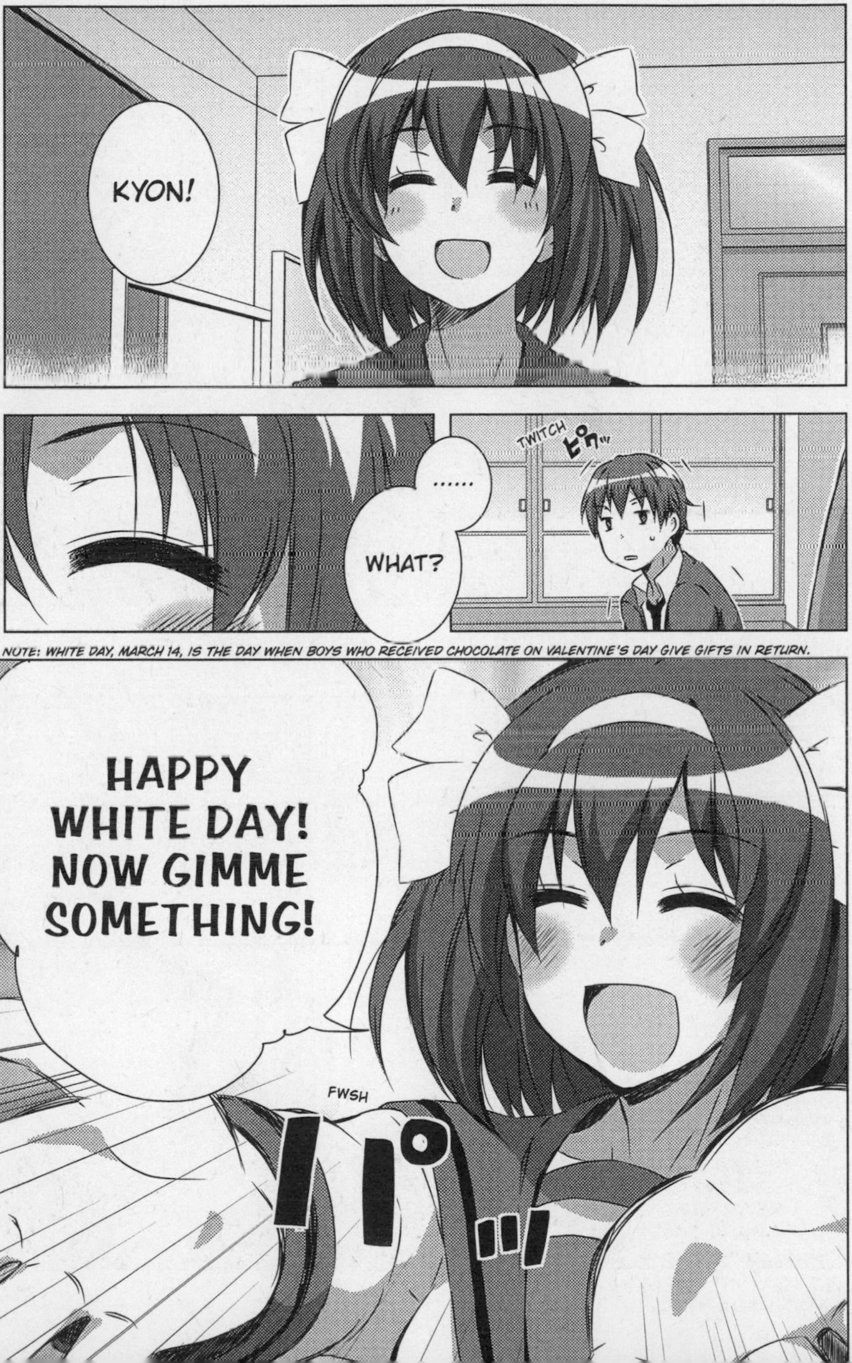
KYON!
TWITCH
......
WHAT?
HAPPY WHITE DAY! NOW GIMME SOMETHING!
FWSH

NOTE: WHITE DAY, MARCH 14, IS THE DAY WHEN BOYS WHO RECEIVED CHOCOLATE ON VALENTINE'S DAY GIVE GIFTS IN RETURN.

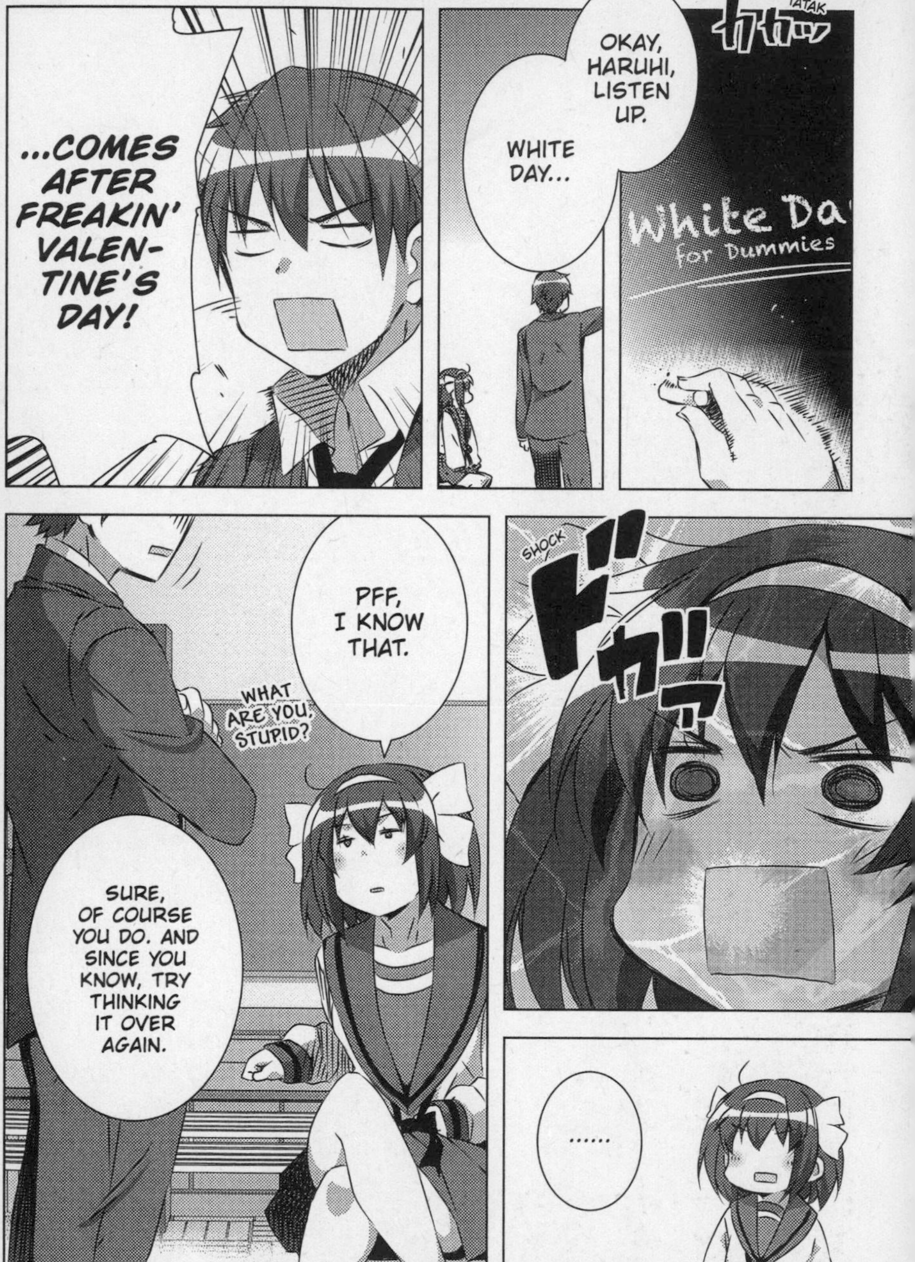
TATAK
White Da
for Dummies
OKAY, HARUHI, LISTEN UP.
WHITE DAY...
...COMES AFTER FREAKIN' VALEN-TINE'S DAY!
SHOCK
......
PFF, I KNOW THAT.
WHAT ARE YOU, STUPID?
SURE, OF COURSE YOU DO. AND SINCE YOU KNOW, TRY THINKING IT OVER AGAIN.

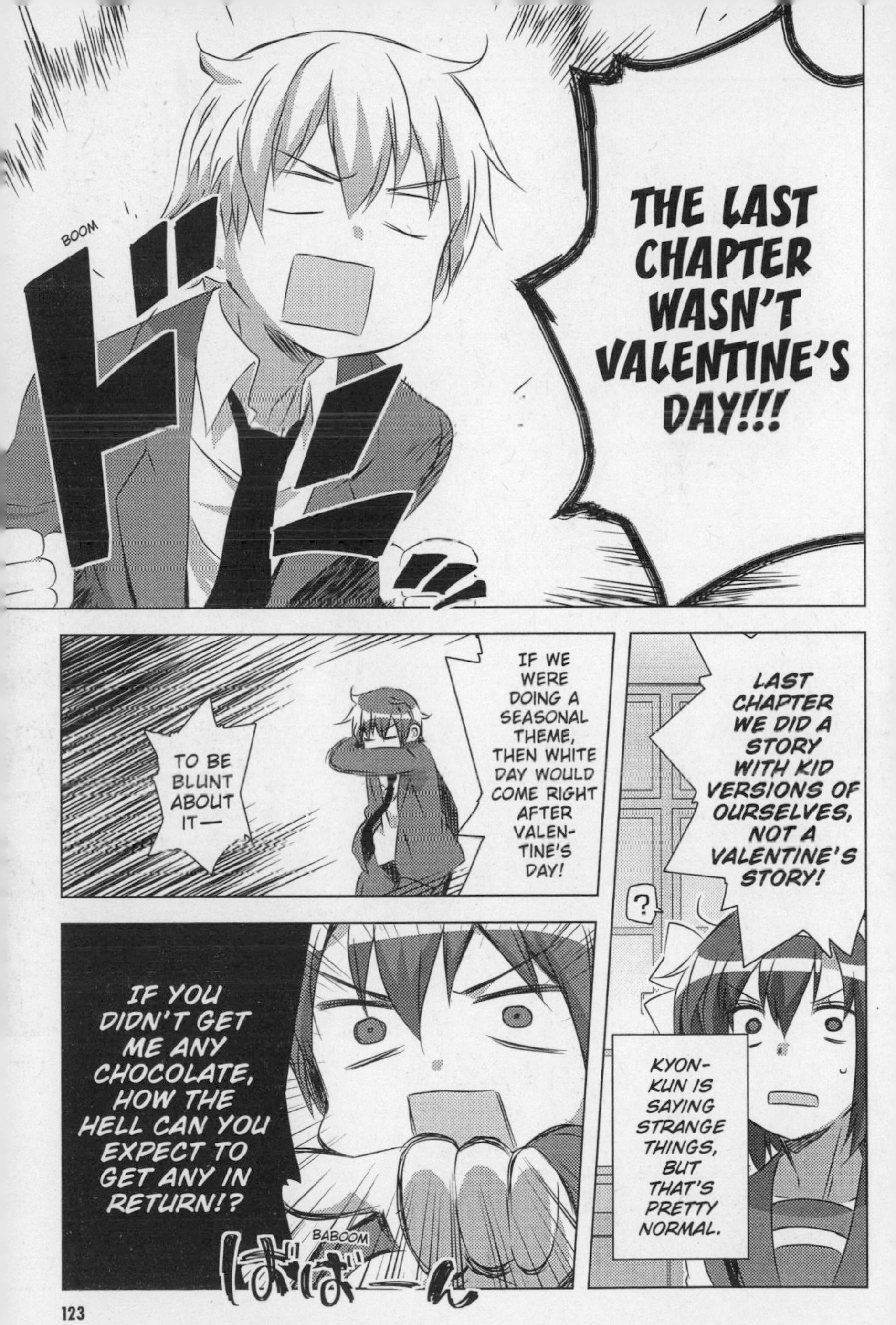
THE LAST CHAPTER WASN'T VALENTINE'S DAY!!!
BOOM
LAST CHAPTER WE DID A STORY WITH KID VERSIONS OF OURSELVES, NOT A VALENTINE'S STORY!
?
KYON-KUN IS SAYING STRANGE THINGS, BUT THAT'S PRETTY NORMAL.
IF WE WERE DOING A SEASONAL THEME, THEN WHITE DAY WOULD COME RIGHT AFTER VALEN-TINE'S DAY!
TO BE BLUNT ABOUT IT—
IF YOU DIDN'T GET ME ANY CHOCOLATE, HOW THE HELL CAN YOU EXPECT TO GET ANY IN RETURN!?
BABOOM

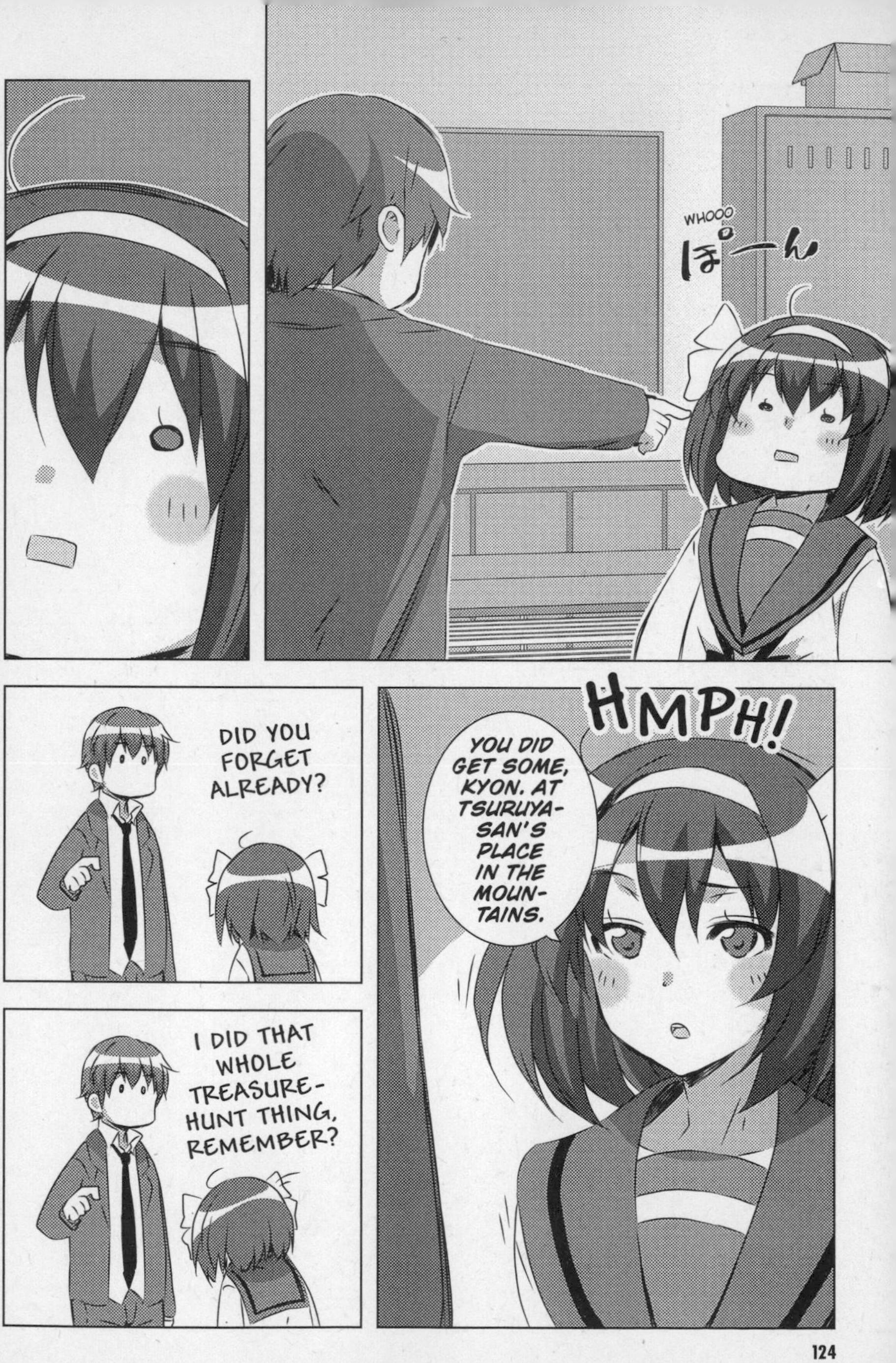
WHOOO
ぽーん
HMPH!
YOU DID GET SOME, KYON. AT TSURUYA-SAN'S PLACE IN THE MOUN-TAINS.
DID YOU FORGET ALREADY?
I DID THAT WHOLE TREASURE-HUNT THING, REMEMBER?

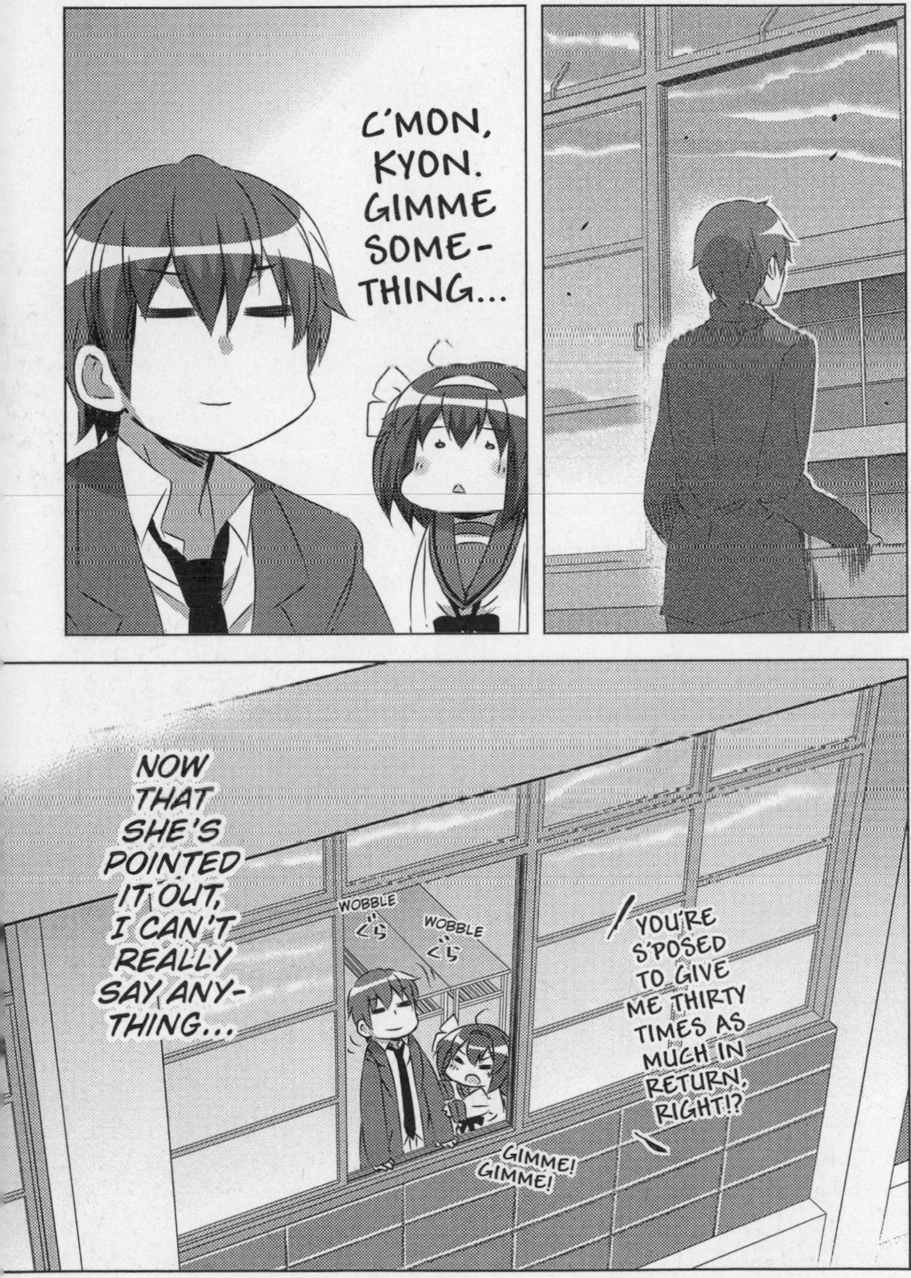
C'MON, KYON. GIMME SOME-THING...
YOU'RE S'POSED TO GIVE ME THIRTY TIMES AS MUCH IN RETURN, RIGHT!?
WOBBLE ぐら
WOBBLE ぐら
GIMME! GIMME!
NOW THAT SHE'S POINTED IT OUT, I CAN'T REALLY SAY ANY-THING...

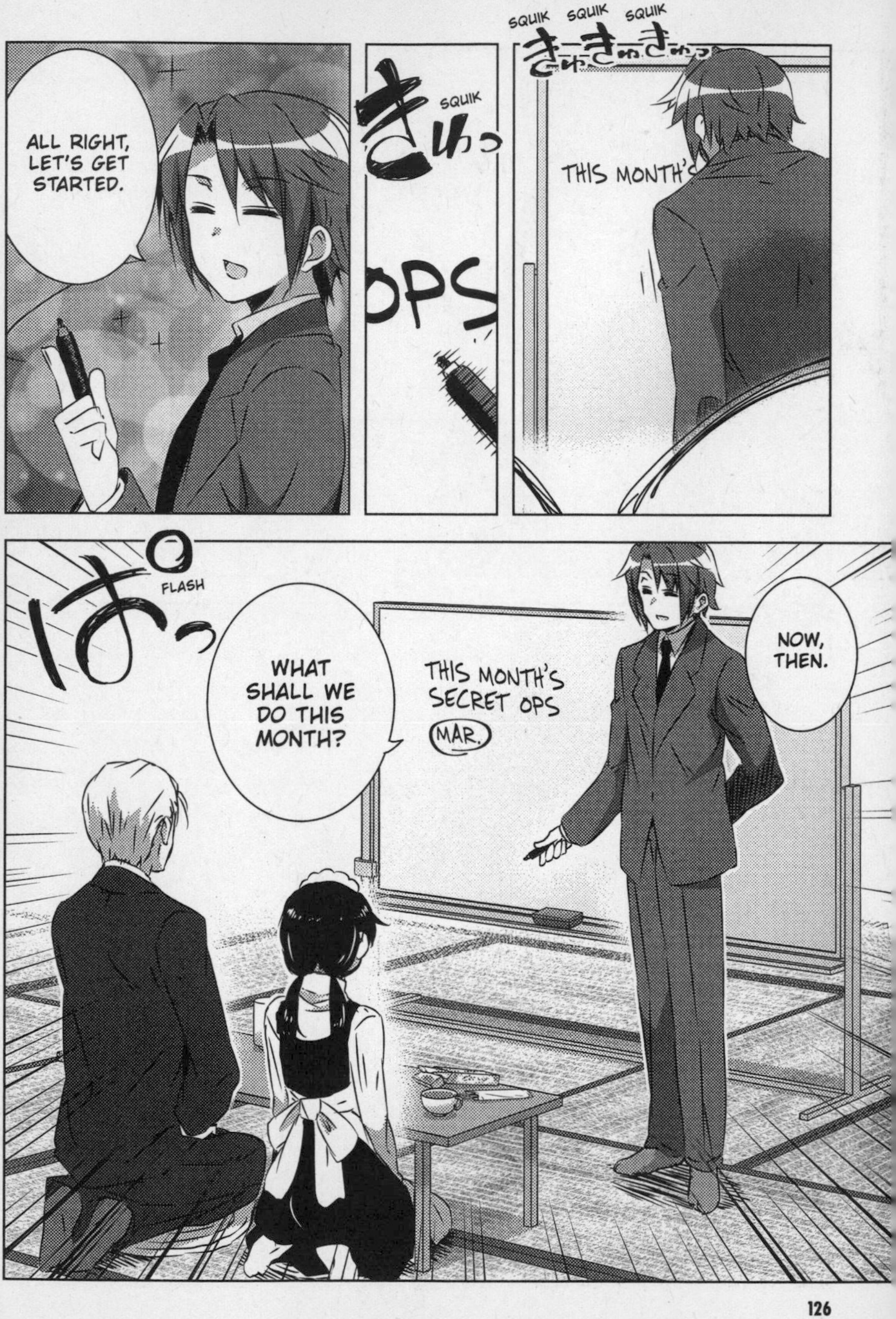
SQUIK SQUIK SQUIK
きゅきゅきゅっ
THIS MONTH'S
きゅっ
SQUIK
OPS
ALL RIGHT, LET'S GET STARTED.
NOW, THEN.
THIS MONTH'S SECRET OPS MAR.
WHAT SHALL WE DO THIS MONTH?
ぱっ
FLASH

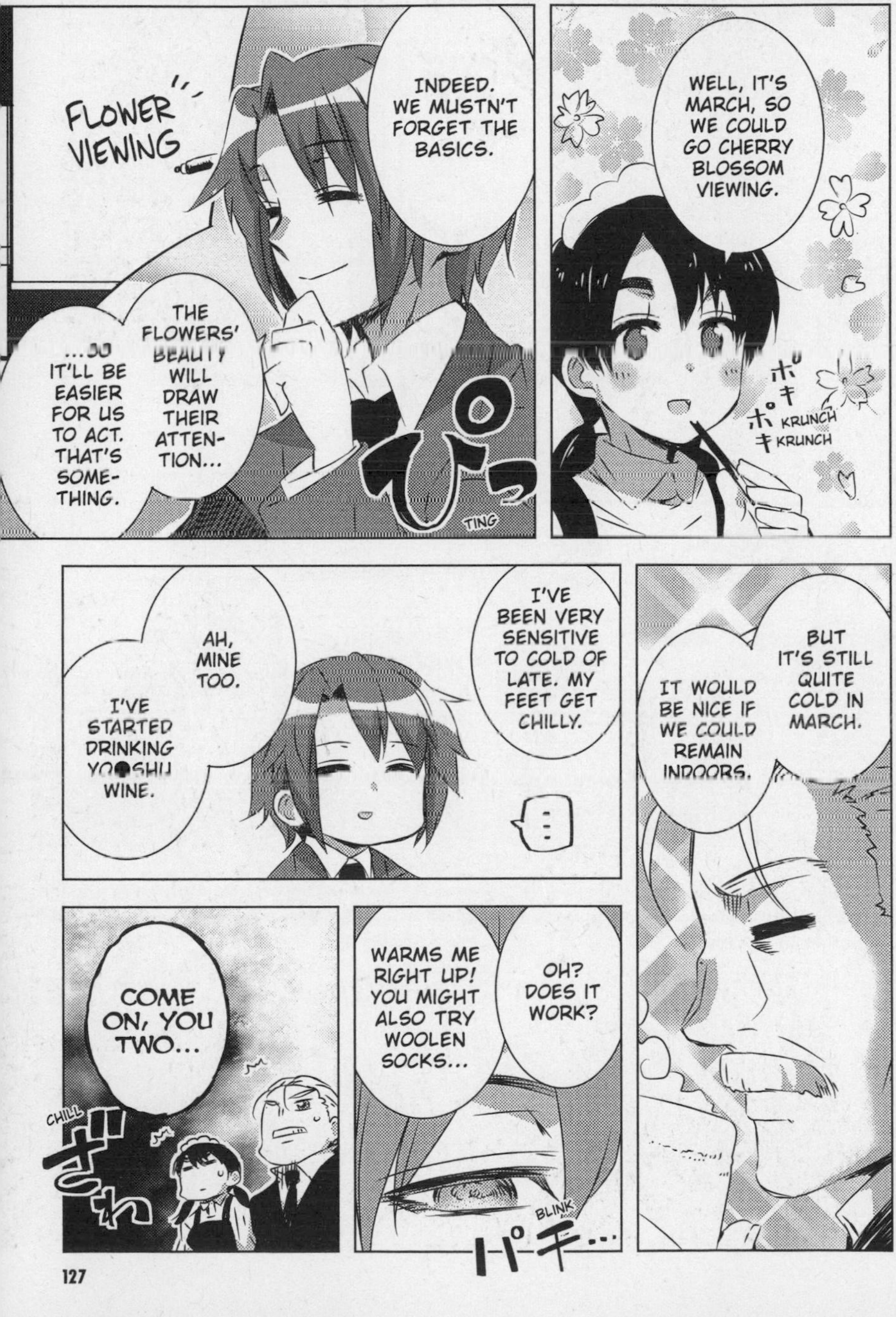
WELL, IT'S MARCH, SO WE COULD GO CHERRY BLOSSOM VIEWING.
ポキポキ KRUNCH KRUNCH
INDEED. WE MUSTN'T FORGET THE BASICS.
FLOWER VIEWING
THE FLOWERS' BEAUTY WILL DRAW THEIR ATTENTION...
...SO IT'LL BE EASIER FOR US TO ACT. THAT'S SOMETHING.
ぴっ TING
BUT IT'S STILL QUITE COLD IN MARCH.
IT WOULD BE NICE IF WE COULD REMAIN INDOORS.
I'VE BEEN VERY SENSITIVE TO COLD OF LATE. MY FEET GET CHILLY.
...
AH, MINE TOO.
I'VE STARTED DRINKING YO SHU WINE.
OH? DOES IT WORK?
WARMS ME RIGHT UP! YOU MIGHT ALSO TRY WOOLEN SOCKS...
BLINK パチ...
COME ON, YOU TWO...
CHILL ざわ

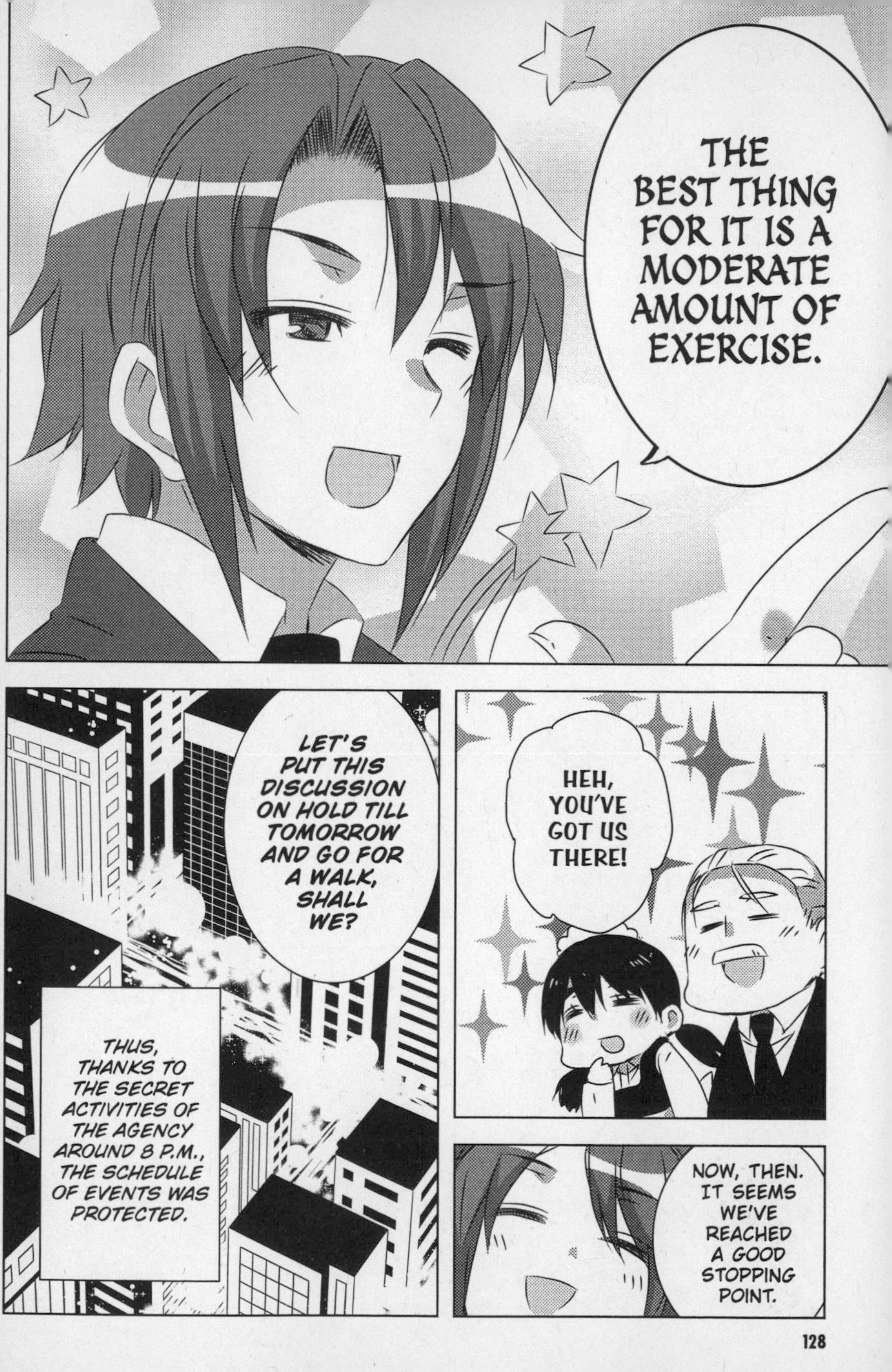
THE BEST THING FOR IT IS A MODERATE AMOUNT OF EXERCISE.
HEH, YOU'VE GOT US THERE!
NOW, THEN. IT SEEMS WE'VE REACHED A GOOD STOPPING POINT.
LET'S PUT THIS DISCUSSION ON HOLD TILL TOMORROW AND GO FOR A WALK, SHALL WE?
THUS, THANKS TO THE SECRET ACTIVITIES OF THE AGENCY AROUND 8 P.M., THE SCHEDULE OF EVENTS WAS PROTECTED.

—NEW SERIES—
THE INTRIGUES OF
KOIZUMI ITSUKI-KUN

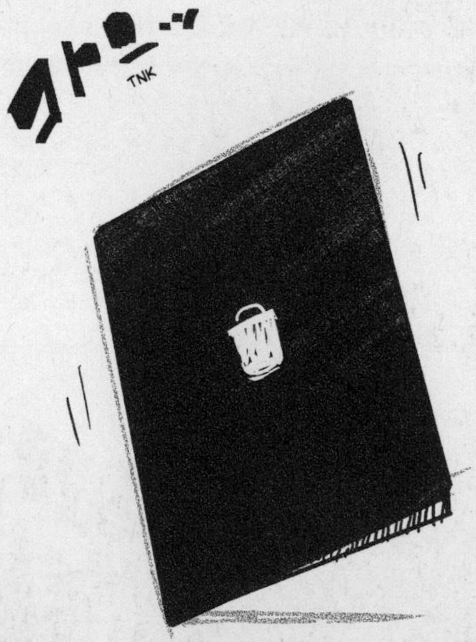
TNK

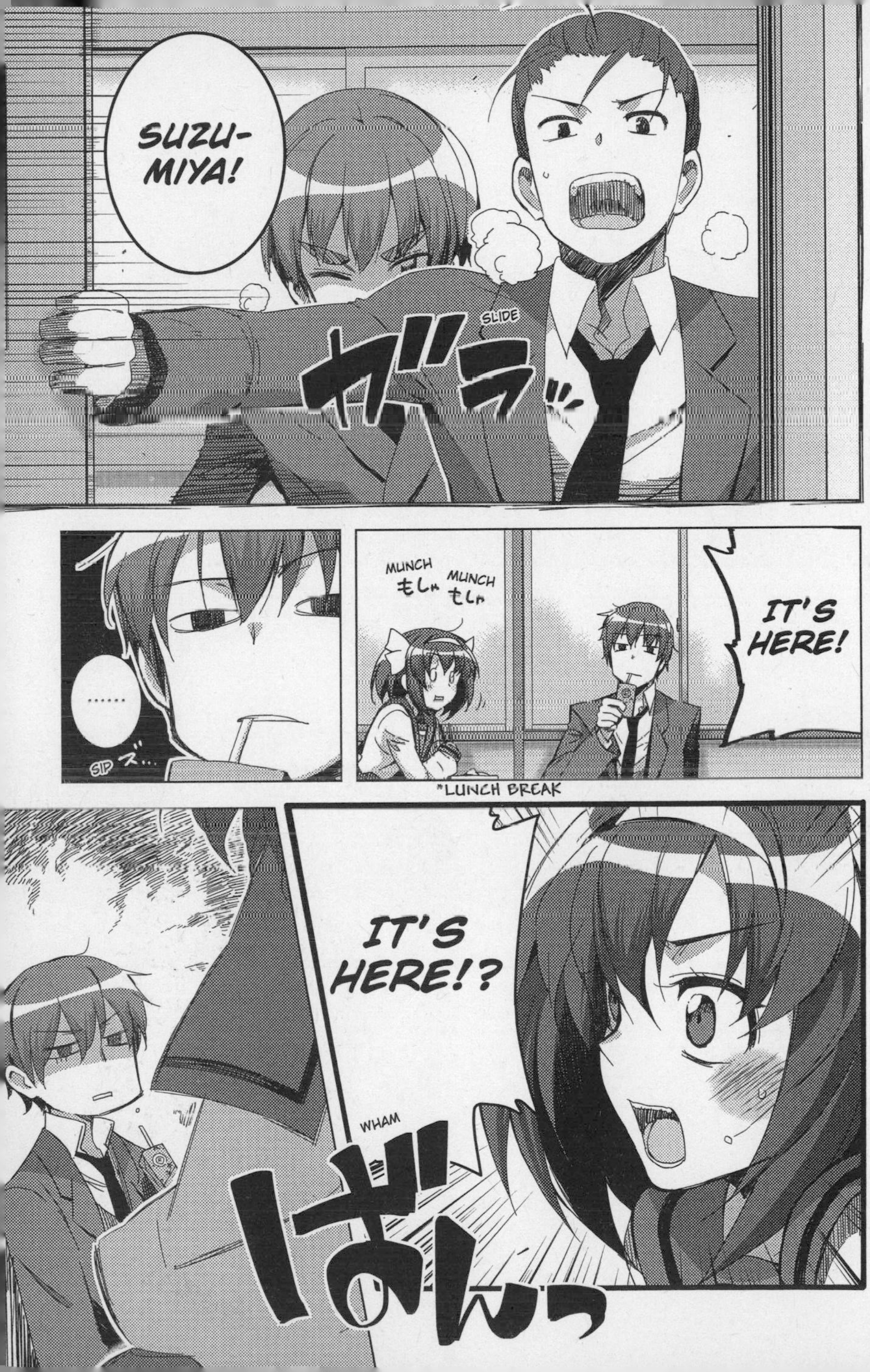
SUZU-MIYA!
SLIDE
ガラ
IT'S HERE!
MUNCH もしゃ
MUNCH もしゃ
*LUNCH BREAK
......
SIP ズ...
IT'S HERE!?
WHAM
ばんっ

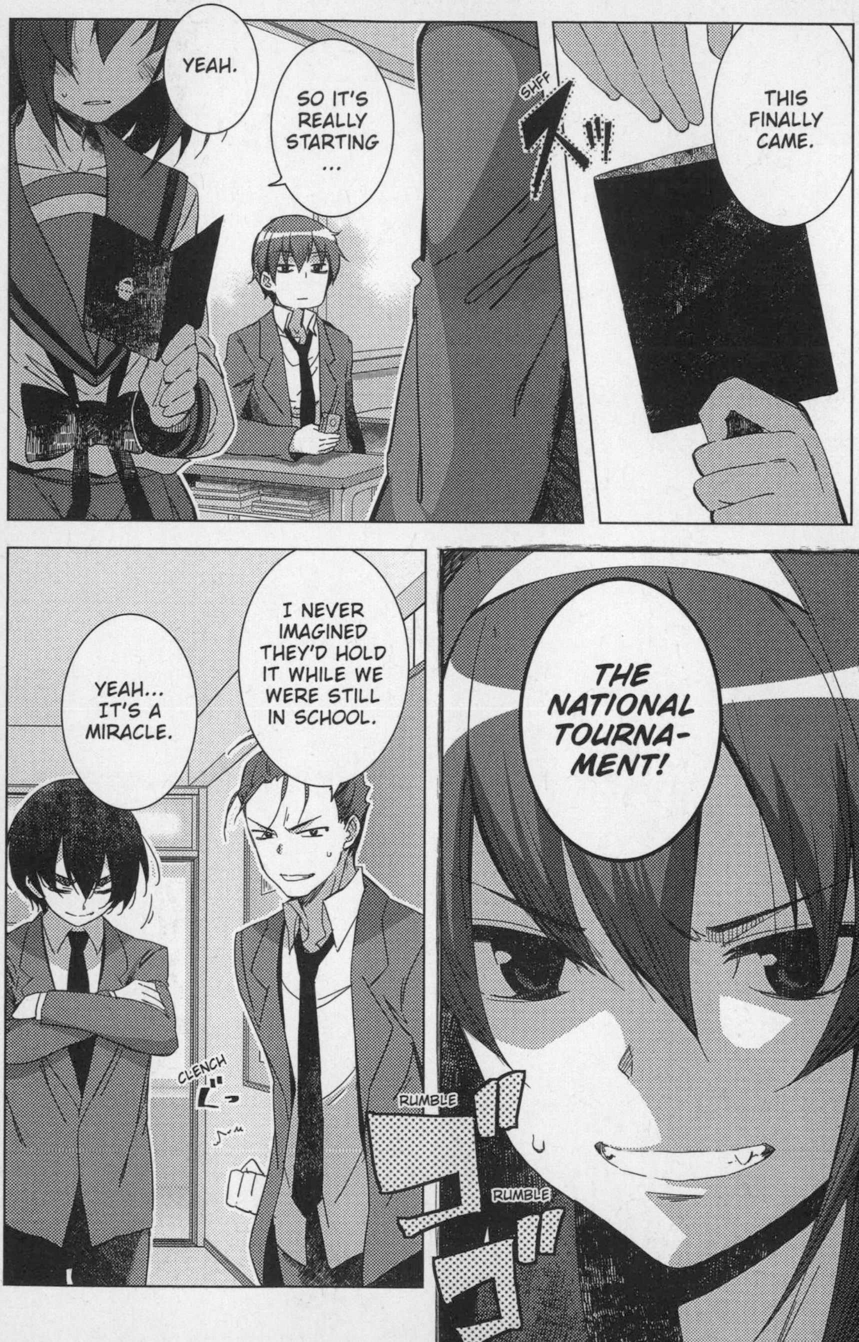
THIS FINALLY CAME.
SHUFF
SO IT'S REALLY STARTING...
YEAH.
THE NATIONAL TOURNAMENT!
RUMBLE
RUMBLE
I NEVER IMAGINED THEY'D HOLD IT WHILE WE WERE STILL IN SCHOOL.
YEAH... IT'S A MIRACLE.
CLENCH

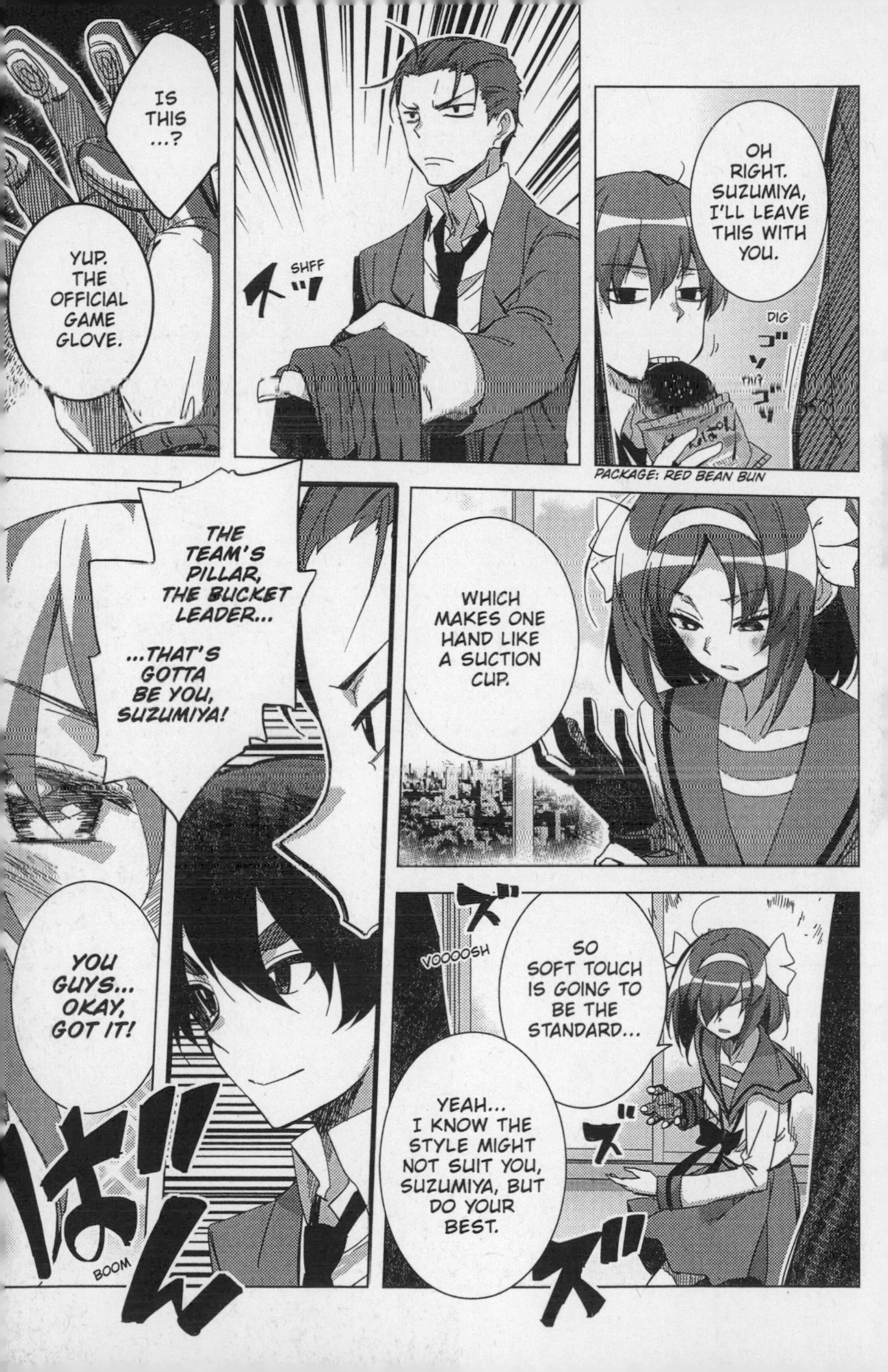
OH RIGHT. SUZUMIYA, I'LL LEAVE THIS WITH YOU.
DIG
PACKAGE: RED BEAN BUN
SHFF
IS THIS ...?
YUP. THE OFFICIAL GAME GLOVE.
WHICH MAKES ONE HAND LIKE A SUCTION CUP.
VOOOOSH
SO SOFT TOUCH IS GOING TO BE THE STANDARD...
YEAH... I KNOW THE STYLE MIGHT NOT SUIT YOU, SUZUMIYA, BUT DO YOUR BEST.
THE TEAM'S PILLAR, THE BUCKET LEADER...
...THAT'S GOTTA BE YOU, SUZUMIYA!
YOU GUYS... OKAY, GOT IT!
BOOM

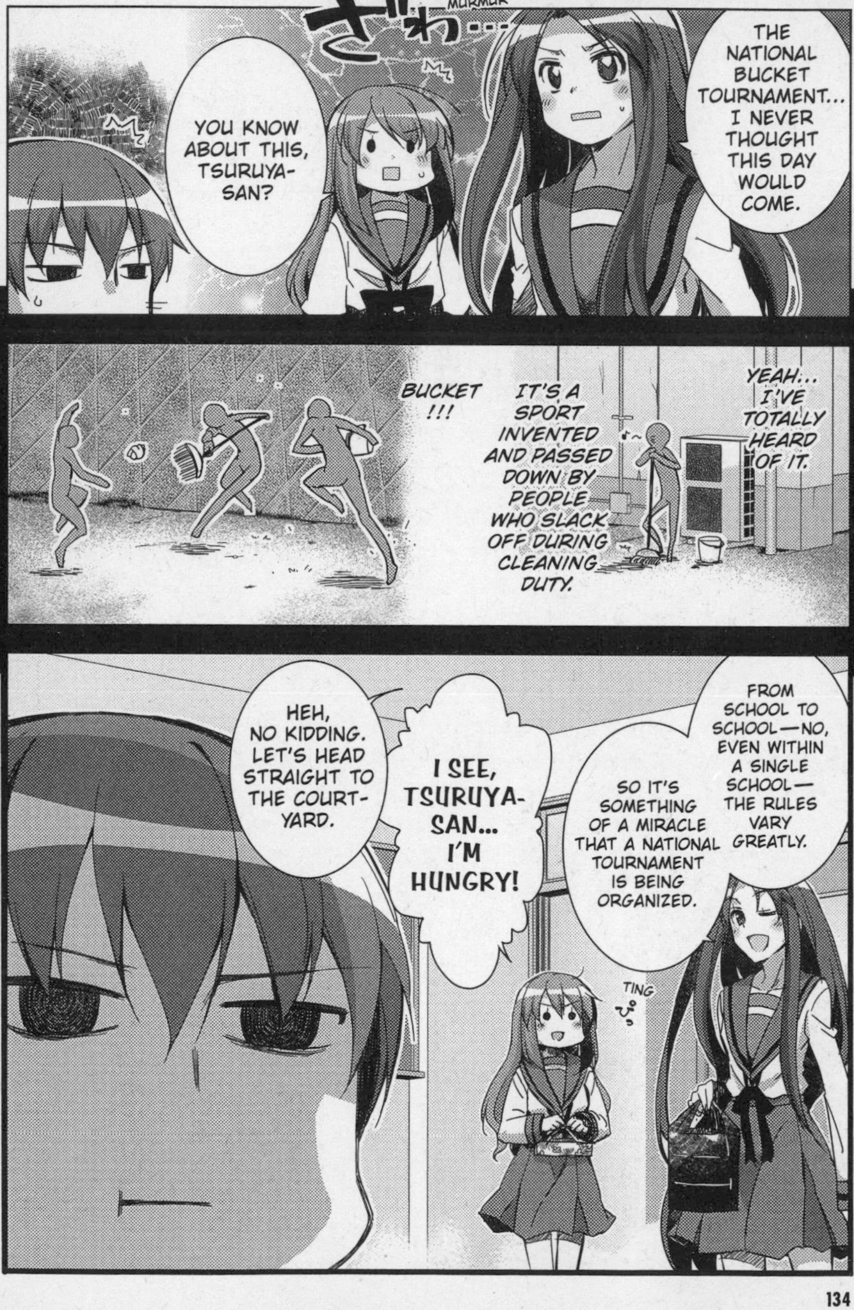

THE NATIONAL BUCKET TOURNAMENT... I NEVER THOUGHT THIS DAY WOULD COME.
ざわ...
MURMUR
YOU KNOW ABOUT THIS, TSURUYA-SAN?
YEAH... I'VE TOTALLY HEARD OF IT.
IT'S A SPORT INVENTED AND PASSED DOWN BY PEOPLE WHO SLACK OFF DURING CLEANING DUTY.
BUCKET!!!
FROM SCHOOL TO SCHOOL—NO, EVEN WITHIN A SINGLE SCHOOL—THE RULES VARY GREATLY.
SO IT'S SOMETHING OF A MIRACLE THAT A NATIONAL TOURNAMENT IS BEING ORGANIZED.
TING
I SEE, TSURUYA-SAN... I'M HUNGRY!
HEH, NO KIDDING. LET'S HEAD STRAIGHT TO THE COURT-YARD.

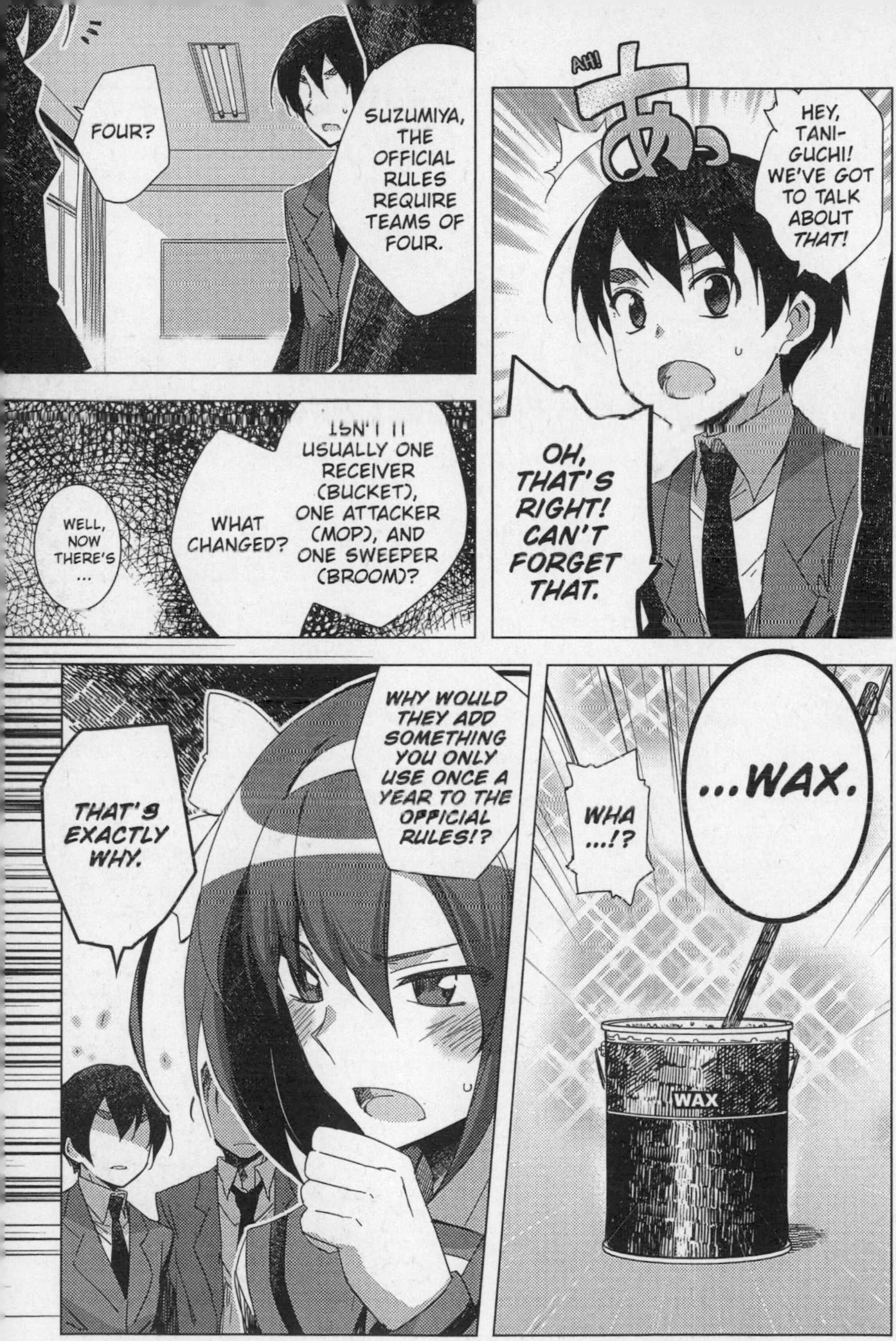
AH!
HEY, TANI-GUCHI! WE'VE GOT TO TALK ABOUT THAT!
OH, THAT'S RIGHT! CAN'T FORGET THAT.
SUZUMIYA, THE OFFICIAL RULES REQUIRE TEAMS OF FOUR.
FOUR?
ISN'T IT USUALLY ONE RECEIVER (BUCKET), ONE ATTACKER (MOP), AND ONE SWEEPER (BROOM)?
WHAT CHANGED?
WELL, NOW THERE'S ...
...WAX.
WHA ...!?
WAX
WHY WOULD THEY ADD SOMETHING YOU ONLY USE ONCE A YEAR TO THE OFFICIAL RULES!?
THAT'S EXACTLY WHY.

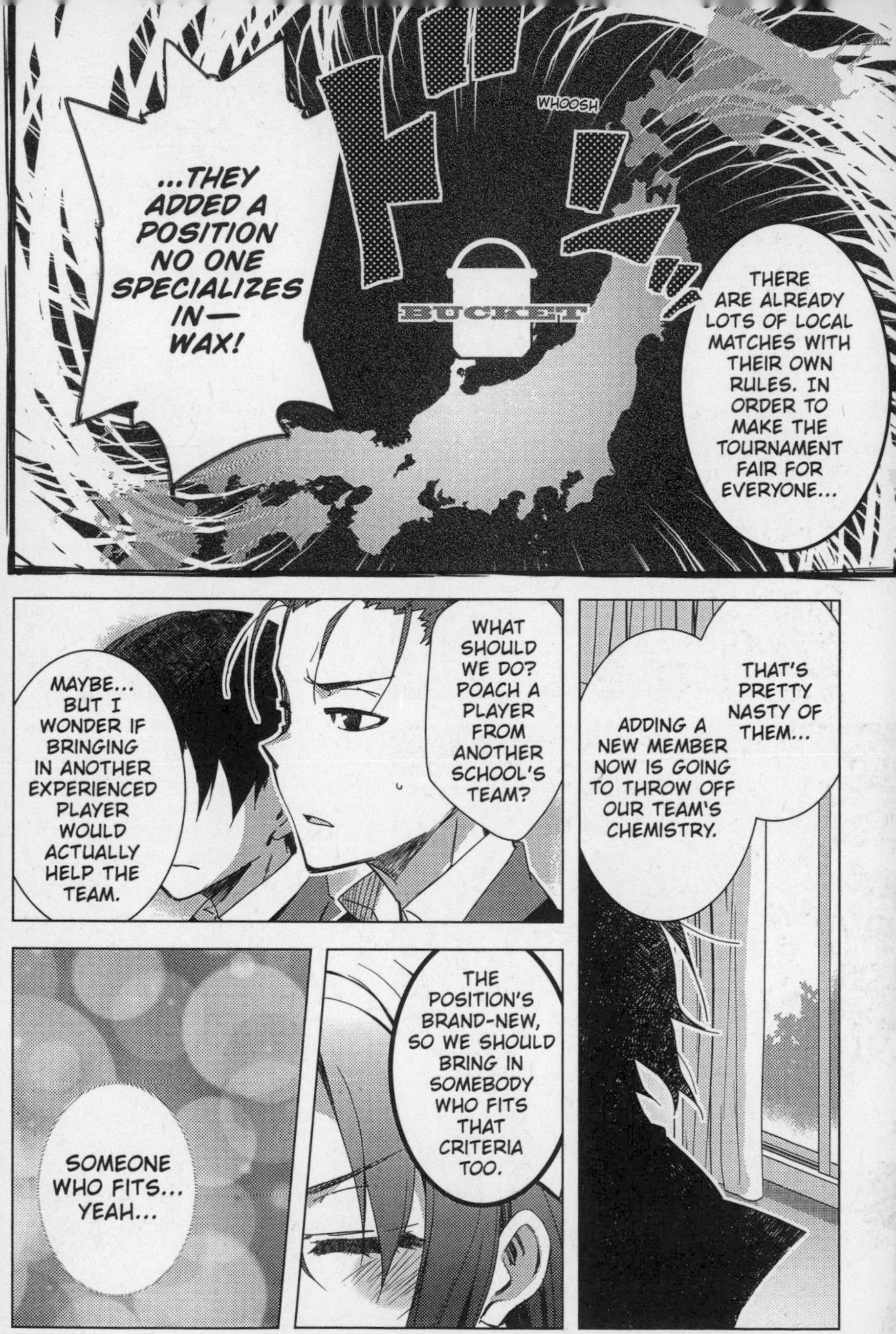
THERE ARE ALREADY LOTS OF LOCAL MATCHES WITH THEIR OWN RULES. IN ORDER TO MAKE THE TOURNAMENT FAIR FOR EVERYONE...
WHOOSH
BUCKET
...THEY ADDED A POSITION NO ONE SPECIALIZES IN—WAX!
THAT'S PRETTY NASTY OF THEM...
ADDING A NEW MEMBER NOW IS GOING TO THROW OFF OUR TEAM'S CHEMISTRY.
WHAT SHOULD WE DO? POACH A PLAYER FROM ANOTHER SCHOOL'S TEAM?
MAYBE... BUT I WONDER IF BRINGING IN ANOTHER EXPERIENCED PLAYER WOULD ACTUALLY HELP THE TEAM.
THE POSITION'S BRAND-NEW, SO WE SHOULD BRING IN SOMEBODY WHO FITS THAT CRITERIA TOO.
SOMEONE WHO FITS... YEAH...

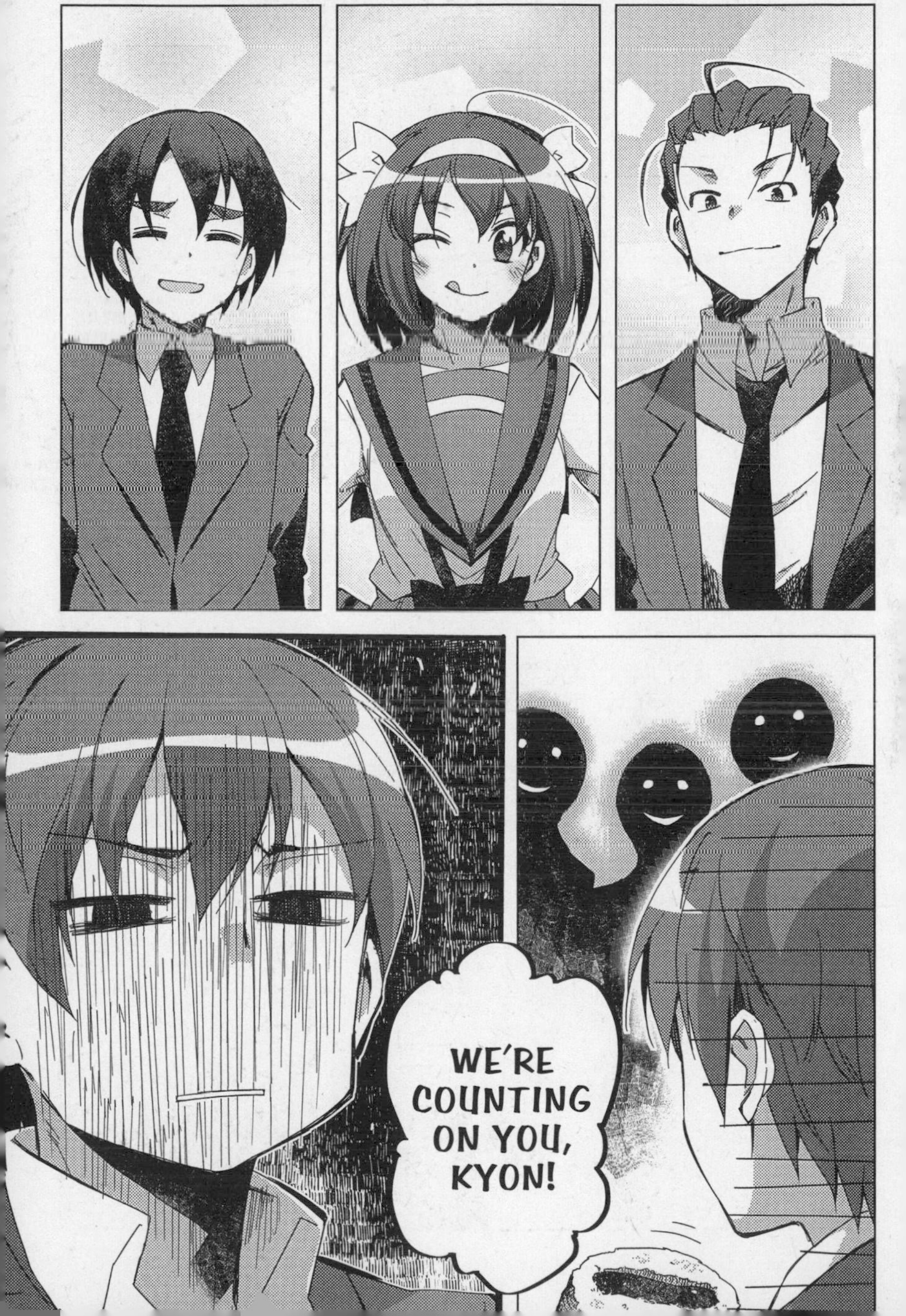
WE'RE COUNTING ON YOU, KYON!

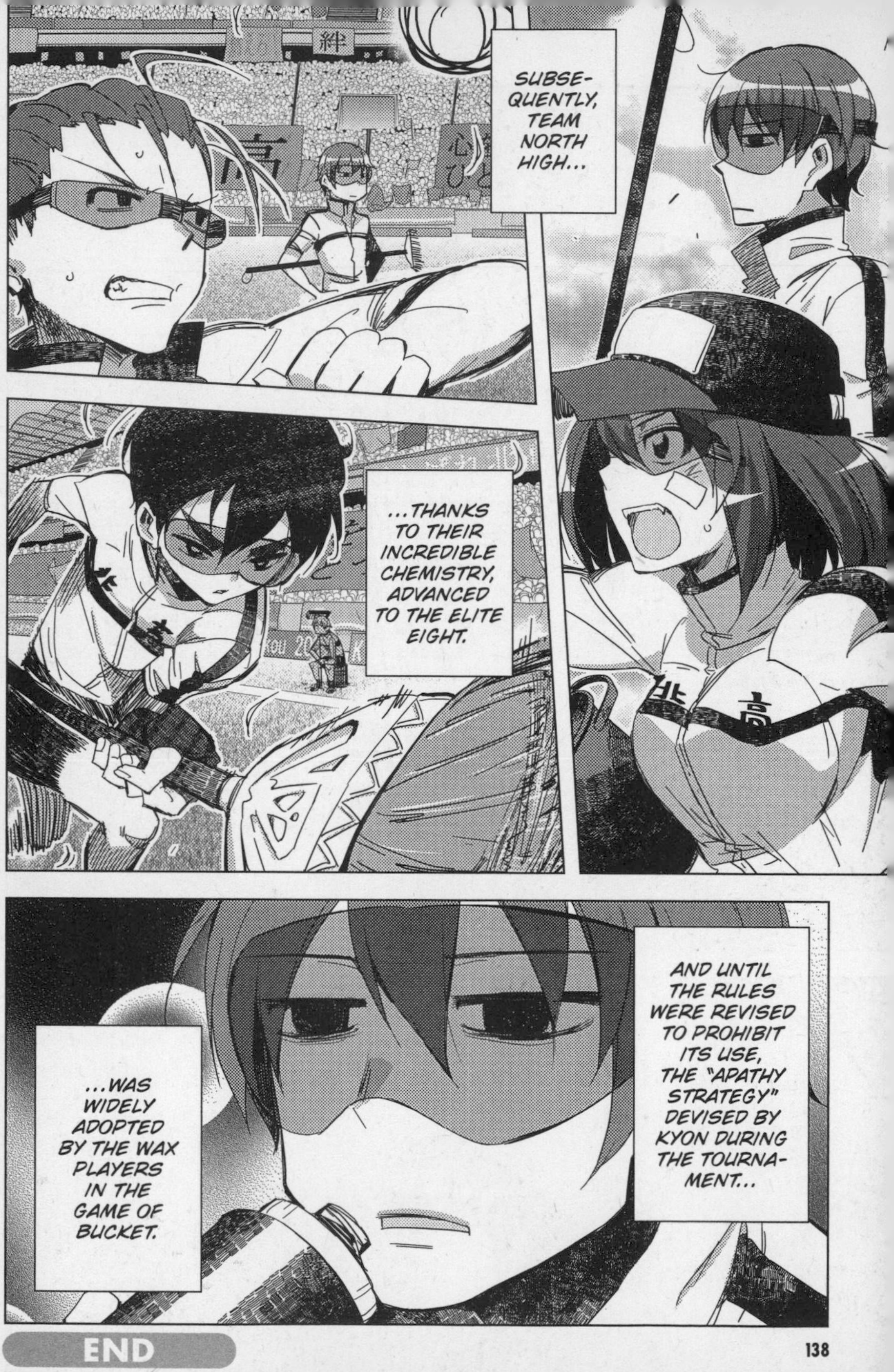

SUBSEQUENTLY, TEAM NORTH HIGH...
...THANKS TO THEIR INCREDIBLE CHEMISTRY, ADVANCED TO THE ELITE EIGHT.
AND UNTIL THE RULES WERE REVISED TO PROHIBIT ITS USE, THE "APATHY STRATEGY" DEVISED BY KYON DURING THE TOURNAMENT...
...WAS WIDELY ADOPTED BY THE WAX PLAYERS IN THE GAME OF BUCKET.


END

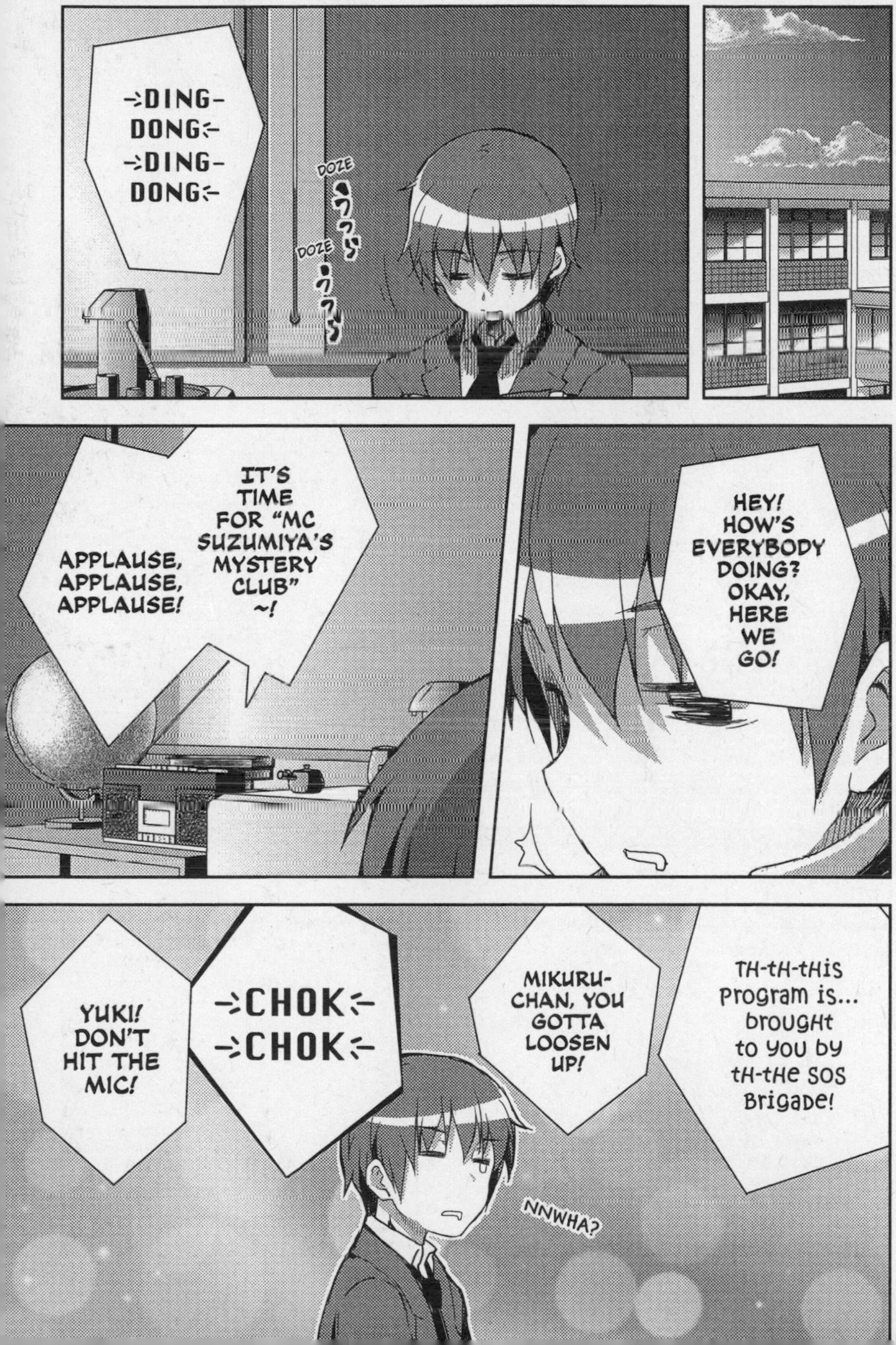

DING-DONG DING-DONG
DOZE DOZE
HEY! HOW'S EVERYBODY DOING? OKAY, HERE WE GO!
IT'S TIME FOR "MC SUZUMIYA'S MYSTERY CLUB" ~!
APPLAUSE, APPLAUSE, APPLAUSE!
TH-TH-THIS PROGRAM IS... BROUGHT TO YOU BY TH-THE SOS BRIGADE!
MIKURU-CHAN, YOU GOTTA LOOSEN UP!
CHOK CHOK
YUKI! DON'T HIT THE MIC!
NNWHA?

# 00:00 - OPENING MONOLOGUE

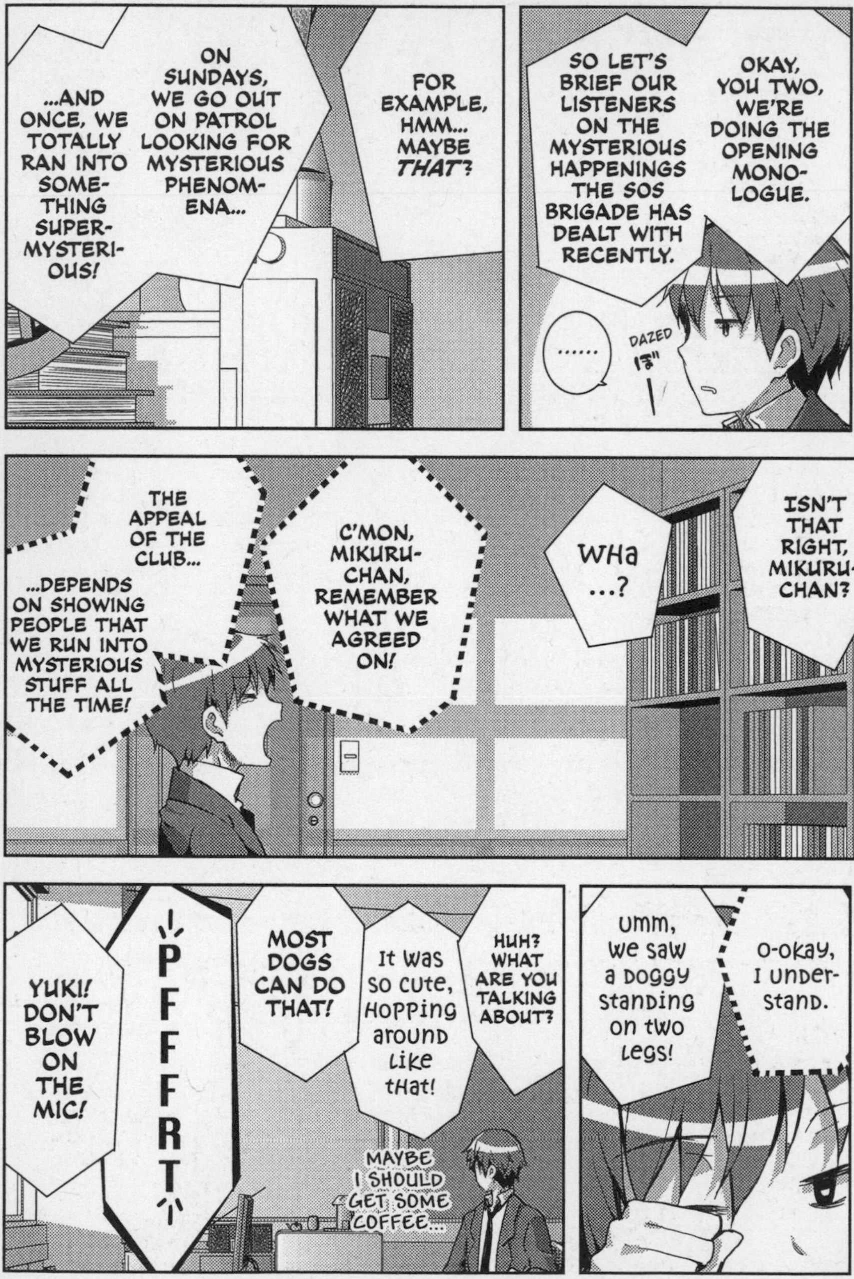
OKAY, YOU TWO, WE'RE DOING THE OPENING MONO-LOGUE.
SO LET'S BRIEF OUR LISTENERS ON THE MYSTERIOUS HAPPENINGS THE SOS BRIGADE HAS DEALT WITH RECENTLY.
DAZED
......
FOR EXAMPLE, HMM... MAYBE *THAT*?
ON SUNDAYS, WE GO OUT ON PATROL LOOKING FOR MYSTERIOUS PHENOM-ENA...
...AND ONCE, WE TOTALLY RAN INTO SOME-THING SUPER-MYSTERI-OUS!
ISN'T THAT RIGHT, MIKURU-CHAN?
WHA ...?
C'MON, MIKURU-CHAN, REMEMBER WHAT WE AGREED ON!
THE APPEAL OF THE CLUB...
...DEPENDS ON SHOWING PEOPLE THAT WE RUN INTO MYSTERIOUS STUFF ALL THE TIME!
O-OKAY, I UNDER-STAND.
UMM, WE SAW A DOGGY STANDING ON TWO LEGS!
HUH? WHAT ARE YOU TALKING ABOUT?
IT WAS SO CUTE, HOPPING AROUND LIKE THAT!
MOST DOGS CAN DO THAT!
PFFFRT
YUKI! DON'T BLOW ON THE MIC!
MAYBE I SHOULD GET SOME COFFEE...

## 00:10 - FIRST SONG, LISTENER REQUEST

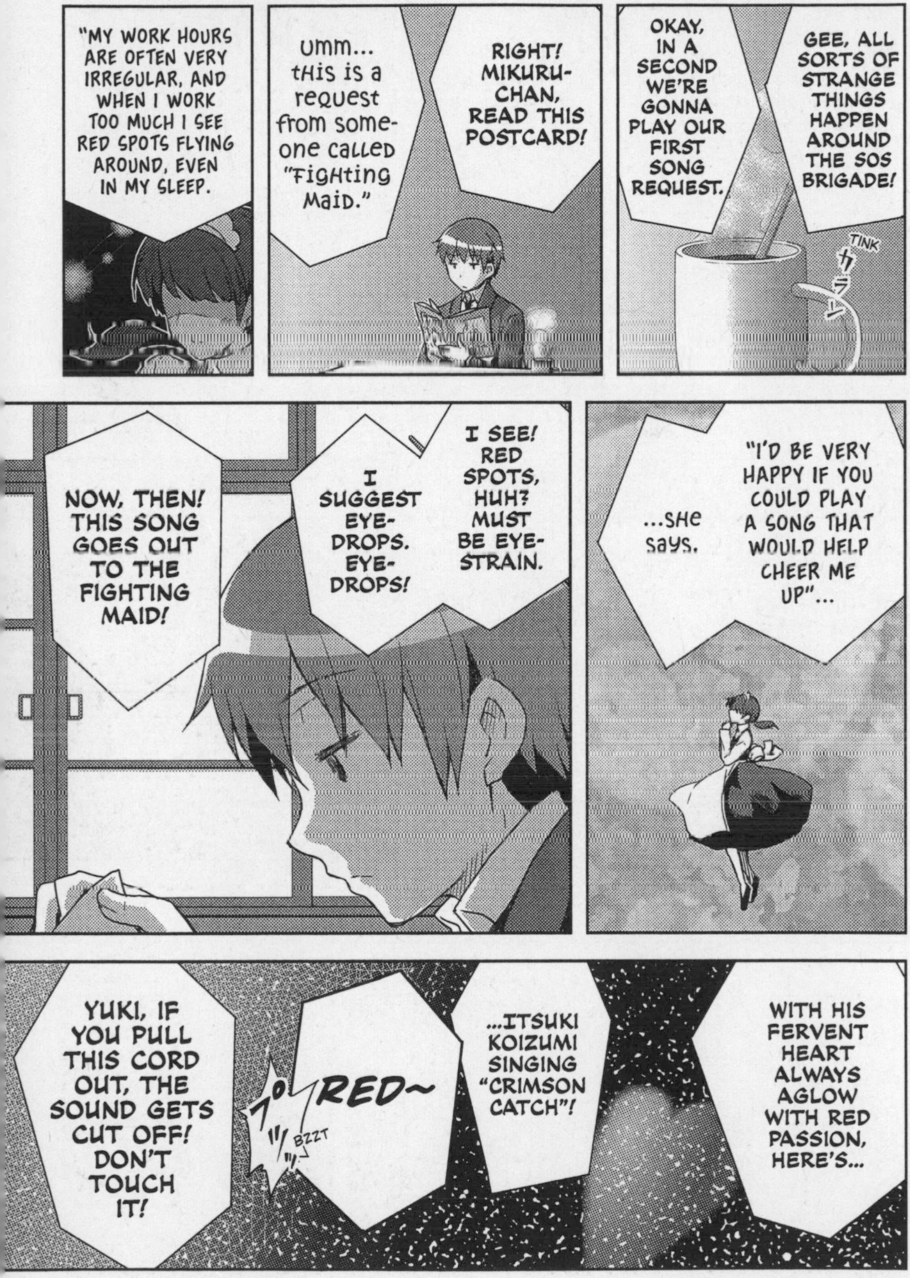
GEE, ALL SORTS OF STRANGE THINGS HAPPEN AROUND THE SOS BRIGADE!
OKAY, IN A SECOND WE'RE GONNA PLAY OUR FIRST SONG REQUEST.
TINK
RIGHT! MIKURU-CHAN, READ THIS POSTCARD!
Umm... this is a request from some-one called "Fighting Maid."
"MY WORK HOURS ARE OFTEN VERY IRREGULAR, AND WHEN I WORK TOO MUCH I SEE RED SPOTS FLYING AROUND, EVEN IN MY SLEEP.
"I'D BE VERY HAPPY IF YOU COULD PLAY A SONG THAT WOULD HELP CHEER ME UP"...
...she says.
I SEE! RED SPOTS, HUH? MUST BE EYE-STRAIN.
I SUGGEST EYE-DROPS. EYE-DROPS!
NOW, THEN! THIS SONG GOES OUT TO THE FIGHTING MAID!
WITH HIS FERVENT HEART ALWAYS AGLOW WITH RED PASSION, HERE'S...
...ITSUKI KOIZUMI SINGING "CRIMSON CATCH"!
RED~
BZZT
YUKI, IF YOU PULL THIS CORD OUT, THE SOUND GETS CUT OFF! DON'T TOUCH IT!

# 00:15 - COMMERCIAL BREAK, POSTCARD CORNER INTRO

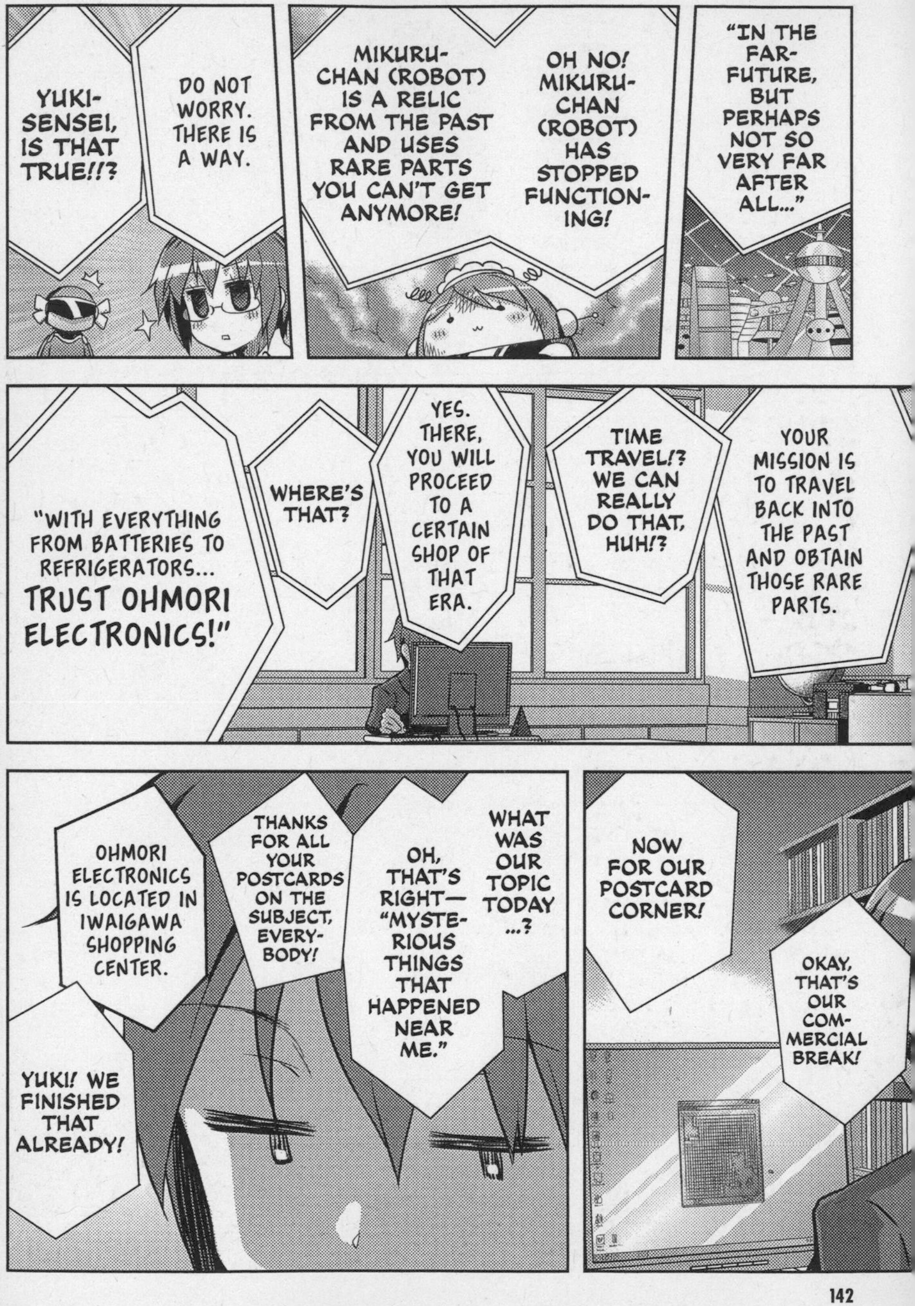
"IN THE FAR-FUTURE, BUT PERHAPS NOT SO VERY FAR AFTER ALL..."
OH NO! MIKURU-CHAN (ROBOT) HAS STOPPED FUNCTION-ING!
MIKURU-CHAN (ROBOT) IS A RELIC FROM THE PAST AND USES RARE PARTS YOU CAN'T GET ANYMORE!
YUKI-SENSEI, IS THAT TRUE!!?
DO NOT WORRY. THERE IS A WAY.
YOUR MISSION IS TO TRAVEL BACK INTO THE PAST AND OBTAIN THOSE RARE PARTS.
TIME TRAVEL!? WE CAN REALLY DO THAT, HUH!?
WHERE'S THAT?
YES. THERE, YOU WILL PROCEED TO A CERTAIN SHOP OF THAT ERA.
"WITH EVERYTHING FROM BATTERIES TO REFRIGERATORS... TRUST OHMORI ELECTRONICS!"
OKAY, THAT'S OUR COM-MERCIAL BREAK!
NOW FOR OUR POSTCARD CORNER!
OHMORI ELECTRONICS IS LOCATED IN IWAIGAWA SHOPPING CENTER.
YUKI! WE FINISHED THAT ALREADY!
WHAT WAS OUR TOPIC TODAY ...?
OH, THAT'S RIGHT— "MYSTE-RIOUS THINGS THAT HAPPENED NEAR ME."
THANKS FOR ALL YOUR POSTCARDS ON THE SUBJECT, EVERY-BODY!

**TODAY'S THEME: "MYSTERIOUS THINGS THAT HAPPENED NEAR ME."**

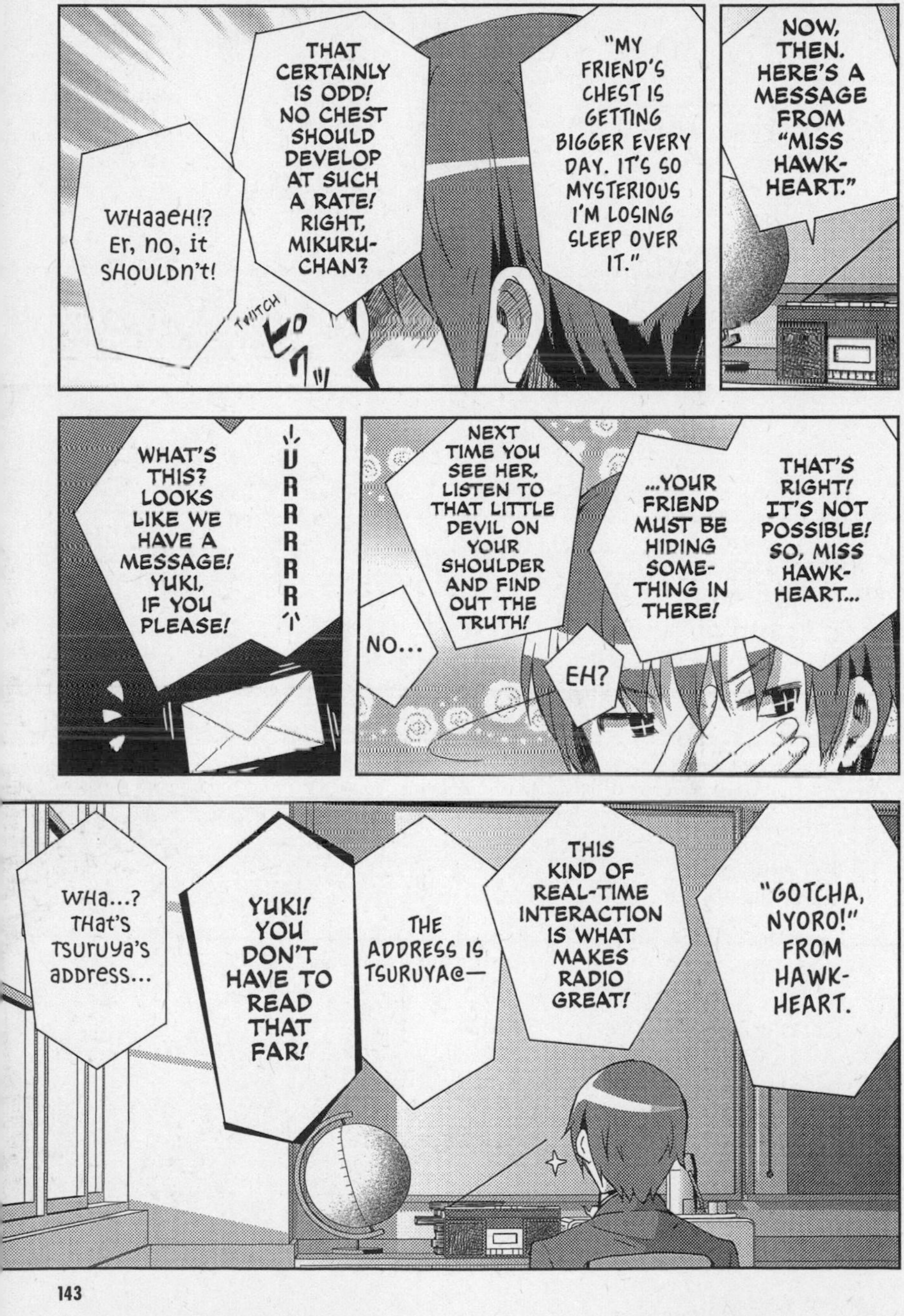

NOW, THEN. HERE'S A MESSAGE FROM "MISS HAWK-HEART."
"MY FRIEND'S CHEST IS GETTING BIGGER EVERY DAY. IT'S SO MYSTERIOUS I'M LOSING SLEEP OVER IT."
THAT CERTAINLY IS ODD! NO CHEST SHOULD DEVELOP AT SUCH A RATE! RIGHT, MIKURU-CHAN?
WHaaeH!? Er, no, it SHOULDn't!
TWITCH
THAT'S RIGHT! IT'S NOT POSSIBLE! SO, MISS HAWK-HEART...
...YOUR FRIEND MUST BE HIDING SOME-THING IN THERE!
NEXT TIME YOU SEE HER, LISTEN TO THAT LITTLE DEVIL ON YOUR SHOULDER AND FIND OUT THE TRUTH!
EH?
NO...
VRRRRR
WHAT'S THIS? LOOKS LIKE WE HAVE A MESSAGE! YUKI, IF YOU PLEASE!
"GOTCHA, NYORO!" FROM HAWK-HEART.
THIS KIND OF REAL-TIME INTERACTION IS WHAT MAKES RADIO GREAT!
THE ADDRESS IS TSURUYA@—
YUKI! YOU DON'T HAVE TO READ THAT FAR!
WHa...? THat's TSuruya's address...

## CONTINUING TODAY'S THEME: "MYSTERIOUS THINGS THAT HAPPENED NEAR ME"

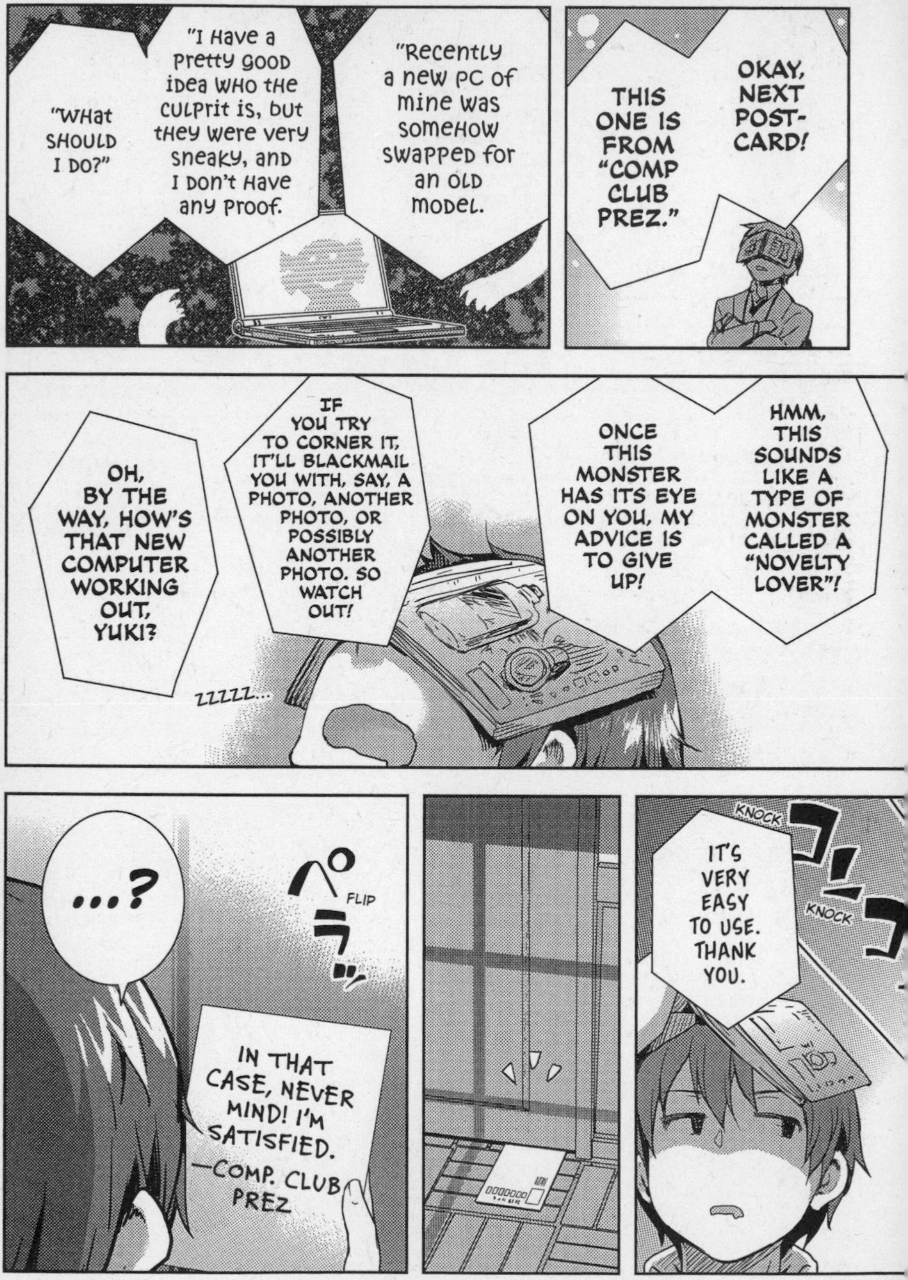
OKAY, NEXT POST-CARD!
THIS ONE IS FROM "COMP CLUB PREZ."
"Recently a new PC of mine was somehow swapped for an old model.
"I have a pretty good idea who the culprit is, but they were very sneaky, and I don't have any proof.
"What should I do?"
HMM, THIS SOUNDS LIKE A TYPE OF MONSTER CALLED A "NOVELTY LOVER"!
ONCE THIS MONSTER HAS ITS EYE ON YOU, MY ADVICE IS TO GIVE UP!
IF YOU TRY TO CORNER IT, IT'LL BLACKMAIL YOU WITH, SAY, A PHOTO, ANOTHER PHOTO, OR POSSIBLY ANOTHER PHOTO. SO WATCH OUT!
OH, BY THE WAY, HOW'S THAT NEW COMPUTER WORKING OUT, YUKI?
ZZZZZ...
KNOCK
KNOCK
IT'S VERY EASY TO USE. THANK YOU.
FLIP
...?
IN THAT CASE, NEVER MIND! I'M SATISFIED. —COMP. CLUB PREZ

## 00:55 - PROGRAM WRAP-UP, SECOND SONG, LISTENER REQUEST

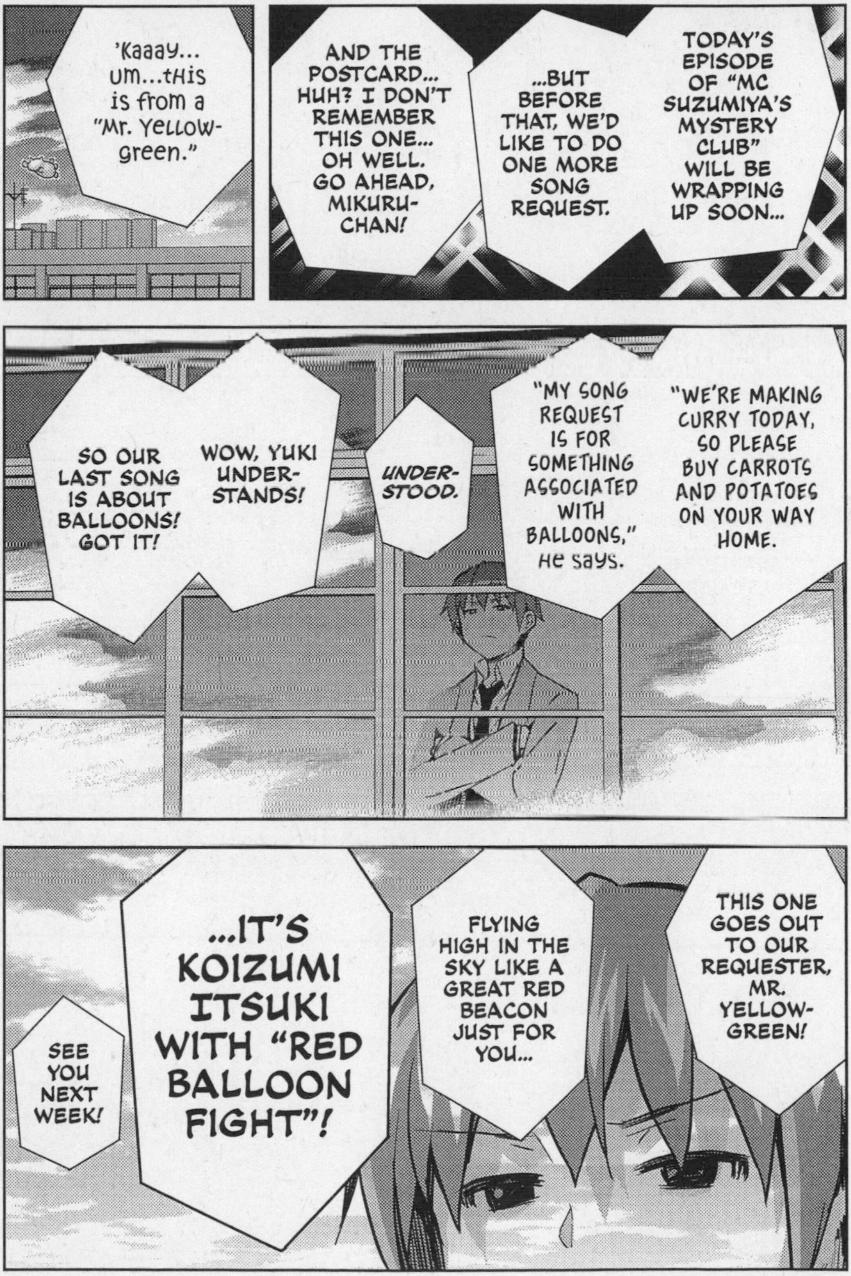
TODAY'S EPISODE OF "MC SUZUMIYA'S MYSTERY CLUB" WILL BE WRAPPING UP SOON...
...BUT BEFORE THAT, WE'D LIKE TO DO ONE MORE SONG REQUEST.
AND THE POSTCARD... HUH? I DON'T REMEMBER THIS ONE... OH WELL. GO AHEAD, MIKURU-CHAN!
'Kaaay... um...this is from a "Mr. Yellow-green."
"WE'RE MAKING CURRY TODAY, SO PLEASE BUY CARROTS AND POTATOES ON YOUR WAY HOME.
"MY SONG REQUEST IS FOR SOMETHING ASSOCIATED WITH BALLOONS," He says.
UNDERSTOOD.
WOW, YUKI UNDERSTANDS!
SO OUR LAST SONG IS ABOUT BALLOONS! GOT IT!
THIS ONE GOES OUT TO OUR REQUESTER, MR. YELLOW-GREEN!
FLYING HIGH IN THE SKY LIKE A GREAT RED BEACON JUST FOR YOU...
...IT'S KOIZUMI ITSUKI WITH "RED BALLOON FIGHT"!
SEE YOU NEXT WEEK!

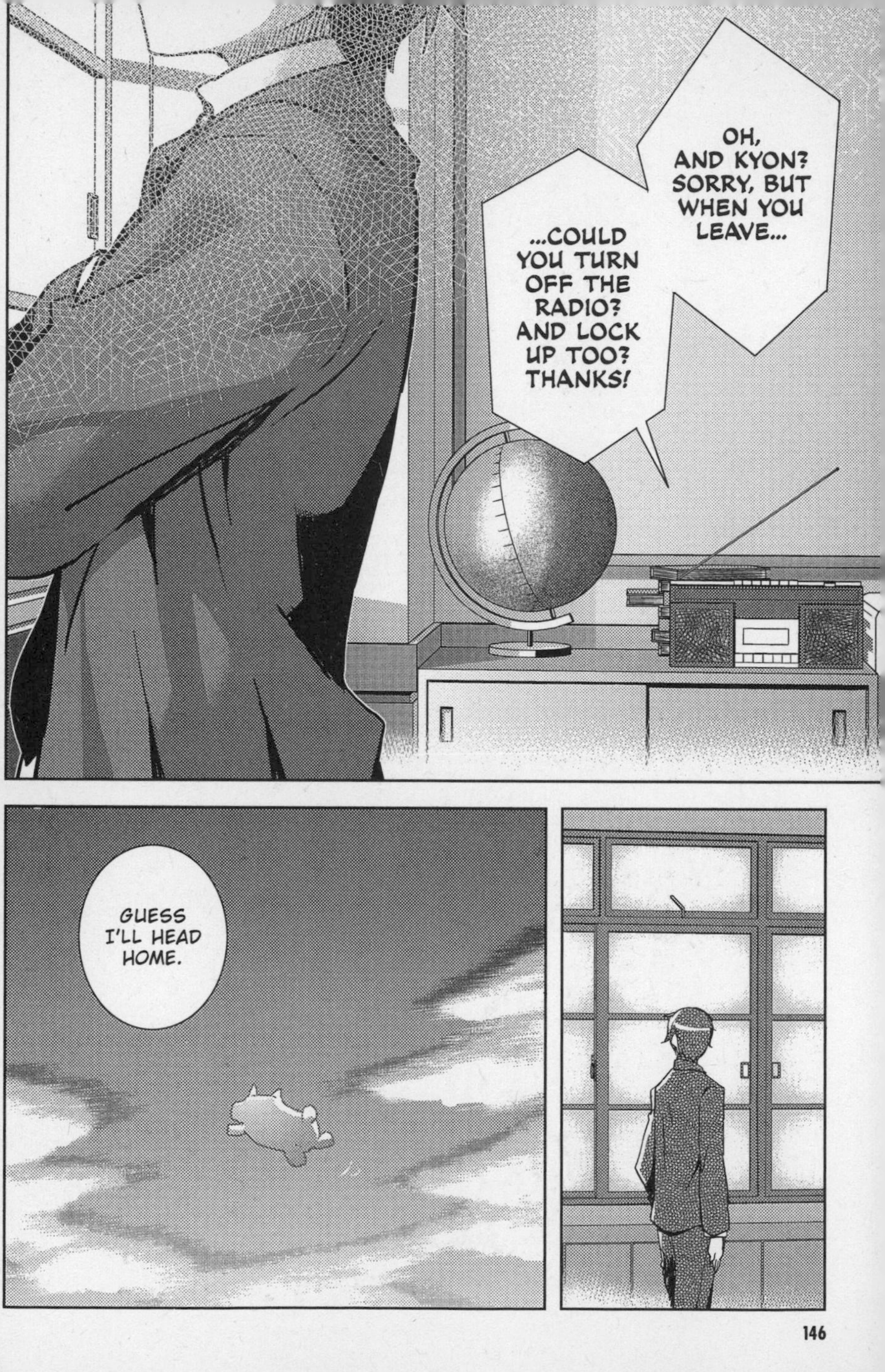
OH, AND KYON? SORRY, BUT WHEN YOU LEAVE...
...COULD YOU TURN OFF THE RADIO? AND LOCK UP TOO? THANKS!
GUESS I'LL HEAD HOME.

AND SOME
CABBAGE...

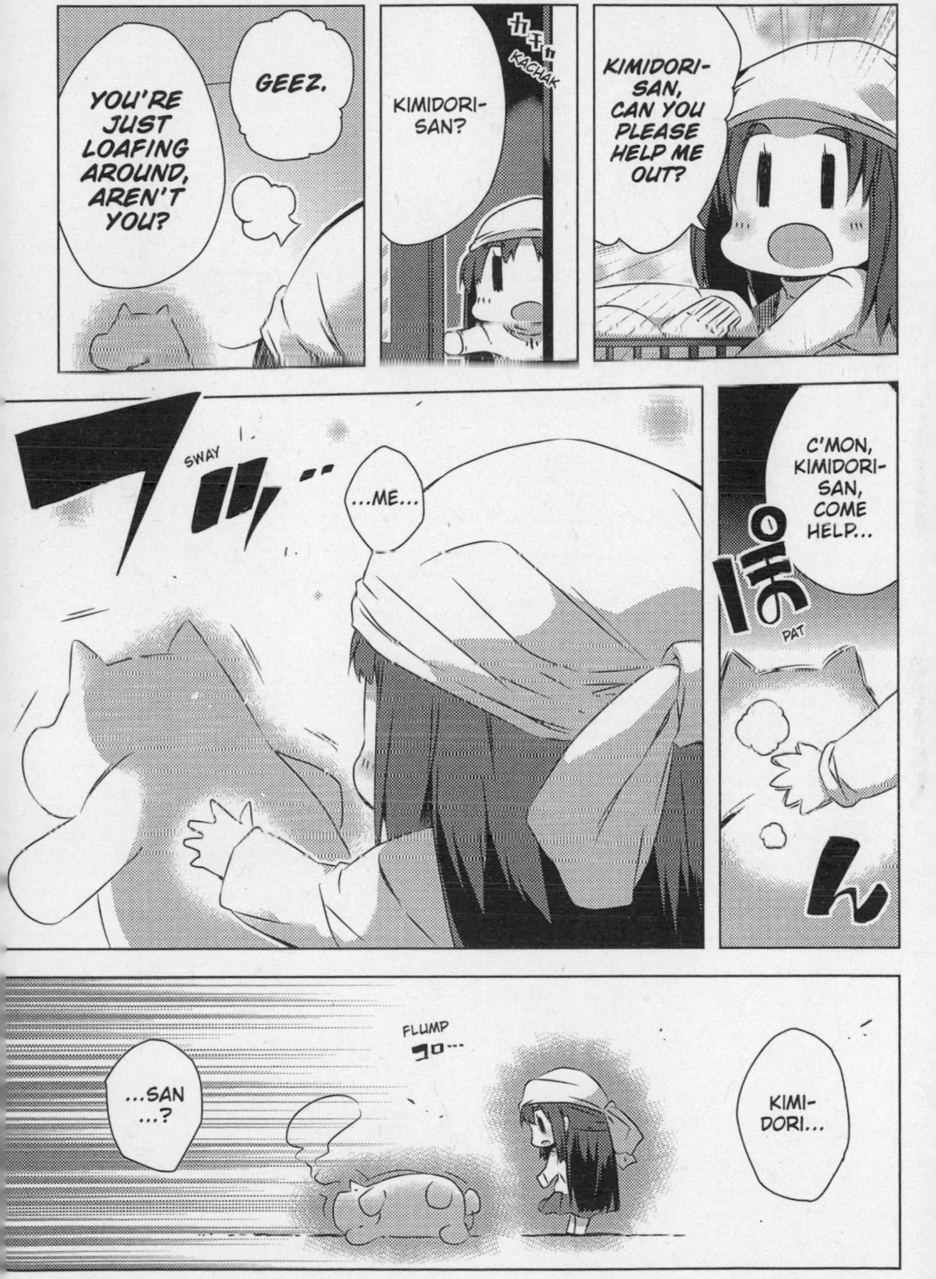
KIMIDORI-SAN, CAN YOU PLEASE HELP ME OUT?
KACHAK
KIMIDORI-SAN?
GEEZ.
YOU'RE JUST LOAFING AROUND, AREN'T YOU?
C'MON, KIMIDORI-SAN, COME HELP...
PAT
...ME...
SWAY
KIMI-DORI...
FLUMP
...SAN ...?

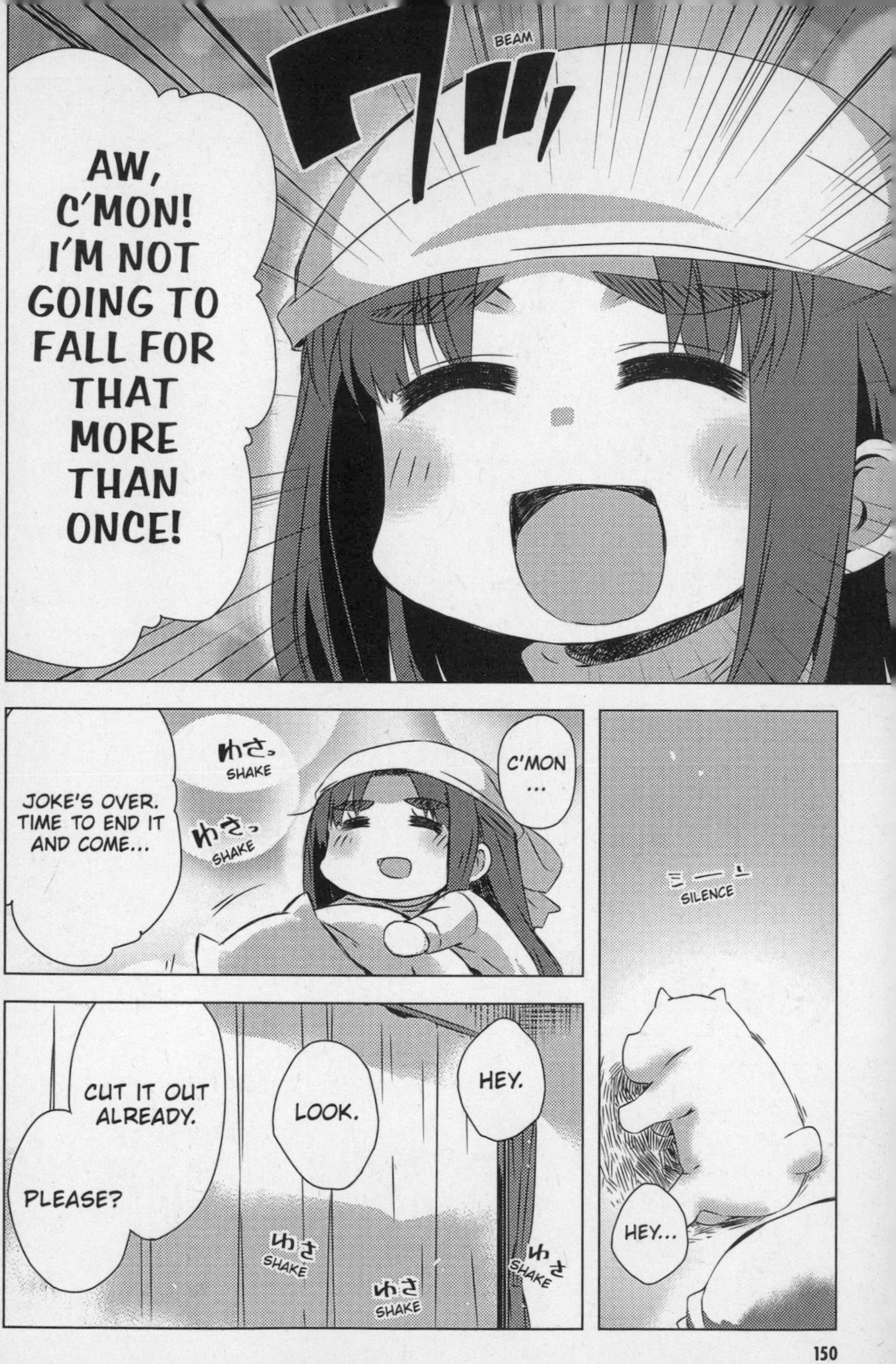

ワッ
BEAM
AW, C'MON! I'M NOT GOING TO FALL FOR THAT MORE THAN ONCE!
シーン
SILENCE
HEY...
C'MON...
ゆさっ
SHAKE
ゆさっ
SHAKE
JOKE'S OVER. TIME TO END IT AND COME...
HEY.
LOOK.
CUT IT OUT ALREADY.
PLEASE?
ゆさ
SHAKE
ゆさ
SHAKE
ゆさ
SHAKE

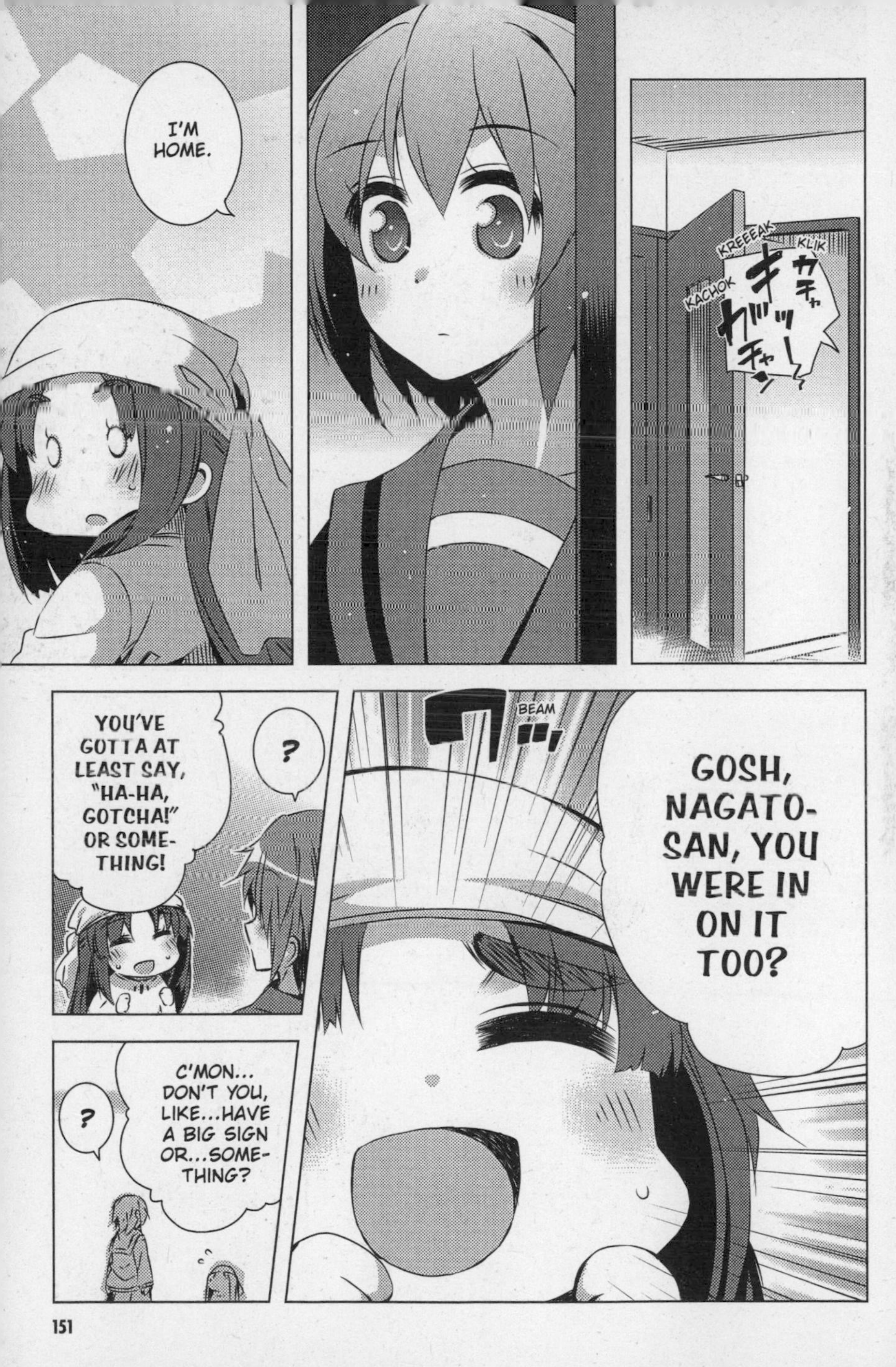

KREEEAK
KLIK
KACHOK
I'M HOME.
BEAM
GOSH, NAGATO-SAN, YOU WERE IN ON IT TOO?
?
YOU'VE GOTTA AT LEAST SAY, "HA-HA, GOTCHA!" OR SOMETHING!
C'MON... DON'T YOU, LIKE...HAVE A BIG SIGN OR...SOMETHING?
?

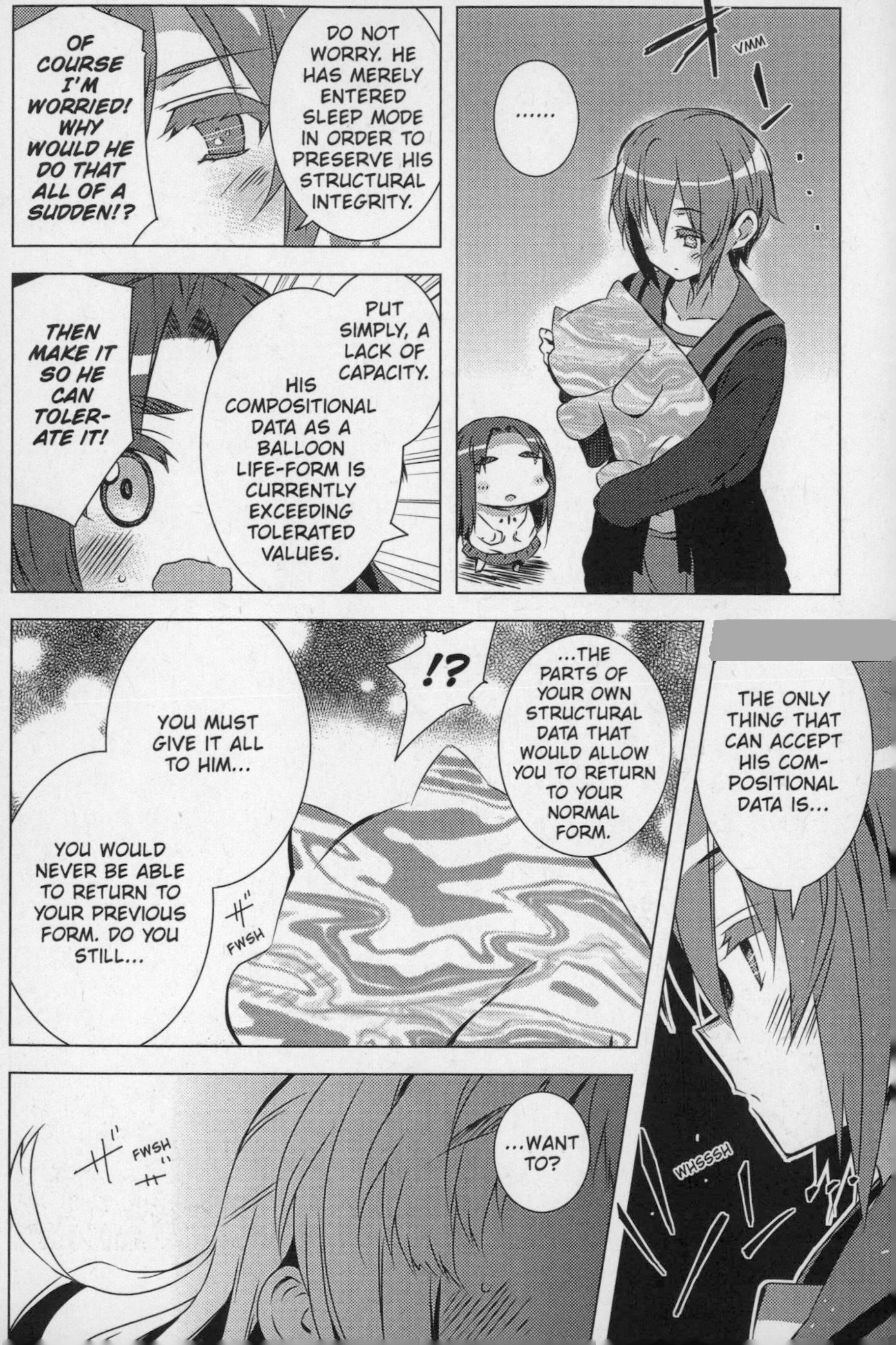
VMM
......
DO NOT WORRY. HE HAS MERELY ENTERED SLEEP MODE IN ORDER TO PRESERVE HIS STRUCTURAL INTEGRITY.
OF COURSE I'M WORRIED! WHY WOULD HE DO THAT ALL OF A SUDDEN!?
PUT SIMPLY, A LACK OF CAPACITY.
HIS COMPOSITIONAL DATA AS A BALLOON LIFE-FORM IS CURRENTLY EXCEEDING TOLERATED VALUES.
THEN MAKE IT SO HE CAN TOLER-ATE IT!
THE ONLY THING THAT CAN ACCEPT HIS COM-POSITIONAL DATA IS...
...THE PARTS OF YOUR OWN STRUCTURAL DATA THAT WOULD ALLOW YOU TO RETURN TO YOUR NORMAL FORM.
!?
YOU MUST GIVE IT ALL TO HIM...
YOU WOULD NEVER BE ABLE TO RETURN TO YOUR PREVIOUS FORM. DO YOU STILL...
FWSH
WHSSSH
...WANT TO?
FWSH

FWSHHH

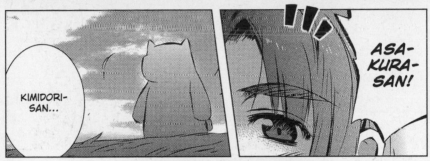

KIMIDORI-SAN...

ASA-KURA-SAN!

SMACK

!?

OH, GOOD... IT LOOKS LIKE IT WORKED.

SHF

SHF

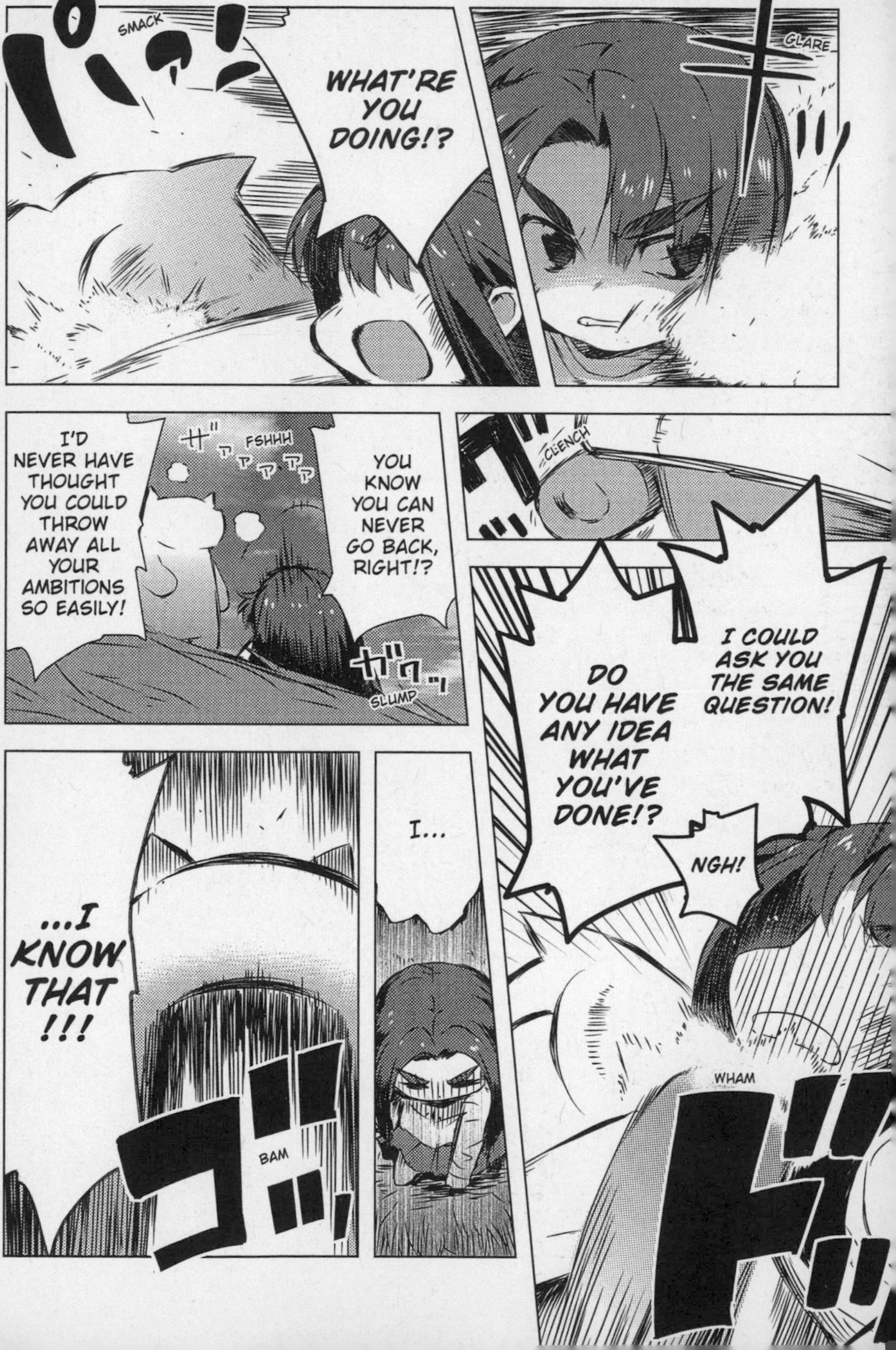
GLARE
WHAT'RE YOU DOING!?
SMACK
CLENCH
FSHHH
I'D NEVER HAVE THOUGHT YOU COULD THROW AWAY ALL YOUR AMBITIONS SO EASILY!
YOU KNOW YOU CAN NEVER GO BACK, RIGHT!?
SLUMP
I COULD ASK YOU THE SAME QUESTION!
DO YOU HAVE ANY IDEA WHAT YOU'VE DONE!?
NGH!
WHAM
I...
...I KNOW THAT!!!
BAM

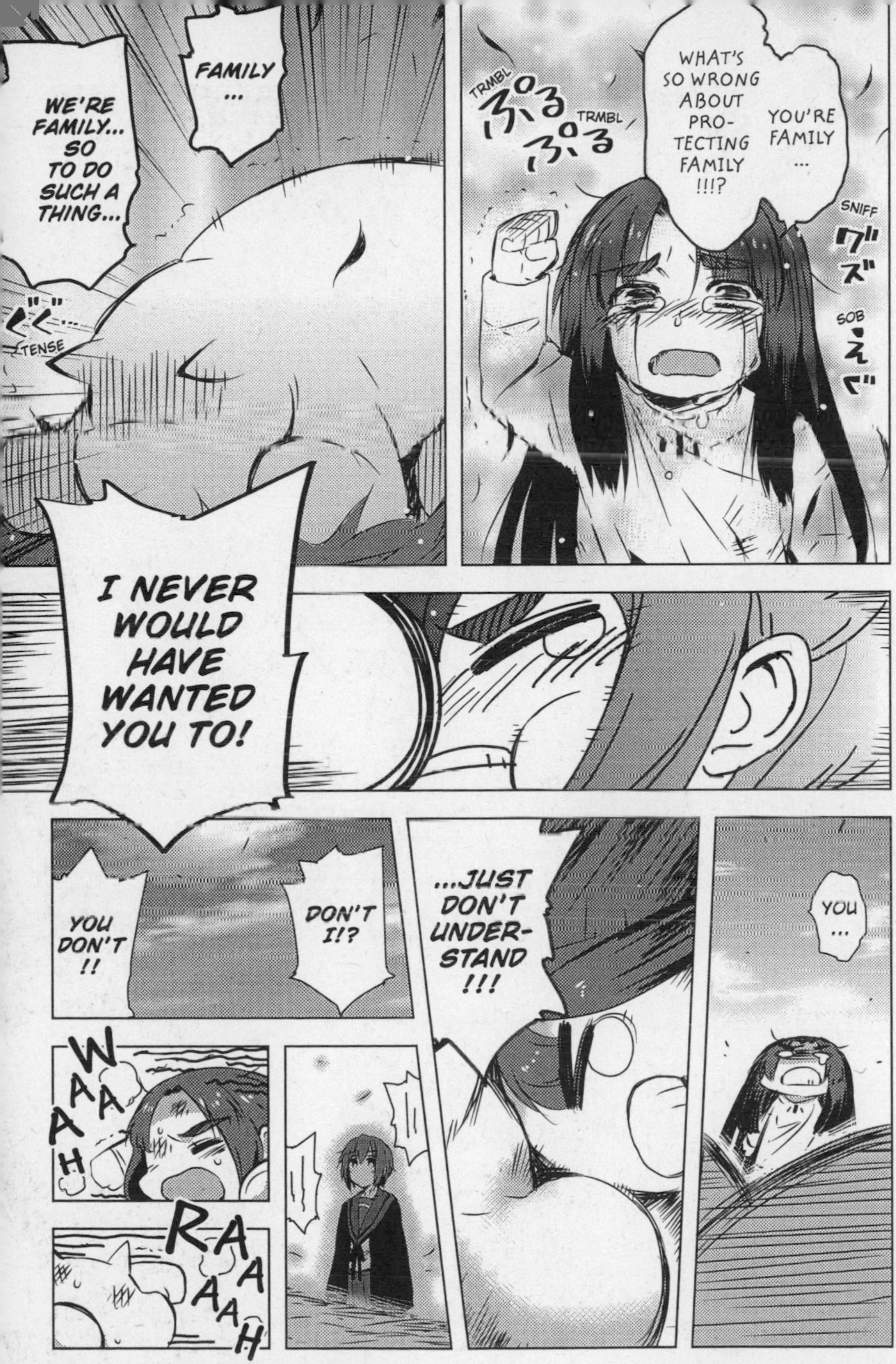
YOU'RE FAMILY ...
WHAT'S SO WRONG ABOUT PRO-TECTING FAMILY !!!?
TRMBL ぷる
TRMBL ぷる
SNIFF グズ
SOB えぐ
FAMILY ...
WE'RE FAMILY... SO TO DO SUCH A THING...
TENSE ぐぐ...
I NEVER WOULD HAVE WANTED YOU TO!
YOU ...
...JUST DON'T UNDER-STAND !!!
DON'T I!?
YOU DON'T !!
WAAAH
RAAAAAH

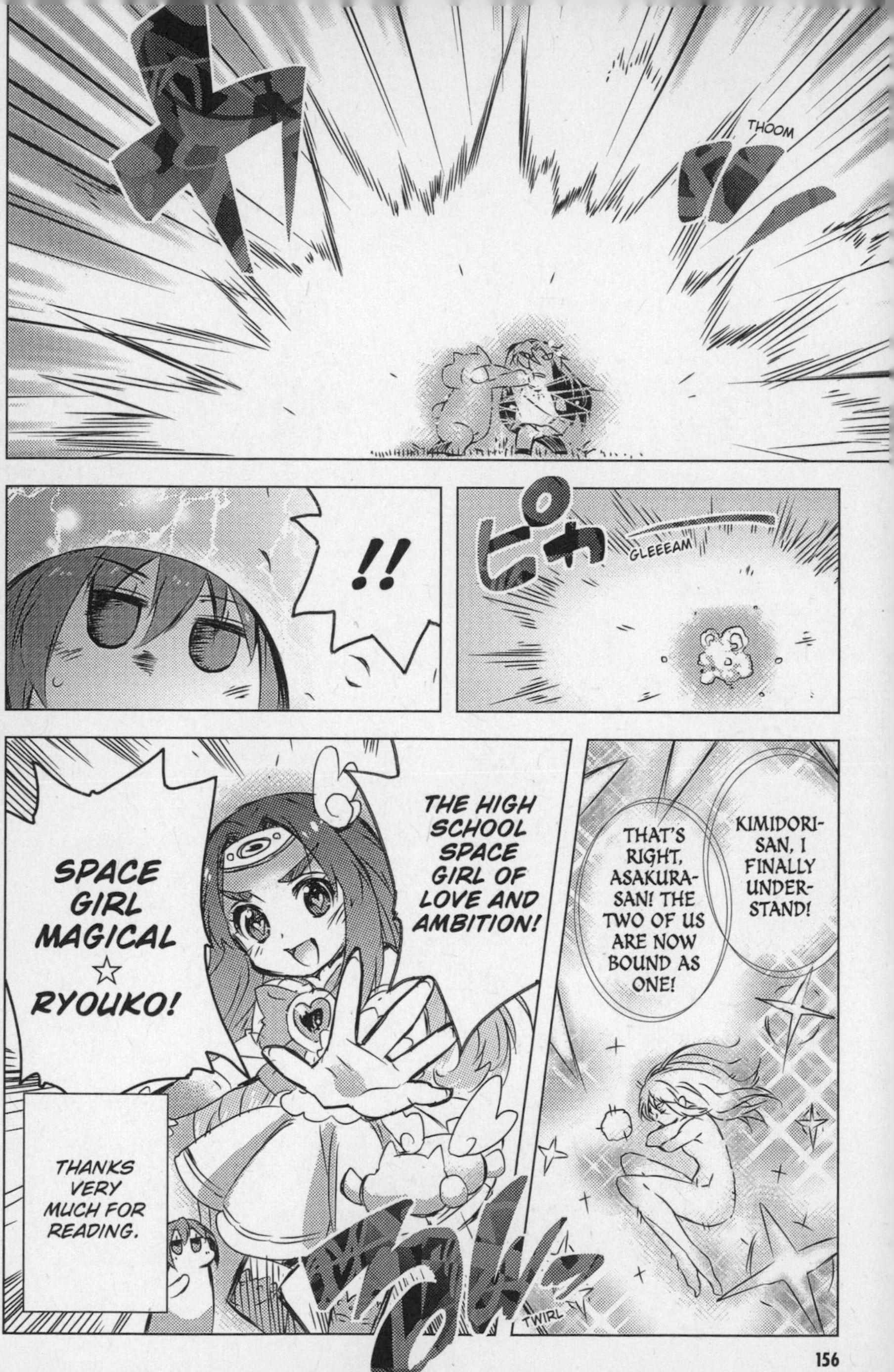
THOOM
GLEEEAM
!!
KIMIDORI-SAN, I FINALLY UNDERSTAND!
THAT'S RIGHT, ASAKURA-SAN! THE TWO OF US ARE NOW BOUND AS ONE!
TWIRL
THE HIGH SCHOOL SPACE GIRL OF LOVE AND AMBITION!
SPACE GIRL MAGICAL ☆ RYOUKO!
THANKS VERY MUCH FOR READING.

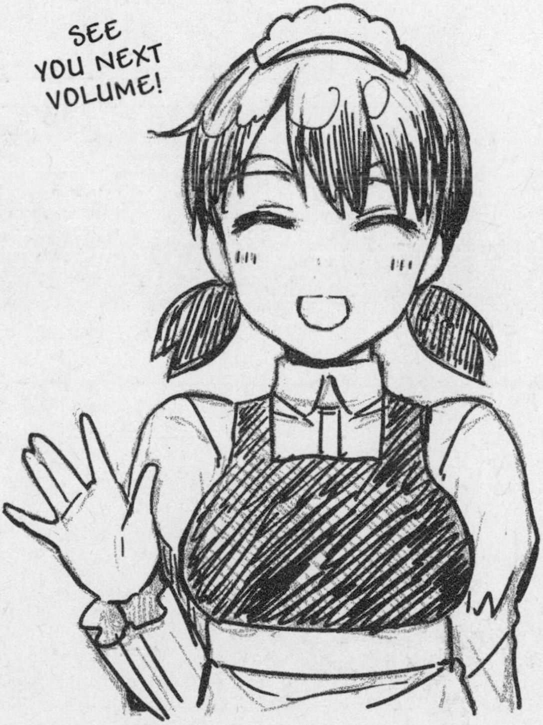
SEE YOU NEXT VOLUME!

WE'RE NOT THINKING ABOUT OUR OWN GAIN.
THEY'VE FINALLY BEGUN TO MOVE.
WE ONLY DESIRE THE SAFETY OF THE WORLD.
IT DOESN'T REALLY MATTER.
SPACE-TIME MANIPULATION. THAT'S THE ONLY THING WORTH SEEING.
NEXT VOLUME, ENTER...

THIS TIME...
IT IS... YOU.
..."THE SURPRISE"!
...THERE IS NO MISTAKE.
HEYA, KYON. LONG TIME NO SEE.

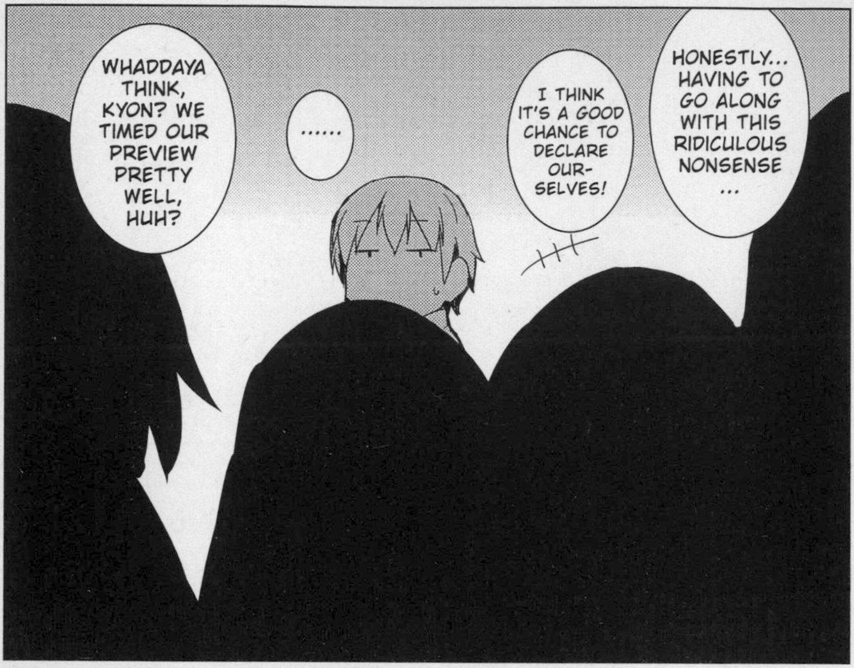
HONESTLY... HAVING TO GO ALONG WITH THIS RIDICULOUS NONSENSE ...
I THINK IT'S A GOOD CHANCE TO DECLARE OUR-SELVES!
......
WHADDAYA THINK, KYON? WE TIMED OUR PREVIEW PRETTY WELL, HUH?

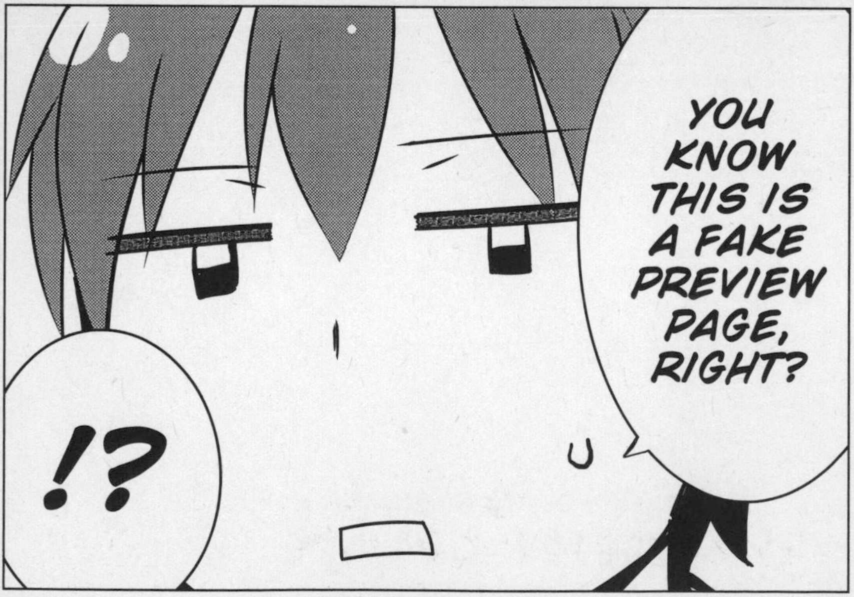
YOU KNOW THIS IS A FAKE PREVIEW PAGE, RIGHT?
!?

THE MELANCHOLY **of** SUZUMIYA
# HARUHI-CHAN
The Untold Adventures of the SOS Brigade

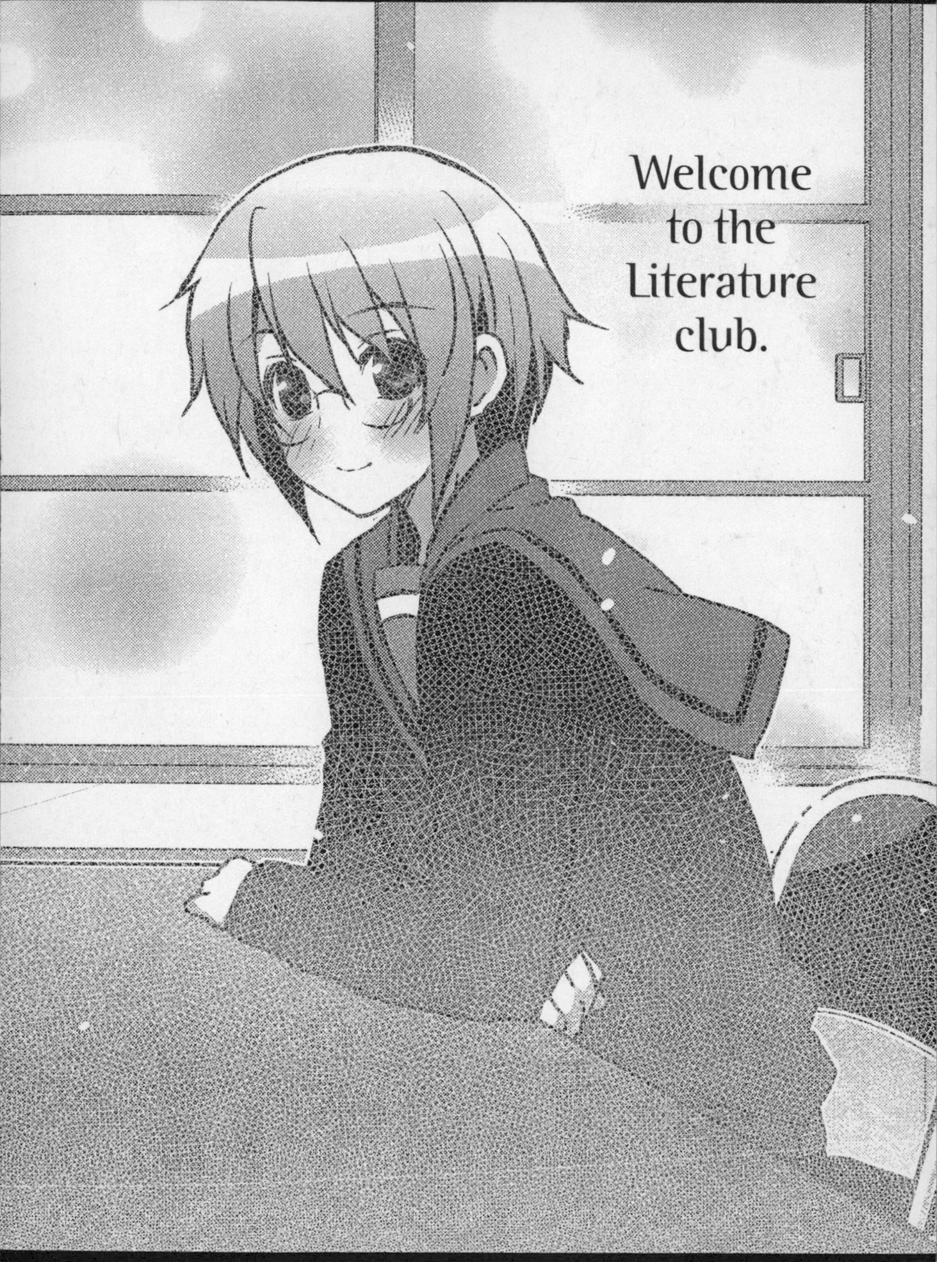
Welcome to the Literature club.

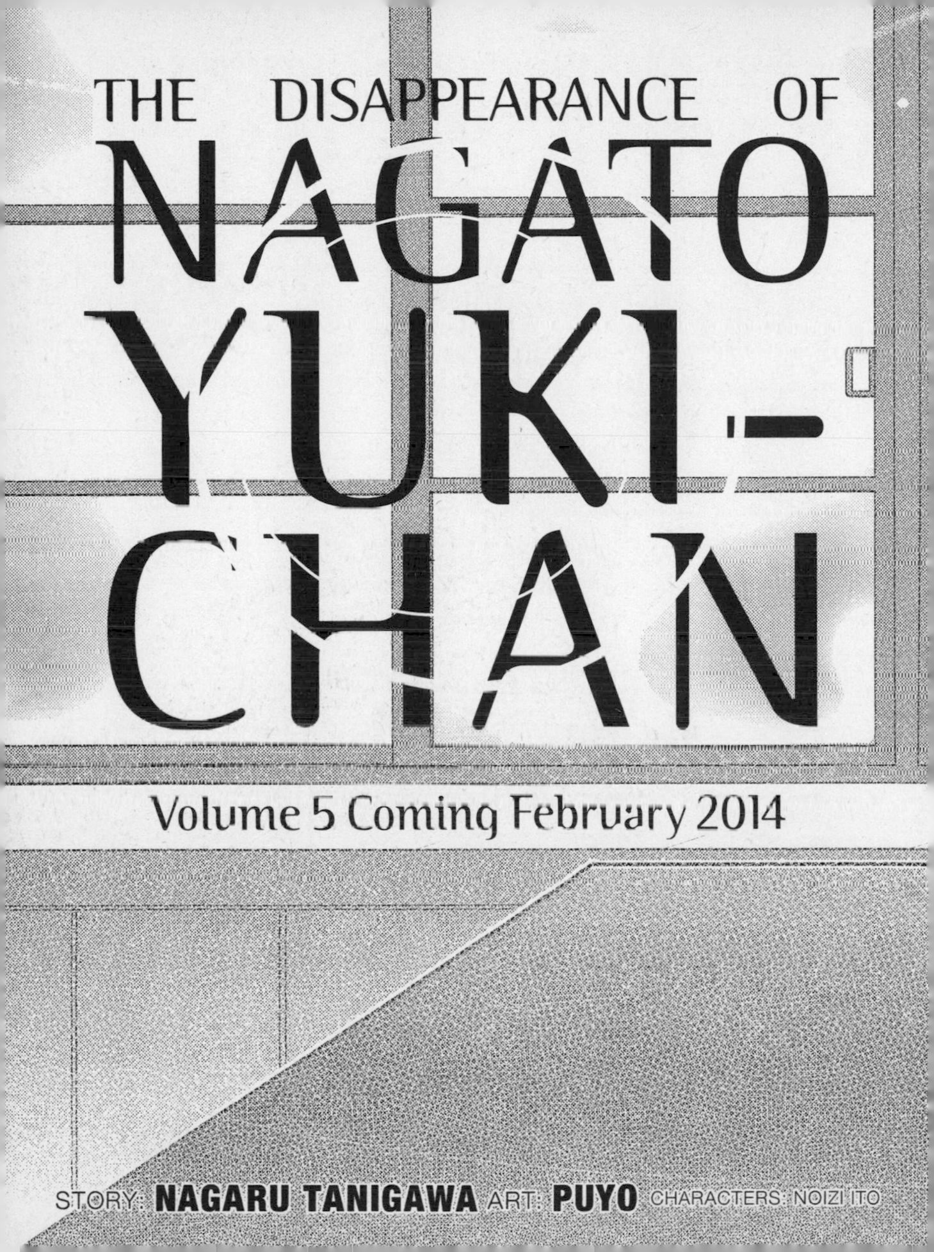
THE DISAPPEARANCE OF
NAGATO YUKI-CHAN
Volume 5 Coming February 2014
STORY: NAGARU TANIGAWA ART: PUYO CHARACTERS: NOIZI ITO

# THE MELANCHOLY OF SUZUMIYA
# HARUHI-CHAN

Original Story: Nagaru Tanigawa
Manga: PUYO
Character Design: Noizi Ito

Translation: Paul Starr
Lettering: Abigail Blackman

The Melancholy of Suzumiya Haruhi-chan Volume 7
© Nagaru TANIGAWA • Noizi ITO 2012 © PUYO 2012. First published in Japan in 2012 by KADOKAWA SHOTEN Co., Ltd., Tokyo. English translation rights arranged with KADOKAWA SHOTEN Co., Ltd., Tokyo through TUTTLE-MORI AGENCY, INC., Tokyo.

English translation © 2013 by Hachette Book Group, Inc.

Yen Press
Hachette Book Group
237 Park Avenue, New York, NY 10017

www.HachetteBookGroup.com
www.YenPress.com

Yen Press is an imprint of Hachette Book Group, Inc.
The Yen Press name and logo are trademarks of Hachette Book Group, Inc.

First Yen Press Edition: September 2013

ISBN: 978-0-316-24310-0

10 9 8 7 6 5 4 3 2 1

BVG

Printed in the United States of America

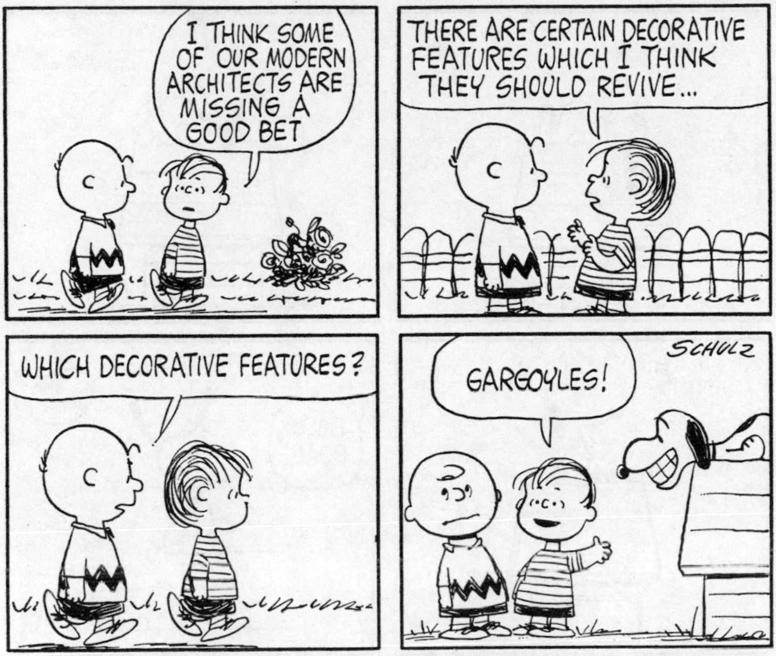
I THINK SOME OF OUR MODERN ARCHITECTS ARE MISSING A GOOD BET
THERE ARE CERTAIN DECORATIVE FEATURES WHICH I THINK THEY SHOULD REVIVE...
WHICH DECORATIVE FEATURES?
GARGOYLES!
SCHULZ

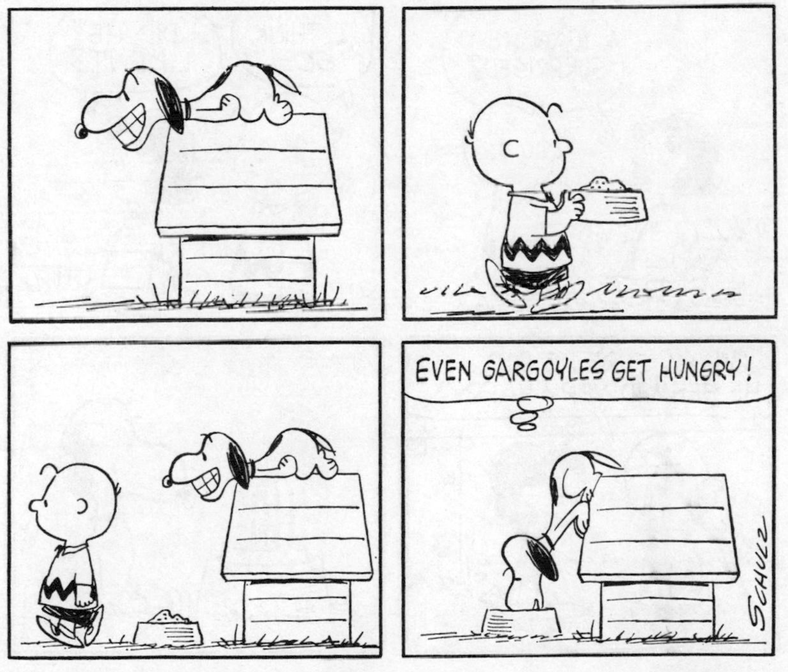
EVEN GARGOYLES GET HUNGRY!
SCHULZ

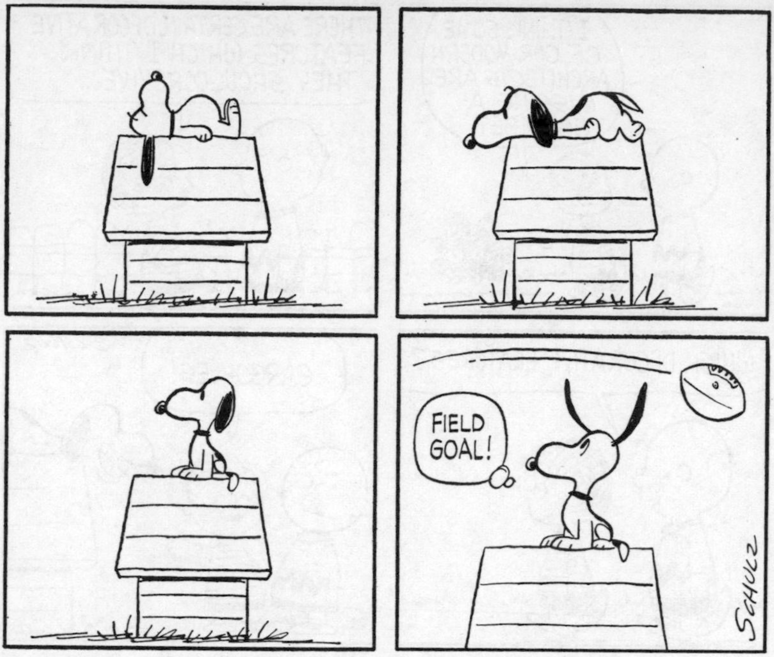
FIELD GOAL!
SCHULZ

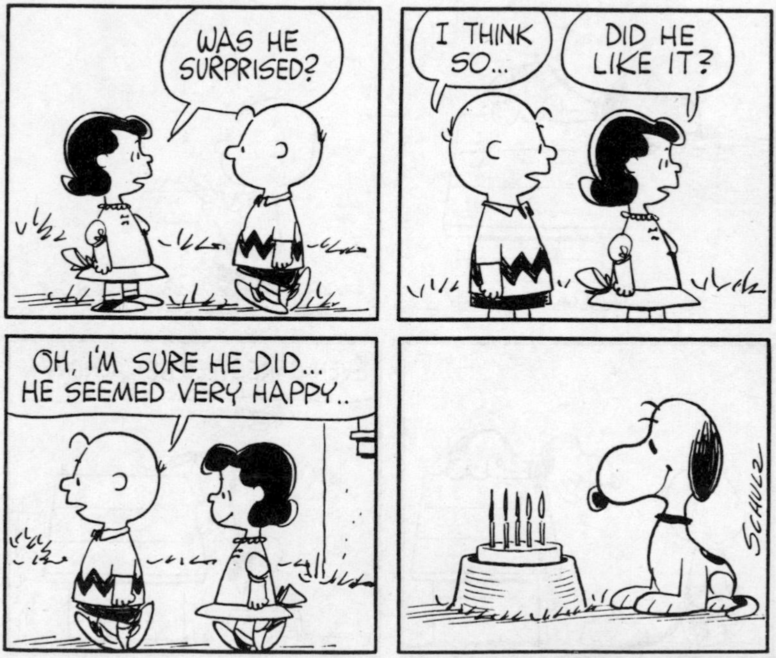
WAS HE SURPRISED?
I THINK SO...
DID HE LIKE IT?
OH, I'M SURE HE DID... HE SEEMED VERY HAPPY..
SCHULZ